4

ADVANCE PRAISE FOR *BRANDS & ROUSERS*

"You've probably heard the saying "think globally, act locally." This popular phrase encourages people to consider the impact on the entire world when making choices while at the same time acknowledging that real change starts from small acts within local communities. Luis Gallardo takes "think globally, act locally" one step further with his own point of view – "think holistic, act personal." This philosophy suggests that there are two elements in a successful business: taking actions that promote sustained profit and growth and addressing your customers' personal needs so that your message is relevant and timely. In other words: for your business to succeed, you must simultaneously think about things in the largest way possible and in the smallest way possible. To fulfill the "think holistic act personal" creed, we must also remember to act personal in ways that bring meaning to peoples' lives. Not only will it help your business, but it might also just start a revolution."

Jennifer Aaker, General Atlantic Professor of Marketing at Stanford University's Graduate School of Business. She is the co-author, together with Andy Smith, of *The Dragonfly Effect*.

"Reputation building and Revenue generation here go hand in hand and are inter-related. That is to say it is widely accepted today that your best revenue base multiplier is your current customer base. Really perform for them and they'll reward you with more (higher order quantity, more frequently) and they'll lead you to other customers by recommending you to them. So, revenue generating well from your current base will strengthen your reputation and grow revenues. I see them both as indispensable tools for the contemporary manager as Luis Gallardo does in his book. A must read!"

Seán Meehan, Martin Hilti Professor of Marketing and Change Management at IMD in Lausanne, Switzerland. and bestselling author of *Beyond the familiar* and *Simply Better*.

"Those businesses driven by a higher ideal or a higher purpose, what Luis Gallardo calls Reason in his book, not only outperformed their competitors by a wide margin, but often created entirely new sectors, and businesses which experienced rapid and sustainable growth. This makes a compelling case for those businesses that don't simply treat its brand as part of the marketing or public relations department, but espouse its core values to all stakeholders, both internal and external."

Tim Wragg, CEO of Millward Brown in Europe

"Despite the challenges of 2011, let us not forget that we have as many, if not more, opportunities ahead of us. We have many choices. Perhaps the biggest test we face is in developing the capacity to look beyond short-term pressures to make sense of change – and to take action today. Looking ahead, it will not be business as usual, or society as usual. We will have to question how we think, work together and act to seize opportunities and address challenges. We need a point of view on the future, a way to move from data overload to informed action. Executives today spend too much time looking at the world from inside their business and responding to short-term pressures. Understanding our current and future reality requires inverting this lens and looking from the outside-in. Frameworks such as the one developed by Luis Gallardo help business managers to make that sense of change."

Tracey Keys, Director of Strategy Dynamics Global Limited, publisher of www.globaltrends.com

"Think Holistic, Act Personal, the platform created by Luis, is a powerful concept. At its best, brand is a key tool to make people think holistically, but you also need to act personally and tailor the message content and voice to the audience. Thinking holistically means capturing synergies across the organization and thinking outside in: a strategically well-defined brand is a rallying point for all across the organization and a filter to bring in an outside perspective to all decisions. Acting personal means considering people and the human element in all you do. A brand platform should be all-encompassing but also expressed and messaged to be relevant to the interests and needs of individual audiences. In order to think holistically, you need a framework, and in order to act personal, you need freedom. These terms are not as opposed as they first may seem, and are essential elements in the process of building a successful global brand."

Brian Rafferty, Global Director, Customer Insights at Siegel + Gale

"In life, as it is in business, it is not enough seen the big picture, it is about understanding the full picture. Brands & Rousers, the book written by Luis Gallardo, is all about interconnections and their meaning, it is about multi-dimensions and dynamic systems. Really helpful! if managing a multinational brand such as Tetra Pak."

Elisa Nistri, Marketing Director of Tetra Pak in Italy

BUILDING BRANDS

BUILDING BRANDS

Strategy and Tactics

Luis Gallardo

Viva Books

New Delhi | Mumbai | Chennai | Kolkata | Bengaluru | Hyderabad | Kochi | Guwahati

First Indian Edition 2014
Reprinted 2015

VIVA BOOKS PRIVATE LIMITED

- 4737/23 Ansari Road, Daryaganj, New Delhi 110 002
  E-mail: vivadelhi@vivagroupindia.net, Tel. 42242200
- 76, Service Industries, Shirvane, Sector 1, Nerul, Navi Mumbai 400 706
  E-mail: vivamumbai@vivagroupindia.net, Tel. 27721273, 27721274
- Megh Towers, Old No. 307, New No. 165, Poonamallee High Road, Maduravoyal
  Chennai - 600 095 E-mail: vivachennai@vivagroupindia.net, Tel. 23780991, 23780992
- B-103, Jindal Towers, 21/1A/3 Darga Road, Kolkata 700 017
  E-mail: vivakolkata@vivagroupindia.net, Tel. 22836381, 22816713
- 7, Sovereign Park Apartments, 56-58, K. R. Road, Basavanagudi, Bengaluru 560 004
  E-mail: vivabangalore@vivagroupindia.net, Tel. 26607409, 26607410
- 101-102 Mughal Marc Apartments, 3-4-637 to 641, Narayanguda, Hyderabad 500 029
  E-mail: vivahyderabad@vivagroupindia.net, Tel. 27564481, 27564482
- Beevi Towers, First Floor, SRM Road, Kaloor, Kochi 682 018, Kerala
  E-mail: vivakochi@vivagroupindia.net, Tel: 0484-2403055, 2403056
- 232, GNB Road, Beside UCO Bank, Silpukhuri, Guwahati 781 003
  E-mail: vivaguwahati@vivagroupindia.net, Tel: 0361-2666386

www.vivagroupindia.com

Published by arrangement with
LID Publishing
6-8, Underwood Street
London N1 7JQ
UK

ISBN : 978-81-309-2683-4

Published by Vinod Vasishtha for Viva Books Private Limited, 4737/23, Ansari Road, Daryaganj, New Delhi - 110 002.

Printed and bound by Thomson Press, New Delhi.

Contents

To Magui, Mario and Ivan, my life team and secure base.

To Deloitte's more than 3,000 marketing, communications and business development professionals worldwide, an amazing community that strives to be always one step ahead.

To my parents, and all those Rousers that are making an impact around the world, with hard work and big hearts.

Welcome

When I became the global marketing and brand leader for Deloitte, I was sure of only two things: there was much that I needed to learn quickly, and I could minimize typical learning curve mistakes by following the conventional wisdom – Think Global, Act Local.

Eight years and 3,000,000 air miles later I was still sure of two things. First, I could never learn enough. Second, conventional wisdom no longer goes far enough. These conclusions reflect a fundamental shift in how I think about building and operating global businesses.

The change didn't happen overnight. It was a process accelerated when I moved from my native Madrid to live in New York City, a place that in many ways is a microcosm of our exciting, tumultuous, and diverse world. The relocation jolted my perception that operating a business across many countries required only an overall strategy, some acknowledgement of local differences and world-class logistics. Nothing could be further from the truth.

In fact, when I arrived at Deloitte almost a decade ago, the brand was willing to challenge other industry giants to achieve the market recognition that we deserved. That goal became my mission. I am proud to say that today, Deloitte is today one of the pre-eminent global professional services networks, having outperformed competitors for the first time by both revenue and size during fiscal year 2010.

As a result of this experience, and after advising CEOs in many companies around the world, I have since altered my view of Think Global, Act Local to a new approach, Think Holistic, Act Personal (THAP), which I believe has enabled businesses to better operate, communicate and work together productively across borders.

I invite you to learn more about Think Holistic, Act Personal in the following pages. Though it may sound simplistic on paper, I can assure you that implementing it requires discipline and commitment. To begin with, it requires the will to lead and step ahead. Once it works – and it does work – everyone feels like a respected, contributing member of the organization and the approach becomes self-reinforcing.

So yes, it takes work. Lots of it. But honestly, it's not that complicated. Let me show you how and why Think Holistic, Act Personal is the management philosophy driving the growth of high performance brands today.

Sincerely,

Luis M. Gallardo

Luis Gallardo

Chapter One

Leading in Turbulent Times

"It is not the strongest of the species that survives, nor the most intelligent, but the one most responsive to change."

CHARLES DARWIN, *THE ORIGIN OF SPECIES*

There are two things we can say for certain about the future: it will be different and it will surprise. Given the competitiveness of global and local markets, the pace of change in business and the sudden emergence of unprecedented challenges and opportunities, there is an overriding need for leadership that is flexible, capable and dynamic. If there is one lesson for organizations to learn from the events of the late 20th century and the first decade of the 21st it is this: it is not simply what we know that matters, but how we react to what we do not know. The time of the all-

WHAT DO THE MOST SUCCESSFUL BUSINESSES HAVE IN COMMON? OF THE WIDE RANGE OF POSSIBLE ANSWERS, AN ABILITY TO ADAPT TO CHANGE IS SURELY ONE OF THE MOST SIGNIFICANT. THIS QUALITY IS MORE IMPORTANT NOW THAN EVER, WITH TURBULENCE INCREASINGLY BECOMING THE NORM FOR BUSINESSES, BRANDS AND EXECUTIVES WORLDWIDE.

knowing leader is gone. Certainty is ephemeral and elusive: even if it is achieved, it soon becomes clouded and overtaken by events.

This book is based on a simple premise: that to succeed in these circumstances, leaders need to think holistically but act personally. It is this balance between strategy and tactics, big picture and detail, planning and action, corporate direction and personal responsibility that helps to ensure progress and resilience for the organization. In practice, this means succeeding in six broad areas: leading with a purpose and reason, generating and maximizing revenues, rousing people and dreams, building relationships, maximizing a strong reputation and becoming resilient.

In this chapter we set the scene and highlight the pressures that are now routinely encountered by executives. We believe that the implication is clear: executives can only resolve these challenges by learning to think holistically and act personally.

THE NEW REALITY

Certainty is a thing of the past. Companies no longer have the luxury of assuming that they can survive glitches in the market with a few last-minute tweaks: markets are now too changeable from too many angles for that to be a sustainable approach. It is not enough to simply develop an ad hoc, last minute response as changes occur; strong companies have a mindset and approach that anticipate change and have systems in place that can deal with any changes quickly and efficiently.

Change comes from so many different directions that companies and leaders can be forgiven for feeling overwhelmed or blindsided. Every day, we are facing a multitude of changes that affect every aspect of running a business. Laws, regulations, compliance requirements, customer preferences, technologies, competitors, changing demographics and shifts in lifestyles are only some of the forces at work. All of these present an immense challenge for any business, but when magnified by the many other countries, businesses and customers entering the global marketplace having different legal requirements, customs, cultures and consumer preferences, the challenge is truly immense. Time moves on and markets evolve. Success will only follow for those organizations that respond effectively and swiftly to the only constant left in business: change.

IT IS A TIME OF CHANGE, INSTABILITY AND UNCERTAINTY AND THE NATURE AND IMPLICATIONS OF THIS NEW REALITY NEED TO BE PROPERLY UNDERSTOOD IF THEY ARE TO BE SUCCESSFULLY INCORPORATED INTO BUSINESS STRATEGY.

It's hard to dispute the view that during the first years of the 21st century the world has experienced a frenetic pace of change and witnessed massive upheaval. Although change has always been with us, what makes this situation different is the realization that chaos and upheaval are now the norm rather than the exception. Companies need to desensitize themselves to the sensationalist, headline-grabbing scaremongering about recent events – from share prices tumbling and climates warming to threats to employment and governments defaulting on debts – and just accept the new reality that these things are here to stay; they will continue to occur. In particular, we need to be wary of falling into the trap of thinking that the need to cope with such drastic changes is only a temporary requirement. What we need to do is better prepare for the likelihood of change, control our responses and get better at anticipating and shaping events. Instead of assuming that there will be a resumption of business-as-usual and that 'things' will settle down soon, we now need to view change and the ability to adapt as an essential business skill.

Leaders need to ask themselves: what are we doing to ensure the long-term success of the company? While dealing with uncertainty is hardly a new concept for businesses, it is the sheer scale of change that we now have to deal with that presents such immense challenges and that leaves the unprepared company vulnerable and such easy prey to their more battle-ready competitors.

A CHANGING WORLD

In recent decades, several themes have shaped business life as a whole and executives' thinking in particular. These issues include the rise of technology and its impact both on what customers want and what business can achieve. Interestingly, history suggests that the impact of technology is often overestimated in the short-term and underestimated in the long-term. The rise of globalization is another recurring theme, highlighted by the value of being both global and local. Closely linked with globalization is the need to appreciate difference and the implications of diversity, an issue long recognized by business executives and reflected in the concept of segmentation.

Another constant theme among customers, employees, shareholders and societies is the desire for an ethical approach to business with greater social awareness and responsibility. The need for an ethical approach crucially resembles the need for a clear customer focus: it has to be genuine and felt throughout the organization. The understanding of behavior, people and relationships is now an established mainstay of modern business and is an area that has grown rapidly in credibility. Issues of trust, engagement, loyalty and connection have become increasingly relevant. Managing for the long-term as well as the short-term is another recurring theme. The case for developing relationships with customers and greater shareholder value through intangible assets (such as brands) is nothing new, but it has grown in relevance in the 21st century.

These inexorable shifts in business are clearly significant, but change is taking place in other areas as well, ranging from economics and politics to society and attitudes to the future. Of all the changes that are taking place, perhaps the one with the most significant implications for the future – and certainly the most striking – is the world's changing demography. At the time of Christ the global population has been estimated to have been around 150 million people, and it didn't reach one billion until around 1800. By 1900 it had grown to 1.6 billion, and by 2000 it had almost quadrupled to 6.1 billion. Incredibly, by 2011 it had reached 7 billion. In other words, in the 12 years from 2000 to 2011, global population rose by

900 million; a figure that the entire global growth in population from the time of Christ to the year 1800. These changes combine with a significant decline in mortality, increased international migration and the growth of urbanization.

In addition, the composition of households and family structures are changing in the developing world, with the result that the influence of women is increasing and consumption patterns are changing. The trend is for future populations to be older, and this will have considerable implications for businesses and governments. As if that weren't enough, urbanization is spreading like wildfire and in 2006, for the first time, the world's urban population exceeded its rural population.

Other forces shaping the future include tribalism, an ever-present aspect of the human condition that cannot be ignored. We need to recognize the implications of this and adapt our businesses accordingly. In addition, the innate universalism and interconnectedness that is present in many societies affects our response to sudden changes. For example, a sudden event or disaster such as a tsunami in Japan or a virus outbreak in Hong Kong could easily move markets and swiftly impact other issues, such as exchange rates, legal requirements and consumer spending.

The consequence of all these changes cannot be ignored. For many, many reasons, the only thing companies can be sure of is that things will change quickly. Adaptable processes and a flexible strategy will become the basic, essential requirements for the successful businesses of the future. It is in navigating this new, volatile business world that fortunes will be made or lost.

VOLATILITY AND CHANGE AT WORK

Changes in society as a whole are, of course, leaving an indelible mark on business and organizations. The last decade has been tumultuous by anyone's standards and it is understandable that so many leaders are feeling battered and are looking forward to the resumption of an easier time; a time when countering a hostile takeover was simple in comparison to facing financial meltdown and market turmoil. This would be a mistake. The fields of battle, both for today and the future, have been permanently redrawn. The harsh truth is that running a business is never going to be the same, and we all need to accept this fact and adapt. It is no longer enough to be the strongest or even the most intelligent: only those able to deal well with the vast array of changes, from constantly changing legal requirements to volatile markets, will survive and prosper. By definition, the survival of the fittest is the prosperity of the most adaptive companies.

IF YOU THOUGHT PREDICTING THE FUTURE WAS DIFFICULT, TRY IGNORING IT.

Dealing with volatility is no easy task. Investments are unreliable and usual sources of revenue are unpredictable. It is worth remembering that markets are not driven solely by cold, hard facts and, because of this inherent irrationality, cannot be predicted with any great accuracy. One only has to look at the price of crude oil to appreciate this. Despite a recession, crude oil jumped from a record high of $100 per barrel in January 2008 to $147 per barrel just a few months later. This may seem an arbitrary example but it matters because the price of oil affects so many other markets. As the high price of gas at the pump raises the end price of most other goods, it also affects consumers' reluctance (or inability) to spend. In addition to the usual assessment of facts and figures underlying this volatility is the human factor: investors are no different from the rest of us; they are influenced by hopes, ambitions, feelings, insecurities, fears and uncertainties. At best, we can make approximations and plan accordingly. However, we also need to prepare for the unexpected, as the unexpected is exactly that: it has a nasty habit of blindsiding even the strongest of companies and catching us off guard.

Of course, it seems trite to say that the world is changing: it always has and always will. But this statement is not as simple as it may seem as it comes with one very important caveat: if you don't adapt, and quickly, you will be left behind. Like the inattentive wildebeest at the back of the herd, the inevitable result of not paying attention is, to be frank, not going to be pretty.

This simple fact has caught out many leading businesses – firms such as Kodak, Bethlehem Steel, Chrysler, Daewoo, Firestone, Digital Equipment Corporation and others. In most of these cases, complacency and a commitment to the status quo escalated in a smooth, undisturbed fashion. The danger for any business is that their lack of awareness and connection to the outside world will increase gradually, incrementally and sometimes almost imperceptibly. This simple fact provides the foundation for most business difficulties. Firms that declined or failed simply did not do enough to understand or prepare for the future during the good times and suffered as a result. In retrospect, countless executives recognize that good is the enemy of great – meaning their firms were doing well, so they saw no reason to change. By the time they came to realize that the world around them had changed (notably customers, competitors and regulators and sometimes even their employees) it was too late to respond.

APPLE AND GOOGLE

If this talk of disaster seems distant or unlikely, then consider two issues. First, all businesses are affected by external views of the brand, and this can result from the action (or inaction) of only a few. Also, no one ever moved from good to great – or sustained leadership in their sector – by being complacent or failing to move with the times. Proving these points is the example of two giants of 21st century business: Apple and Google.

Apple

Apple is an iconic and rare business indeed, a technology business that is not only able to generate genuine passion among its customers but has come roaring back since being on the brink of near disaster in 1997. The renowned developer of the Apple Mac reinvented itself as a consumer electronics firm with the iPod and iPhone and is consistently ranked as one of the world's most innovative firms. The story of its rise has several lessons for aspiring innovators.

First, Apple uses an approach known as **network innovation** – this is the process of acquiring good ideas from outside the business as well as from within. For example, Apple has been described by *The Economist* as, "an orchestrator and integrator of technologies, unafraid to bring in ideas from outside but always adding its own twists." Highlighting this point is the development of the iPod. Originally conceived by an external consultant recruited to manage the project, the iPod was designed to work with Apple's iTunes software (which was itself acquired from outside and then overhauled) and was prototyped in-house. Network innovation is achieved by cultivating external expert contacts, constantly searching for new ideas and avoiding the 'not-invented-here' syndrome.

Next, Apple **emphasizes simplicity** – chiefly by designing the product around the needs of the user. When introducing technology the temptation is to overcomplicate, often with technical experts including technical enhancements that appeal to them. This introduces a layer of cleverness and complexity that may seem genius in theory but leaves customers cold. So, the iPod was not the first digital music player but it was the first to make buying, transferring and organizing music fun. Similarly the iPhone was not the first cell phone to include a music player, web browser and email, but it was the first to be simple, cool and highly appealing.

Apple's approach relies on its ability to **understand customers** – this is much more than 'user-centric' innovation or simply listening to customers. Apple believes that from time to time it is necessary to actually ignore what customers say they want today. This is clearly hazardous, but the risks can be reduced by understanding what customers value, how they typically work and what they want to achieve. It is important to innovate using a sophisticated approach to knowing your customers: understand them better today to predict what they will want tomorrow.

Fail wisely is another hallmark of Apple's approach to innovation. Failure is disappointing and far from ideal but it is also an opportunity to learn and, most important of all, it is inevitable.

Consequently, anyone worried about failure needs to get over it: we all fail at some time so it may as well be viewed positively. The alternative is, at best, staleness, timidity and incremental improvements – at worst, it can provoke blame, recrimination and a cycle of despair. For example, the iPhone resulted from the failure of Apple's original music phone developed with Motorola. Apple learned from its mistakes and tried again. The leadership challenge is to overcome the concerns that successful, talented employees may have about failure and to make sure that failure is not stigmatized. Instead, employees should persist with new ideas, secure in their own expertise, ability to learn and improve with the support of colleagues.

Google

Google is dominating the market for online searching and advertising. At times it is hard to discern which aspect of its business is most innovative: its ambition and ability to organize the world's information, or its commercial ability to make money from its services. In fact, both are vital and reflect an important feature of the business: Google's use of simple, clear directives. For example, paramount among these is the principle that information should be organized by analyzing users' intentions.

Several other factors underpin Google's remarkable rise and popularity.

Develop an infrastructure that is 'built to build.' Google has invested billions in its internet-based operating platform and its proprietary technology. This enables the business to guarantee service levels, respond to searches in fractions of seconds and swiftly develop new services. For users, Google's service is simple and highly effective. These advantages result from its infrastructure. There are several attributes of Google's infrastructure that aspiring innovators need to understand:

• Scalability – the business shares information globally to meet customers' changing demands. It also has another characteristic of world-class businesses: a willingness to take risks and invest heavily in proprietary technology (and nearly one million computers) to meet customers' needs.

• A fast product development cycle – Google engineers quickly develop prototypes and beta versions of products; those that are popular with users are then accelerated and emphasized, with Google's enormous computing capability making room for them. Testing and marketing follows next and are almost simultaneous. This creates a close, unique relationship with customers, who become part of the development team. It also relies on a confident, listening approach and the ability to act quickly.

• Support for mashups and new developments – Google has a flexible infrastructure described as 'an innovation hub' where third parties can share access and create new applications incorporating Google's functionality.

Few companies can match Google's massive infrastructure investments, but that misses the point: its can-do attitude and the way that resources are gathered, shared and organized is what makes Google successful, not simply its technology.

Control your world. Google's success and sheer size and ubiquity mean it dominates the industry. This fact, combined with its technology and flexible, sharing attitude, provides it with the ability to control its world. People come to it because they are the market leaders and Google responds by involving these third parties and customers in its business. It's almost as if the firm has learned from other business giants and is ensuring that their rapid growth does not mean they become complacent or out of touch. The lessons are clear: have the confidence to be open and share expertise with customers and other third parties as far as possible.

Recognize vulnerabilities and deliver the essentials. Clearly, there are several fundamentals that must be delivered by Google, not just for it to succeed but more accurately, to ensure it avoids failure. For example, the business needs to protect customers' data and preserve their trust. Innovation and dynamic, continuous improvement are vital but this needs to be balanced with an ability to execute and deliver the fundamentals.

Make time for innovation. Technical employees are required to spend 80 percent of their time on the core search and advertising businesses and 20 percent on technical projects of their choosing. New ideas are often generated from the bottom up by employees at Google. Their time is specifically allocated for innovation and the improvisational, empowering, can-do culture positively demands it.

Improvise and improve. People at Google have the authority to act on their own initiative and are encouraged to make improvements and to work on new developments. The result is that the firm is able to attract and retain driven people who enjoy improving and developing things and who value their freedom and autonomy. This situation then becomes a self-sustaining cycle: autonomy and empowerment lead to success and attract more talented people, and these people are then encouraged and empowered to succeed.

Finally, it can be argued that Google's greatest strength is its ability to **recognize the value of failure and chaos.** This is shown, most notably, in its approach to product development. Google releases a wide range of products with the expectation that some will become blockbusters. (Clearly, this also relies on an ability to spot and then maximize a blockbuster as soon as it appears.) This way of working provides valuable insights that can then be fed back into future developments. While this strategy may not be sustainable or even desirable in the long-term, it is resulting in an impressive array of new products and enhancements. Google's product development process has been described by *The Economist* as "frenzied and low friction." As well as directly resulting in new products, the creative frenzy also has the indirect benefit of building a culture that is not only innovative but also dynamic, well-informed and determined. That, it seems, is surely one of the most elusive innovations of all.

Many industries are replete with examples of newcomers that virtually or literally destroy incumbents. Whether you are a newcomer wanting to assert your dominance or an incumbent wanting to protect your position, in very quick order the battle line will inevitably be fought over the ability to adapt, survive and dominate. For example, technological changes have changed the playing field leading to new companies, such as Microsoft, Google and Facebook, coming to dominate markets and leaving older companies behind.

TO SUCCEED, INDIVIDUALS AND ORGANIZATIONS ARE BEST SERVED BY TAKING A BROAD, SYSTEMS APPROACH AND BALANCING THIS WITH A DEEP HUMAN UNDERSTANDING AND A PRACTICAL, 'CAN'DO' DESIRE TO MAKE THINGS HAPPEN. THAT'S WHAT WE MEAN WHEN WE SAY WE NEED TO THINK HOLISTICALLY BUT ACT PERSONALLY.

We do not live in a fair, equal world where we all have access to the same information and opportunities. But neither do we live in a world where we can rely on being the sole beneficiary of potentially lucrative information or market preferences. We must anticipate the unlikely, the unexpected and the unfair. We must be ready, perhaps despite being the current top dog, to deal with better competitors wanting to usurp us or new legislation that could undermine us. The only way forward, the only way to ensure our long-term survival, is to put in place the right processes, culture and leadership to equip us for the myriad of changes that our companies will have to deal with.

This may sound like an easy-to-achieve instruction. It isn't. Changing a whole company, from culture to logistics, is no small task, but is the only true means of survival for the companies of tomorrow. Leaders can no longer rely on the view that they have proven their worth. It is not an individual's reputation or ability that matters anymore: it is only a company's intrinsic, structural ability to adapt to change that counts.

THINK HOLISTICALLY, ACT PERSONALLY

So, why do companies persistently fail to adequately prepare for change when they know that change is such an inevitable, essential aspect of doing business? I would suggest that it is not because they are unaware of the constancy of volatility, ever-changing legal requirements and market conditions; it is more likely because they do not know how to best fit their companies for this new challenge.

There are some companies, however, that stay the course. In fact, there are those that thrive through the years: entities of every size in industries and geographies across the board that fend off challenges of all kinds. The insights from these firms are revealing as they suggest several actions that are needed to fortify your business. In other words, they highlight how to position your company for distinctive, long-running, profitable progress.

In summary, it's a matter of Rs. To be precise there are six Rs that, when used together, help businesses achieve their objective of sustained, gainful growth. These are explained in detail in later chapters but they are based on several key elements, including: focusing on the reason behind the business, generating and maximizing revenues, rousing people, developing a reputation, building business relationships and ensuring resilience.

Focusing on the reason

Everyone, at every level of the business, needs to understand the company's vision, values and mission. Taken together with other related issues such as its culture – the way things are done – and strategy, form the firm's reason for existence. If people explicitly understand these issues then they are much more likely to consistently pull together, and in the right direction.

Maximizing revenues

Every major business is a significant, long-term investment. Shaping and managing it requires the right strategy and the right structure. Keeping it fresh and vital requires a mix of entrepreneurial and innovative input. And all elements, including the tactics employed, must support the organization's mission, underlying values, and, of course, its growth.

Resources are also vitally important because these are needed to generate a return. That return can take various forms. In can be tangible or intangible, financial or non-financial. Each offers the promise of the same fundamental attribute: value. This can take the form of the ka-ching of a cash register or may be qualitative and socially oriented in character. The point is that value creation is central to an organization's growth and sustainability.

Rousing people

The next building block of corporate success is the ability to set the wheels of a business in motion so that it generates the necessary revenue and value. After all, strategy, structure, operations, what an organization stands for, and how it wishes to be perceived both inside and outside its walls, must resonate with its stakeholders. This happens by actively engaging and rousing people and the path is from the top down. Martha Maznevski, professor of organizational behavior at IMD (International Institute for Management Development) business school highlights this point, saying, "The leader's role is to create direction and meaning and to encourage autonomy. This requires clarity, curiosity and courage."

A responsible leader serves as the champion of an organization. This person is the one who articulates the right messages, supports the right postures and provides the funding for the organization to achieve its goals. This advocate provides an understanding of mission and brand and, most of all, ignites and excites stakeholders. This person sets the tone, guides activities and is the force to be known here as the Rouser.

Building reputation

Rolf Classon, former CEO of Bayer HealthCare, likes to talk about how to manage change in today's dynamic environment. He focuses his remarks on the major trends taking place worldwide. He closely follows that with comments on how the firm's partners and their teams can address these developments. In linking the two, he provides the context and content for another critical ingredient in the R growth mix: reputation. "Why do we use a preferred supplier? Because you know our industry and our issues. You continuously bring us ideas and perspectives that our organization would not come up with on our own. You deliver – and exceed – excellence in service. You help us and add to our success. At my company, you often need five signatures just to buy a chair. Thanks to your brand, I don't have to explain to my people why we should use you. You have earned our trust with your reputation."

Building relationships

What drives transactions in the B2B and B2C sectors? The 'B' letters used may give the impression that exchanges in the marketplace come about through brick and mortar, e-commerce, or some other inanimate object. That would be a mistake. It is people who generate receipts and ensure value creation. The best people build relationships, engage clients, share with them, take an interest in them and show it. When you know your clients and they know you and the good work you and your teams do, the result is a much greater willingness to remain loyal, buy more and improve your business. Our organization relies on people: the people who work here and those who receive our services.

Ensuring resilience

As this chapter has highlighted, the capacity of an organization to respond quickly and effectively to opportunities, threats and changes is vital – now, more than ever. This capacity or skill is the last of the six Rs: resilience. Organizations need to know how to handle both disaster and triumph.

In fact, these six Rs, Reason, Revenues, Rousers, Relationships, Reputation and Resilience, provide the foundation for developing high-performing businesses, brands and careers. Subsequent chapters present research-based evidence, experiences and examples to show why this works and how it can work for you and your business. Before exploring these issues in detail, the next chapter highlights several firms that have weathered the storms of business, as well as those that have merely managed to survive and others that have faded into business history. The point is simple: an illustrious history may be an asset, but it is absolutely no guarantee of future success. What is increasingly significant, however, is the ability to think holistically and act personally. This is the subject of the next chapter.

Chapter Two

Value at Work

"The nature of things has stamped upon corn a real value, which cannot be altered by merely altering its money price."

ADAM SMITH, *THE WEALTH OF NATIONS*

VALUE: WHAT IT MEANS ...

Having seen previously the way the world is changing, it is clear that there is an antidote that will help to sustain success through even the toughest of turbulent times: that is the ability to create value. In fact, as Adam Smith recognized, the ability to create value lies at the heart of successful business and commerce. For a price to be paid the object has to be valued; this underpins the theory of supply and demand that lies at the heart of market economics. Profitability requires that something is valued and this is increasingly provided by the uniqueness of knowledge. The more abundant the supply of a good or service, the lower its price will be, even to the extent that it may not be profitable to be produced and sold. Whereas the more scarce the supply (or when

"VALUE ISN'T THE NEXT BIG THING; IT'S THE ONLY THING ... THE PATH TO VALUE MAY NOT BE EASY, BUT IT SHOULD, AT LEAST, BE CLEAR."

***The Value Habit*, Deloitte**

competition is held back by barriers such as patents, expertise or other forms of knowledge), the more likely the good or service is to generate a profit. Where there are such barriers, the price of a good or service no longer relates directly to its cost of production but rather to its customer value, which in turn relates to its uniqueness or the costs that buyers would incur if the product were not available.

For example, in the pharmaceuticals industry, if there is a high demand for a product for which you have a patent and no alternative exists, the future is a lucrative one, even if the development costs have been high. This is the second point, recognized in the quote by Adam Smith: people and prevailing conditions, through the mechanism of the market, determine the value of something, and this value cannot be altered simply by changing the price. Organizations should therefore focus on those opportunities where they can create value and benefit from scarcity, keeping a special eye on the future.

... AND WHY IT MATTERS

Several other points about value are also vitally important:

- **Every company's mission is to create and protect value.** It is at the core of an organization's purpose and, potentially, it sets it apart from others. It is a source of competitive advantage and it generates profit.

- The way to create financial value in a business is simple, well-documented and unchanged since the days of Adam Smith: **the firm earns an appropriate return on the capital that has been provided.** In today's global environment, shareholder value and total shareholder return (TSR) are driven by market expectations of future cash flows, and these are based on the company's ability to sustain performance and grow over the long-term.

- Before we can build a profitable company that can secure sustainable growth, we need to consider how we are going to create value – **and value creation starts by understanding the purpose of the organization.**

SHAREHOLDERS PROVIDE THE CAPITAL. OTHERS MAXIMIZE ITS LONG-TERM VALUE.

So, the very first thing we must do is simply ask: why is the company here and what is it trying to achieve? Only by consciously and directly answering these questions is it possible to identify what the company needs to do to achieve its aims. A vague idea is not good enough. A company's success is completely dependent on a clear understanding of why it is there. This is why Reason is the first of the six Rs that we will be looking at in this book (see Chapter 4) – because when companies forget the reason why they exist, it is usually a good indicator that trouble is brewing. Those that don't lose sight of their purpose are better placed to know what they need to do to prosper.

What is significant, therefore, is the ability to create value – an issue that lies at the heart of this book. This chapter highlights several fundamental truths for firms that are creating value and weathering the storms of business.

FINDING YOUR PURPOSE

It is easy to frame business issues in terms of the activities that need to be done. While this is necessary, it is missing one key ingredient: purpose. Without knowing the purpose, it is highly likely that business plans and actions will miss the mark. Leaders need to step back from everything else, from all the day-to-day distractions and simply think. By this I mean spend some time deciding what your company is for – and then see all other business activities through this lens. By doing that, you will ensure everything from strategic development to managing operations, be correctly focused and aligned to deliver real value and growth and to build a strong, resilient and successful company.

Before you dismiss this as a waste of time, given the mountain of other more immediate tasks you have to attend to, consider the following point. All buildings are made of similar materials; knowing how to put them together relies on knowing two things: what the building is to be used for, and what you want the building to look like. Without knowing the purpose of the building, how would you know how to put all those building materials together correctly? This is why all business issues ultimately rest on the reason for its existence: it is the foundation on which the rest of the company is built.

Essentially, business is about maximizing profit – perpetually – and as we mentioned earlier, to achieve this, an organization has to offer something that other businesses or consumers want. Yet focusing on profit is only part of the equation. For some organizations, profit is not their primary focus and for others, such as charities, it is of little or no concern at all. By looking at the motivations of these not-for-profit companies, we will see how pivotal it is to know the purpose of the organization for achieving aims. This is something that the for-profit sector should learn from, ironically, in order to boost profits.

Although these organizations operate on a social rather than a profit-driven basis, they do seek to maximize something. In this regard, they are no different from their for-profit counterparts – they are both seeking to maximize their respective 'somethings.' In the case of not-for-profit entities that 'something' is the contribution they make to society. Of course money is a factor, as the more donations and revenue they raise and the better they manage their costs, the more benefit there will be for society. An interesting case that blends the approaches of charitable and for-profit sectors successfully is Grameen Bank. Significantly, their case reveals how much can be achieved by placing all business issues within the context of the organization's purpose, and this can be applied to any business in any sector.

GRAMEEN BANK

Working as an economist at Chittagong University in Bangladesh in the 1970s, Muhammad Yunus witnessed the extreme poverty people were living in. He could see that one of the major reasons for people being trapped in poverty was that either they had no access to credit or the rates charged were so high that it forced them to always live hand-to-mouth and be unable to grow their businesses or improve their standard of living.

The story began when Muhammad Yunus visited a poor village with his students. There, a woman who made bamboo stools explained how she had to borrow money to buy the bamboo and by the time she had paid back the loan after selling the stool, there was very little money left for her to live on – and this process continued over and over, as the woman could never get enough money to buy the bamboo without getting another expensive loan. It was clear that the exorbitant rates of interest being charged (often 10 percent per week) were preventing people from being able to rise out of poverty and build a secure future.

With no money to invest in their future, the cycle of poverty could never be broken. Yunus decided to use his own money and offer microloans at affordable rates so that people were able to keep more of the revenue, which enabled them to invest in the future, raise their standard of living and break the poverty cycle. The sums were very small, amounts that other banks would not have been interested in – small returns on small sums would be considered as not worth all the effort. Moreover, the loans were given to people that other banks would have dismissed as too great a risk – they had no reliable credit history, no collateral and no obvious means of paying the loans back (quite simply, banks believed poor people could not be trusted to repay the loans). Yet Yunus believed it could work; not only did he feel it was the right thing to do, he believed he could minimize the risks and run the business successfully. Other banks and even the government advised him not to pursue this route. He ignored them and, in 1983, formed the Grameen Bank – which means village bank.

The reason for founding Grameen Bank was to help poor people escape from poverty by providing small, long-term loans at low interest rates. Key to making this work was trust and knowing who to lend to and what conditions should be put in place. As a condition of taking a loan, borrowers were given financial advice. By insisting on this, it was more likely that ventures would be successful, which also minimized the risk to the bank. Yunus believed poor people could be trusted to manage their finances and he knew that it was the women who could be relied upon to run their business and personal affairs efficiently and responsibly and to repay loans. Another important reason for its success is solidarity: 95 percent of the bank is owned by the borrowers themselves, giving everyone a shared responsibility and commitment.

Today, the size of the bank is truly impressive: it has loaned over $9 billion through 2,564 branches to over 8 million borrowers in over 80,000 villages. Grameen has the highest rate of successful repayments – 97 percent of all loans are repaid. An important reason for this results from the fact that the bank mainly gives the loans to women (97 percent of the total). The bank is at the forefront of a world movement that aims to eradicate poverty through microlending, and its methods have now spread to projects in 58 nations, including developed countries such as the U.S., France and the Netherlands.

Grameen has enabled many families to cross the poverty line. In addition to business loans, it helps to improve people's lives in other ways. Housing loans have meant people have been able to build houses – almost 700,000 have been constructed. Loans for education have helped many to improve their chances of getting better jobs. Also, the bank awards educational scholarships to bright children – especially girls, as it is more difficult for them to get access to education in Bangladesh. The bank has been a helpline to millions of poor people, proving that microcredits work. These small loans made all the difference, as Yunus says; they facilitated that "spark of personal initiative and enterprise" that helps get people out of poverty.

The bank provides something that so many people desperately need. Although most years have been profitable, its main purpose is to create something more than money; it is to create a better society – and it certainly does that. Hardly surprising, then, that Muhammad Yunus is known as 'the banker of the poor': he was awarded the Nobel Peace Prize in 2006 for his work helping people to rise out of poverty.

The example of Grameen Bank highlights an important theme: the need for work to have meaning, which is increasingly significant and links with the fact that successful organizations have a clear purpose and create value. Grameen Bank also highlights the fact that issues of value and purpose are as relevant in the not-for-profit sector as they are in the commercial environment – and possibly more so.

So, how do organizations find their purpose?

Understand buyers' motivations

> "VALUE IS AT THE CORE OF AN ORGANIZATION'S BEING AND WHAT POTENTIALLY SETS IT APART FROM OTHERS."
>
> **Bob Dalton and Brent Wortman, *The Value Habit***

Whatever product or service you're selling, it is vitally important to know what the motive is for people to buy. The issues of motivation and behavior lie at the heart of creating value. It is the first place to start. Erich Joachimsthaler, Managing Director at Vivaldi Partners believes that: "People purchase a product or service for one basic reason. They expect it to improve their life. That's why they need to perceive the product/service as 'relevant'." He adds that a successful product adds something for the customer – perhaps, freeing up time, boosting confidence, solving an issue, raising status, improving efficiency and/or making tasks easier. Clearly, the decision to purchase arises from the sense that the product or service will enrich a person's existence in some way. In short, it delivers extra value.

Focus on customers

Success then, relies on a product's attributes of adding value for the customer. This has implications for developing new products and repositioning or redesigning existing ones: a company must consider how it adds value. Michael Raynor analyzes the relationship between new products and purchasing decisions and argues that when a product enriches someone's life, it represents a disruption from the past. This makes sense: if a product offers little extra advantage over what is already offered, then there would be no obvious reason for customers to choose that product over a competitor's. Consequently, businesses can capitalize on this by aiming to disrupt customers from what they are used to with products that break from the norm, thereby adding extra value to enrich their lives. Michael Raynor calls this 'disruptive innovation' (in *The Strategy Paradox*, Crown Business, 2007). He adds that, because the future is uncertain, companies should remain flexible by developing a range of options to prepare for different situations. A useful way to achieve this is through a deep dive. The benefits of this approach, as Michael Raynor points out, are that, "These problem-solving sessions tap the full potential of the existing business [and] identify actionable ideas to enter new realms [and] lead the way to the next wave of growth."

DISRUPTIVE INNOVATION AND DEEP DIVE PROTOTYPING

Disruptive Innovation

Disruptive innovation was first described in the 1997 best-selling business book, *The Innovator's Dilemma* by Clayton M. Christensen working with Michael E. Raynor of Deloitte. This work highlights two different types of innovation: sustaining and disruptive.

- **Sustaining innovations** can be incremental or radical and 'breakthrough' in nature, and they essentially improve performance for a customer in a specific market or segment. An example is the development of the car tire, which has provided steadily improving performance based around improvements in technology.

- **Disruptive innovations** are different: they manage to build a business on customer segments that are under-served or not served: groups that are either ignored or deemed unprofitable. This is possible because customers get left behind as the performance of a product improves since they either can't afford or simply don't value the 'improvements' in performance.

Examples of disruptive innovation include the development of different disk drives: with each successive generation disrupting the one that had gone before, as well as the telephone (which disrupted the telegraph), semiconductors (which disrupted vacuum tubes) and steamships (which disrupted sailing ships).

A classic example of disruptive innovation is provided by the copier industry in the 1960s and 1970s, with market leader Xerox providing large copier machines for use in the print rooms of major corporations or copy shops with teams of engineers servicing their machines. This was challenged by Japanese manufacturer Canon in the mid-1970s, who produced a copier for the mass market with cheap, replaceable parts. Small businesses and individuals who were previously unable to photocopy now had access to cheap, reliable photocopiers and that disrupted the industry. The disruption then spread to large firms as well, causing problems for Xerox.

There are several reasons for disruptive innovation and one crucial factor to understand is the concept of a value network. This is the context within which a firm operates. Notably, the way it responds to customers' needs, solves problems, reacts to competitors and increases profits. The firm's value network or approach matters for two main reasons.

- It can lead a business to 'listen too much' to its main customers. As a result, it will not recognize potentially disruptive innovations that serve only minor customers.
- Large companies will not be interested in small markets because they offer limited growth opportunities. Again, this leads companies to ignore a disruptive innovation or to wait until the market is 'large enough to be attractive.' That is when new entrants attack an incumbent's turf and by that time it is usually too late.

Deep Dive Prototyping

Deep dive prototyping supports disruptive innovation by adopting a team approach to generating ideas or solving specific problems or challenges. It uses the ideas of everyone in a team in a highly creative, focused and energetic way. A deep dive combines brainstorming and prototyping, where an initial potential solution is explored and developed.

In their book, *Virtuoso Teams: Lessons from teams that changed their worlds* (published by FT/Prentice Hall), management writers Andy Boynton and Bill Fischer highlight the different stages involved in deep dive prototyping:

- Understand the main issues – these usually include customers and technology – as well as any constraints.
- Observe customers: how do they approach issues, what are they after and how do they buy?
- Synthesize the themes from the first two phases.
- Frenzy – this involves intensive brainstorming and discussion, as well as visualizing new concepts and ideas around the main themes.
- Prototyping is the next stage, building and further developing an idea.
- Refine and streamline your ideas. Again, brainstorm ways to improve the prototype and overcome obstacles and narrow and focus your concepts. Evaluate and prioritize your ideas and decide how they will be implemented.

Embrace uncertainty and change

The next stage in finding a purpose is to remember the two things we know for certain about the future: it will be different and it will surprise. The key is to recognize how uncertainty creates strategic advantage: it acts as a launching pad for new growth. Many things get in the way of businesses being able to respond well to change, not least, the lack of data at hand to help guide the correct course of action. If companies don't maintain correct information, don't look for signs of change or have never thought about how to deal with possible scenarios, they will be limited in their ability to remain profitable or even survive at all. This is where the right mindset is critical.

In *Marketing Under Uncertainty: The Logic of an Effectual Approach,*[1] Stuart Read and his colleagues point to one group of people with the right mindset to deal successfully with change. He calls them expert entrepreneurs. Unlike others, expert entrepreneurs are always well-positioned and have the flexibility to swing into action and capitalize on the unexpected. As Read explains, "Uncertainty unleashes their imagination, which promotes innovation and new opportunities. They operate on the basis of 'effectuation.' This form of reasoning and set of problem-solving skills runs counter to 'causation,' which is the process most of us rely on."

Understand the difference between cause and effect

When it comes to embracing uncertainty and change, it helps to appreciate the difference between cause and effect.

- Causation means 'if I can predict the future, I can control it.'
- Effectuation means 'if I can control the future, I don't need to predict it.'

CAUSATION IS THE WAY MOST OF US MAKE DECISIONS, WHICH IS BY TRYING TO PREDICT THE FUTURE. 'EXPERT ENTREPRENEURS' OPERATE IN A DIFFERENT WAY, VIA EFFECTUATION.

Most people make decisions using causation, where they try to determine the best course of action – that is, they try to get control of the future by predicting it. Expert entrepreneurs, however, use effectuation, where they take action based on what they know, who they know and the resources they have available rather than by analyzing optimal courses of action. They evaluate opportunities based on whether the risk of the downside is acceptable rather than on the attractiveness of the predicted upside. For these people, they are confident that they can control the future so there is no need to predict it.

CREATING VALUE

Clearly, establishing a purpose is an essential first step to creating value. Creating value is the lifeblood of organizations and is pivotal to the premise of this book. It is not hard to see why. Value is what connects you to your customers and differentiates you from competitors; it builds confidence among all stakeholders and secures the company's long-term growth. As Deloitte's Bob Dalton and Brent Wortman note, "Every company's mission is to create and protect value, but some clearly do a better job of it than others. Value is at the core of an organization's being and what potentially sets it apart from others." Yet this raises a fundamental question: what is value? Without knowing this, how do we know where to focus our efforts?

> CALL IT WHAT YOU WILL OR LOOK AT IT FROM ANY PERSPECTIVE, SUCCESSFUL ORGANIZATIONS DO SOMETHING POWERFUL: THEY DELIVER VALUE.

The Enterprise Value Map

Companies are about making money; they are about providing a healthy return on investment – all investments including time and effort, as well as money. This is not always straightforward, as value is affected by so many things. Still, we can understand its importance if we look at shareholder return. The return shareholders ultimately get will be affected by how the business is expected to perform in the future, which means that it is imperative for companies to demonstrate that they will perform well and grow. This is achieved through four primary levers on The Enterprise Value Map:

1. Revenue growth

2. Operating margin

3. Asset efficiency

4. Expectations

Figure 2.1: Deloitte's Enterprise Value Map

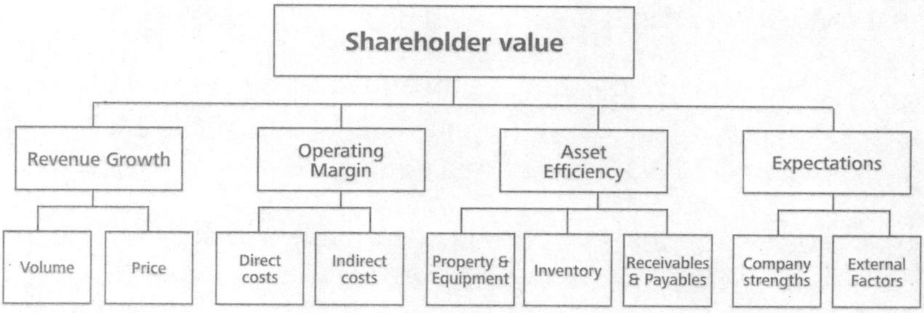

Figure 2.1 highlights how critical creating value is to the long-term growth of a company. Just how critical is emphasized by Bob Dalton and Brent Wortman, "Value isn't the next big thing; it's the only thing." Often, this is not an easy thing to achieve but is an essential task. By assessing your company through the different techniques available – from deep dives to The Enterprise Value Map – and having the right mindset, you will be better able to steer your company toward a successful future. Most importantly, we have to remember that these are not one-off exercises. There is a reason that Bob Dalton and Brent Wortman called their book *The Value Habit*: creating value is a constant requirement.

THE PATH TO VALUE MAY NOT BE EASY, BUT IT SHOULD, AT LEAST, BE CLEAR

Value-creating behaviors

Creating value is a huge topic. It is complex: prone to subjective judgments, easily and swiftly eradicated and subject to unexpected fortunes – both good and bad. It is also manageable; we have the skills and ability to stay in charge and direct our fortunes. There are common attributes that we can follow to help us deliver value and secure long-term success. Several simple, value-creating behaviors that can become habits are:

- Connecting vision, strategy and business processes with what is needed to succeed – putting mechanisms in place to ensure that people work toward the same goal.
- Positioning the company to deal with a range of possible futures, and then being able to hone in on what is needed when a particular future arrives.
- Aligning the range of initiatives with the company's overall objectives and strategies.
- Inspiring the actions you want by leading others appropriately.
- Focusing on the connections between stakeholders that will create value.
- Using the strategies, and their value drivers, to present a credible picture of where the company is headed.
- Making value creation central to evaluating and managing people and to determining how performance is rewarded.
- Appointing one person to align strategies, actions and performance management.

It's useful at this point to return to the issue of shareholder value and stakeholders. In 1986, 'shareholder value' entered the business lexicon with the publication of Alfred Rappaport's book *Creating Shareholder Value* (Free Press, 1997). This term referred to the overriding need to provide those who invest in a company with a higher return than they might have earned in other ways (such as investing in a savings account). The idea focused on long-term gains not limited to the price of shares; it reflected, in essence, The Enterprise Value Map.

From stakeholder analysis to the value constellation

Shareholders are not the only ones that an organization has a vested interest in. All stakeholders count. For example, employees are major stakeholders. Businesses of all kinds want to attract and retain the top talent on the market, and employee attitude has a direct impact on customers and consequently, the success of the company. The same principle applies to customers, suppliers and distributors and even includes the media, special interest groups, regulators and numerous others. Who creates value in this multi-faceted domain? That depends upon where you look and who you ask. Michael E. Porter suggests, "Look to the value chain for the answer." He presented the value-chain theory in *Competitive Advantage: Creating and Sustaining Superior Performance* (Free Press, 1985). The value chain consists of a series of linked value-adding activities, starting with suppliers and extending to end users.

It is time to revisit the value chain. With the passing of time and other influences, points of view about value creation have grown more complex. So have the number of players, their roles and the directional signals that move within the organization between the company and external parties as well as those between others outside the organization. The value chain soon became the value network, and the journey did not stop there. A newer mechanism has introduced even more complexity, paths and participants. From value chain to value network, we have now arrived at the value constellation.

The value constellation looks at value creation differently. Instead of developing products for customers, it develops products with them. Really, this is the natural extension of the recent focus on stakeholders. By viewing customers as stakeholders, it makes sense to consider them 'partners' and listen to their ideas and preferences when developing products and devising strategy. Add to these customers

THE VALUE CONSTELLATION LOOKS AT VALUE CREATION DIFFERENTLY. INSTEAD OF DEVELOPING PRODUCTS FOR CUSTOMERS, IT DEVELOPS PRODUCTS WITH THEM.

all the other stakeholders, and product development is best seen as many points that interact and link that if used properly, is capable of creating something of even greater value. As Stefan Michel, professor of marketing at IMD, explains, "Stakeholders in the largest sense, such as allies, business partners, the media, regulators, suppliers and customers, serve as resources. They band together. They interact. Through their exchanges, they identify unrecognized and unmet needs. This, in turn, leads to integrated solutions with their own value propositions. Value is not produced – it's co-produced.

Value constellations extend the potential to innovate and deliver breakthroughs. I see it as the future of marketing."

Figure 2.2: From Value Chains to Value Constellations

Classical Michael Porter's Value Chain

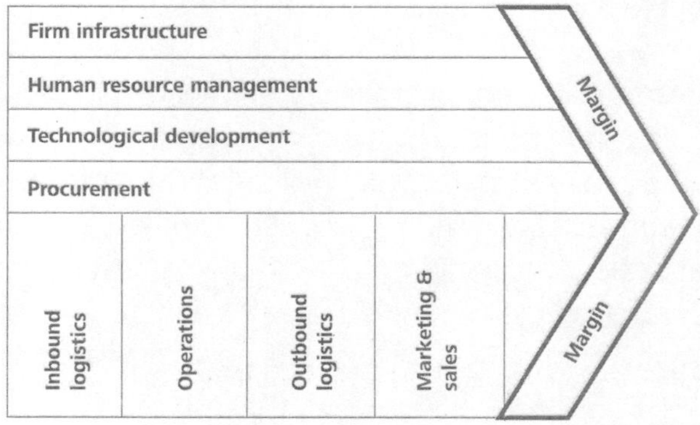

Procter & Gamble's innovation platform Connect and Develop

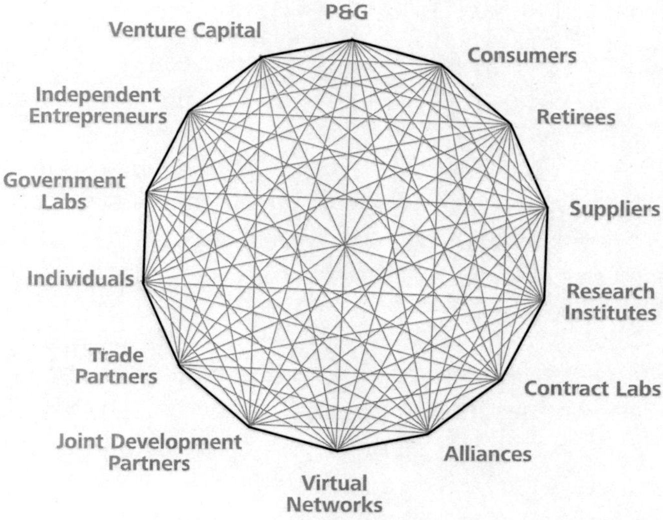

Creating value has to be seen in terms of its impact and significance for all business activities. This is highlighted by an assessment of the qualities that equip a company for long-term success. These include:

- Using a rousing vision and values that inspire.
- Possessing a clear and compelling strategy.
- Being consistent.
- Segmenting markets and brands.
- Being innovative.
- Ensuring employee enthusiasm, and always …
- … Controlling costs.

Significantly, successful companies are defined by their focus on stakeholders and their desire to create outstanding customer value.

Value creation requires leadership

So what can we take away from all of this?

- Value is tangible and can be calculated through a host of financial performance metrics.
- Value is also intangible, where other factors, from brand and corporate social responsibility to developing customer relationships and managing the press, inevitably impact on the real worth of a product in the market.

It is tempting when discussing value and value creation to focus on financial issues, and certainly no one denies the power of financial performance or the importance of financial data. Clearly, good financial performance is a prerequisite if a company is to prosper. However, there is growing recognition that other drivers need to be taken into account when running a company for the long-term, and that these factors are not necessarily captured in the profit-and-loss statement. Of course, this makes the leader's task more difficult: the challenge is to measure and manage something that is, at best, hard to quantify but is so vital that it can't be ignored. The challenge of leadership is an issue that we will return to throughout this book. For now, we will take a brief look at the new information and measures we need to assess those business activities that add the greatest value.

THE NEW BOTTOM LINE: QUALITY, SUSTAINABILITY AND DECENCY

It is clear that successful organizations create both tangible and intangible value. What's more, they manage value creation carefully – very carefully. How do they do this? They focus on generating quality in all things they do, including environmental sustainability and responsible business practices. These are not random terms; they are what customers and other stakeholders increasingly care about. They are the cornerstones of the United National Global Compact, launched in July 2000, which seeks the support of companies to eliminate human rights abuses and corruption and to promote environmental responsibility and decent standards in the workplace. No wonder, then, that they appear in so many organizations' vision and mission statements. Such considerations are now an integral part of business, as they create an intangible value for stakeholders.

As the 20th century passed into the 21st, big business began to spread its wings. Advances in technology served as enablers. Demographic changes were drivers as were economic and regulatory considerations. Companies set their sights on operations in lands far beyond their usual horizon. They globalized – and as they set up shop around the world, activities and practices abroad were highlighted back home. The transparency of business activities has meant companies can no longer afford to focus on short-term gains to the exclusion of all other considerations. Today, the business agenda has to be much broader in its scope – it's what people expect, and transgressions can be swiftly punished.

"WE NEED BUSINESS TO GIVE PRACTICAL MEANING AND REACH TO THE VALUES AND PRINCIPLES THAT CONNECT CULTURES AND PEOPLE EVERYWHERE."

Ban Ki-moon, Secretary-General of the United Nations

This new emphasis has given rise to another way of looking at financial measures. A theoretical, multiple bottom line brings new measures to the fore, assessing more intangible benefits and revealing where companies really create value. This in no way diminishes the importance of traditional financial standards.

However, it is much more useful as it extends the bottom line from a narrow focus to encompass three dimensions of performance. By incorporating more data and taking such a wide-angled view of the economic landscape, this 'triple bottom line' better informs companies about value creation.

The triple bottom line targets three areas of value creation: People, Planet and Profit. This covers a wide area, which is certainly a challenge for any business to deal with. However, by constantly

"WHEN EACH OF THESE THREE ELEMENTS OF VISION – CONCERN FOR EXCELLENCE, FOR PEOPLE, AND FOR THE WIDER ENVIRONMENT – IS PRESENT, BUSINESS IS TRANSFORMED FROM A TOOL FOR MAKING PROFITS INTO A CREATIVE, HUMANE EXPERIMENT FOR IMPROVING LIFE."

Mihaly Csikszentmihalyi, ***Good Business: Leadership, Flow and the Making of Meaning***

evaluating and planning activities through each of the human, natural and financial perspectives, companies will be better-informed and well-positioned. Significantly, when an organization generates capital along all three planes, it will optimize its ability to deliver value and to secure prolonged, meaningful growth.

Delivering value requires many skills and it demands keen insight across all business issues. In the past, a piecemeal, ad hoc approach to adding value may have sufficed, but this is no longer the case. To realize their full potential, companies need to have a holistic approach, where all business activities are seen through the lens of value. This isn't an option; it is the new reality, and we must be ready. The future is all about value creation. Having explained the significance of value creation – what it means, why it matters and where to focus – we now look at how to make it happen in your organization: a challenge that requires the six Rs.

Chapter Three

Introducing the Six Rs

"I believe that for every headwind we confront, there's an equally powerful tailwind to be ridden. The trick is finding it."

MUHTAR KENT, CHAIRMAN AND CEO, COCA-COLA

This advice, from Muhtar Kent, sums up the combination of optimism and realism that drive the most successful companies. The challenges we face in business today are immense, complex and unremitting and require a great deal of skill and energy. Tackling them all is certainly not an easy task. However, by equipping ourselves with the right approach and capabilities, we will be better placed to find that powerful tailwind.

"WHETHER YOU THINK YOU CAN OR WHETHER YOU THINK YOU CAN'T, YOU'RE RIGHT!"

Henry Ford

This chapter introduces the six techniques for successfully building a business, brand and career. These are the six Rs: **Reason, Revenue, Rousers, Reputation, Relationships** and **Resilience.** We will explain why it is important to remember the purpose of the company and to stick to your convictions and never forget the reason you are in business. Generating and maximizing revenues are the engines that drives any business; they are what enable plans to happen. This may seem obvious but time and again, companies do not pay enough attention to these critical aspects of running a business.

The impact of inspiring and rousing people cannot be overstated. Motivation, commitment and support, along with an array of other benefits, all spring from this ability. Building relationships underpins every aspect of running a business, from employee engagement to customer retention. As such, it should be an integral part of guiding all business activities and decisions. Companies can rise or fall on the strength of their reputation, and managing this area requires constant vigilance. In these turbulent times, forging resilient companies is now the number one job for all leaders. Most importantly, these six Rs do not operate in isolation. They are complementary; each supports and mutually reinforces the other. Think of them as part of a holistic framework to help you create value, competitive advantage and sustainable growth.

THE SIX Rs EXPLAINED

The following chapters explore the six Rs in detail. Before we embark on that journey, however, it is useful to first have a brief definition of each one.

Reason

The intention and values of a company must be defined clearly. These values and purpose have to be communicated to employees in order to gain commitment and to ensure your people know they are an important part of the company and that its success relies on them. Everyone, at every level, must understand the company's vision and mission.

Gain commitment for the company's values: When the intention of the company is shared by its workers, their commitment will go a long way in achieving your objectives. To do this, it is useful to encourage participation and actively seek the opinions and new ideas of your employees at all levels. Motivation strategies and compensation, such as economic incentives, recognition or promotion, will also secure commitment.

Always consider the company's values and mission at each stage of pursuing goals: Implementing the company's reason, goals and values is divided into three phases. First, define both the short-term and long-term objectives. Second, communicate the strategic plan to employees so that they understand and share the objectives and so that they will deliver the required results. Third, evaluate and monitor peoples' alignment to the objectives and take action to realign, if necessary.

SUCCESSFULLY BUILDING A BUSINESS RELIES ON THE SIX Rs: REASON, REVENUE, ROUSERS, REPUTATION, RELATIONSHIPS AND RESILIENCE.

Offer the right product or services: The type of product or services your company offers should complement the reason why it is in business. Similarly, the segments you operate in and the quality of your offer should also fit with your company's purpose. This ensures that different aspects of your business work together and do not confuse your strategy, your customers or your employees.

Revenue

Revenue covers a variety of company assets, including financial capital, structural capital, and its portfolio of clients. Examples of financial capital are a company's EBITDA (their Earnings Before Interest, Taxation, Depreciation and Amortization), income and debtors (the money owed to the company). The indicators you choose for assessing the state of revenue will depend on your company's particular situation. Generally speaking, finance is an excellent indicator of the health of the company. It is not the only indicator of health but it is clearly essential for continued survival and prosperity. In fact, there are many elements to a company's structural assets, including the firm's knowledge, information systems, management style and other elements. Essentially, the structural assets are what are left when everyone leaves at the end of the day. They are vital if the firm is to leverage capabilities, intellectual capital and reputation, take advantage of opportunities and provide a solid platform from which to transform an entire company.

Also, the company's client portfolio should not be overlooked when it comes to assessing revenues. Valuable clients make for a highly valued company. Moreover, if your portfolio of clients is strong, it is a good sign that you are already performing well across all of the six Rs. However, this situation should not breed complacency. Many companies have failed by sticking with a backward-looking, historic approach that favors business as usual, fails to notice signs of change or emerging challenges or simply takes their customers for granted.

Rouser

THE COMPANY'S CLIENT PORTFOLIO SHOULD NOT BE OVERLOOKED WHEN IT COMES TO ASSESSING REVENUES. IF THE PORTFOLIO OF CLIENTS IS STRONG THEN IT IS A GOOD SIGN THAT THE FIRM IS PERFORMING WELL ACROSS ALL OF THE SIX Rs.

Being a rouser means inspiring, motivating and gaining the commitment of people for the company's mission and objectives. It lies at the heart of leadership because it is about bringing people along with you to achieve the company's goals. So, what do rousers do and how can they increase commitment to their plans? The answer is by succeeding in several areas.

Focus on achieving results

You should be goal oriented, improve the efficiency of processes and quality of products and services, make sure plans are sustainable and convey the stability of the company to employees. This requires openness, trust and honesty, making the company's results visible to everyone.

Engage others and gain commitment to achieving common objectives

A key skill for a rouser is to ensure that everyone's efforts are aligned. For this reason, the global strategy of the company must be accepted at all levels in the organization. The level of commitment among leaders is especially significant here, as they are in positions to influence the efforts and commitment of others. Conversely, leaders are the ones with the greatest capacity to jeopardize plans if they fail to obtain the employees' commitment for achieving common objectives.

Increase the company's ability to adapt

As we have already seen, there are two things we can say for certain about the future: it will be different and it will surprise. Companies therefore need to update the way they work and the products and services they deliver. In addition, the lifespan of products and services is becoming increasingly shorter and shorter, requiring companies to innovative more rapidly and be ready to respond immediately to new products from other companies. This means that leaders need to motivate their people to accept change and to reorient to new situations quickly. This is achieved by instilling new behaviors and attitudes into the culture of the organization. Therefore, a rouser should encourage people to be adaptable and they should also empower them to be proactive.

Instill an innovative approach

Rousers are not only innovative themselves: they also encourage others to be innovative. This means keeping an eye on what is happening in the business environment and the world at large. It also involves looking to the future, anticipating trends and identifying and creating opportunities to help the company achieve future success.

Reputation

Reputation is an issue that applies both internally – within the organization – and externally. What employees think of the company influences their level of motivation, engagement and commitment. Externally, your reputation among customers, suppliers, retailers, the media, government and public bodies

> "TO THINK IS EASY. TO ACT IS DIFFICULT. TO ACT AS ONE THINKS IS THE MOST DIFFICULT."
>
> **Johann Wolfgang von Goethe**

will all affect both short- and long-term profitability. Factors that come into play include: people's perception of your products and services, the company's perceived 'trajectory' (whether it is felt to be going in the right direction), word-of-mouth, as well as other sources of influence and information. An excellent reputation provides the organization with considerable competitive advantage as it strongly influences customers' preferences. In addition, a strong reputation increases the value of shares and the firm's appeal to investors.

Although a reputation is fairly consistent, an organization can have different reputations with different segments or groups. These include:

- **Employees.** The reputation or 'employer brand' that the company has with its own people greatly influences their productivity. In addition, employees with a positive view of the company have much greater confidence in the future, which in turn improves employee retention. Of course the conditions of work, compensation and recognition are all important in this regard, but other factors matter too – such as the desire to work for a company that is valued by others outside the organization and, increasingly, that it has a sound reputation for corporate social responsibility.

AN EXCELLENT REPUTATION PROVIDES THE ORGANIZATION WITH CONSIDERABLE COMPETITIVE ADVANTAGE AS IT STRONGLY INFLUENCES CUSTOMERS' PREFERENCES. IN THE WORDS OF WARREN BUFFETT, "IT TAKES TWENTY YEARS TO BUILD A REPUTATION AND FIVE MINUTES TO RUIN IT. IF YOU THINK ABOUT THAT, YOU'LL DO THINGS DIFFERENTLY."

- **Clients.** If a company is valued by its clients it increases the likelihood of retaining them as customers for existing products, and it gives the opportunity to sell further products. Also, satisfied customers are more likely to recommend your company to others. Reputation is particularly important in the service industry.

- **Investors.** Reputation is keenly watched by current and prospective investors. Investors will be more willing to invest in a company that has their confidence, and this is invariably because of a strong reputation in several areas, including popularity among customers and clients, vision, stability, appropriate attitude to risk, integrity and sound leadership.
- **Opinion leaders.** In the words of the legendary investor Warren Buffett, "It takes twenty years to build a reputation and five minutes to ruin it. If you think about that, you'll do things differently." This is never truer than in the case of opinion formers and influencers. Given their powerful position to influence others, it is essential that an organization maintains a good reputation with them.

Relationships

All business relationships, both internal and external, are connected with each other. In terms of the whole company, you could no more separate the parts than you could separate a stem from a flower – the whole plant clearly needs both parts. The quality of relationships is a very real asset of the company. The learning, generation of knowledge, improvements and innovations that result from good relationships all contribute to the bottom line.

Internal relations take place between people at all levels within the company. When there is rapport, trust and agreement between employers and employees, it improves the quality of internal relationships and increases the flow of communication.

External relations with clients, suppliers, public and governmental bodies, shareholders, influencers and the media help with creating and sharing knowledge, detecting new opportunities, innovating, improving products and reputation and building customer loyalty. Relations can be at the institutional and group level but they often operate at the individual person-to-person level as well. Relationship capital considerably increases the value of the company.

Resilience

Resilience is the capacity of an organization to respond quickly and effectively to opportunities, threats and changes. Ideally, resilience enables a company to take control and direct its own future before problems occur.

RESILIENCE IS THE CAPACITY OF AN ORGANIZATION TO RESPOND QUICKLY AND EFFECTIVELY TO OPPORTUNITIES, THREATS AND CHANGES.

Learning is a key part of resilience, as the lessons from experiencing difficulties will strengthen your ability to tackle future problems. Resilience needs to be instilled throughout the organization: from its culture and capabilities to its operational decisions and strategic development.

Two key questions can be used to evaluate an organization's resilience:

- **Are the right procedures in place before problems occur?** It is important to develop a business continuity plan to ensure that critical functions adapt successfully to change. Having the right procedures in place and ensuring that they are understood and followed will help to maintain stability, avoid panic and give employees the ability to suggest new ideas.

- **Do you have a culture that emphasizes overcoming problems and that encourages continuous improvement?** The number of crises that an organization successfully overcomes will affect its level of resilience. Organizations with a high level of resilience develop a culture of continuous improvement and innovation, which helps for resolving future problems and for confronting new challenges.

CONNECTING THE SIX Rs

Figure 3.1: Causal diagram

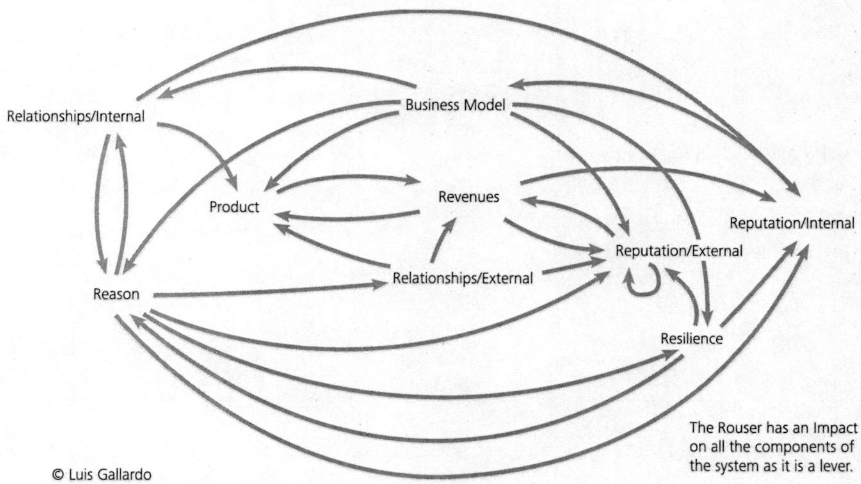

© Luis Gallardo

In figure 3.1 we can see the existing relationships between the different elements. This highlights the fact that the six Rs are best viewed as a whole; they form a complete tool box for running a business. This holistic approach is necessary for dealing with the complexity of doing business in a fast-changing and diverse world. While teamwork has been the hallmark of successful businesses in the last twenty years, such efforts are merely the forerunner of the next round in commercial enterprise. The future requires us to act holistically: no ifs or buts. This task is not an option, it is essential. Survival depends on it as does prosperity. We shall come back to this point in Chapter 10 when we discuss our our THAP framework - how to Think Holistically, Act Personally.

The six Rs …	… and how they connect and support each other
Reason Reason is the most fundamental part of any organization. Why all the other Rs must come together in pursuit of Reason and why this R supports all the others is understandable: it is the raison d'être, the very soul of a company, without which the company would be directionless. Clearly, this matters enormously. Everything springs from intention – it sets the tone for the whole business.	• Reputation and Relationships are led by a company's Reason. • Resilience is strengthened through strong corporate values and commitment to its purpose. • Revenues increase when everyone is dedicated to the fulfillment of objectives as well as being motivated by the company's mission statement and values (Rouser).
Revenues The financial capital of a company includes its portfolio of clients. To improve this portfolio and increase income, the other variables in our six R list must work together, mutually reinforcing each other.	• Revenues are affected by the level of Resilience. Fortunes can be wiped out or made, depending on a company's ability to respond effectively to changes, threats and opportunities. • Internal and external Relationships both have a considerable impact on revenues. For example, improving external relationships with clients, investors and suppliers is critical to increasing income and managing costs. • The Reputation of your company and how it is perceived by customers and others has a direct impact on revenue by affecting income and even costs.

	For example, your reputation with suppliers (which is also affected by their perception of your reputation with yourclients) can make a significant difference to the terms they are willing to agree to. A good reputation enables you to increase the number of customers, in part through word-of-mouth and recommendations. Also, a good reputation motivates and engages your people, who are then more likely to perform better and increase revenue. • In addition to having a popular product, customers are drawn to other factors in a company, including its Reason. Here, the purpose and values of a company have an impact on customers' decisions to buy. • In Rouser terms, inspiring and motivating others and gaining buy-in to the company's objectives sets the stage for increasing revenue, achieving goals and managing costs. Also, by empowering people, you will encourage greater participation, engagement and the generation of useful opinions and ideas, which will improve operations and strategy – and, consequently, revenues.

<table>
<tr>
<td>

Rouser

Rouser involves being goal oriented, committed to common objectives, being adaptable, innovative and seeking the opinions of others. It requires inner strength and encouraging this strength in others.

</td>
<td>

Inspiring people to follow you in pursuit of the company's mission is a key part of what a leader must do – especially during turbulent, insecure times. Leadership will also:

- Improve the level of commitment to corporate values (Reason);
- Enhance the company's Reputation (especially internally);
- Promote good Relationships and …
- … increase Revenues.

Acquiring experience and developing Resilience will enhance the ability to lead others, while excellent leadership skills will build the resilience of the whole company.

</td>
</tr>
<tr>
<td>

Reputation

Reputation operates at an internal level, affecting your own people, as well as externally affecting clients, investors and opinion leaders and others. Clearly, internal reputation is affected by (and also affects) the other Rs.

</td>
<td>

- Internal reputation is influenced by:
    - Compensation, incentives, and employee engagement (Relationships).
    - Commitment to corporate values (Reason).
    - The financial capital and portfolio of clients (Revenues).
- Resilience will increase employees' confidence in the company, improving reputation further.
- Being able to gain commitment to corporate objectives and having an inclusive, positive working environment (Rouser) will enhance the company's reputation.
- As well as being influenced by the quality of internal relationships, these factors also influence external reputation in their own right. Significantly, Revenues are highly susceptible to external reputation.

</td>
</tr>
</table>

Relationships Relationships are divided into internal and external relations. As well as affecting the other Rs, they also affect each other. For example, customer perceptions of the company motivate employees, while engaged employees improve the service to customers.	Leading others well (Rouser) and having a strong corporate mission and values (Reason), will lead to good internal relationships – as well as with other stakeholders. Good relationships with all internal and external stakeholders will improve the company's Reputation and increase Revenues. Strong relationships also build Resilience, as they insulate the company against threats, ensure the whole company pulls together and provide a source of innovation.
Resilience Resilience has to be a total, company-wide activity, which means that it calls on capabilities in all aspects of the business. Resilience should operate at a personal, team and company level, which requires all six Rs to support each other. When all six Rs work well together, not only is a company ideally placed to cope with problems, it is in a position to fix things before they actually break, circumvent threats and take advantage of opportunities.	• Clearly, Resilience and Revenues are interdependent, as revenue is the engine of the business. • The level of commitment to corporative values (Reason) bolsters resilience, as does a culture of adaptability, securing employee engagement and inspiring people (Rouser). • For a company to be resilient, excellent Relationships and Reputation are critical to coping with adversity or change.

SUCCEEDING WITH THE SIX Rs

The six Rs provide a great way to assess the health of your business and the areas of strength and weakness, but for this approach to succeed you need to look at each element in greater detail, something we do in the following chapters. For now, one question dominates: what are the implications of the six Rs for you, your team and your business?

"WHERE THERE IS AN OPEN MIND, THERE WILL ALWAYS BE A FRONTIER."

Charles F. Kettering

With good reason

There is a very good reason why we start with Reason: it underpins everything else – all activities, all strategies, how stakeholders view us, employee engagement and customer loyalty. Our values and purpose should permeate throughout the organization. Employee engagement depends on it and your reputation lives or dies because of it. The reach of your purpose and corporate values is immense, and they have the power to deliver profitable growth or ignominious demise. Customers, employees, investors and other stakeholders will assess what you are offering and judge you accordingly.

As we shall see, what you stand for, as a company, has a critical impact on your fortunes. News travels fast and it may not be the news that you were hoping for. Success demands that we anticipate and stay ahead of ideas and trends. We must remain alert to what matters to customers and adapt accordingly. It is not enough to have an idea of what we value, it is important for these values to coincide with the values that accord with the values of the times. I do not mean to suggest that we should be manipulative, since genuine beliefs are the hallmark of successful companies; rather, I am suggesting that we should evaluate the situation, reassess our values and consider what matters to people – employees, customers and to the world. As we acquire new ideas our perceptions and beliefs change. We should take a big picture view: the world is changing and we should be on the same page and orient our businesses to account for new ideas, new thinking and new demands.

A company's mission is the focal point of all business activities. It is what drives motivation and commitment; it is what draws customers to your brand. While values and mission statements must be genuine, they must also be responsive to change. After all, business is a total, all-consuming enterprise. As such, it is easy to see how important it is to have your company's values and purpose influence every other part of your business. This focus is critical to keeping your company on track. By focusing on your goals, and assuring the commitment of your people to them, you will be better placed to keep your company on the trajectory that will realize these goals. To maintain the course you have set, communicating these ideas to your people and securing buy-in is crucial. This is not easy: it demands a great deal of energy and acumen, but the rewards are similarly great.

Our ambitions for our companies are rooted in our values and beliefs. These are what direct the company's route to success. In the past, we may have focused exclusively on generating profits at all cost. Today, we face a very different scenario: profits result from having the right values. Without the right values, companies will miss the mark and suffer accordingly.

Companies need to encourage participation amongst employees and current and potential customers. This will help to secure employee commitment and generate innovative ideas that could take your company further. Given the impact of your motives on reputation, you should make sure that everything your company does accurately portrays your company in the way that you want. After all, reason supports the other six Rs and the other six Rs support it. This is understandable, as reason is the spark that ignites all other activities.

Re-energizing revenues

> "THE ENEMY OF THE TRUTH IS VERY OFTEN NOT THE LIE – DELIBERATE, CONTRIVED, AND DISHONEST – BUT THE MYTH: PERSISTENT, PERSUASIVE, AND UNREALISTIC."
>
> **John F. Kennedy**

Nothing else the business does will matter if revenue is not put front and center in business plans and operations. All business leaders know that generating, maintaining and protecting revenue streams are what lie at the heart of strategy. This is easier said than done, as the difficulty lies in knowing how to achieve these goals. The six million dollar question is: how can we make sure that revenue enables growth? The answer is look to the six Rs: revenue supports company goals but how we execute policy, operations and strategy will affect the level of revenue.

Adding value and increasing revenue depends on our ability to adapt to changing circumstances – any company enduring the tumult of the past few years will appreciate this basic, if unwelcome, fact. The unprepared will struggle to survive, as business-as-usual is now a fossilized concept. By the same token, companies that are alert to signs of change will be able to respond and adapt to both current and potential changes, gaining the necessary competitive advantage to secure revenues for further growth. Revenue is a factor that must be seen in terms of both the present and the future – also, reputation from the past will undoubtedly impact revenue in other time frames.

Looking to the future is the key to revenue: it is a world of opportunities and threats; it provides the stage upon which we can act out our hopes. We need to detect signs of change and identify trends, in order to take control of our future. This often demands a break from the past, as what worked in the past may not apply today and will almost certainly not apply in the future. Far from allowing fate to be forced upon you, increasing revenue is a question of market awareness, skilled entrepreneurship and self-determination. Taking control is essential and requires fact finding, fine-tuning the company's approach and winning the support of others in the company. Companies are, ideally, aiming to lead change rather than follow it. Basically, we need to re-examine the factors that affect revenue.

Chapter 5 about revenues explores what we need to do to keep our companies on the road to building long-term growth. We will look at a number of issues, including Blue Ocean Strategy, the Star Model, value creation, exploiting adjacencies, creating and entering new markets and how to quantify change. Growing revenues requires a rigorous, analytical, challenging and creative approach throughout the organization and toward markets, competitors and the world at large. In essence, we need to monitor, measure and innovate. Critically, we need a particular mindset: to think outside the box, be ready to challenge assumptions and be adaptable. As we shall see, two key aspects of generating revenues are having a flexible working environment that encourages innovation and ideas, and aligning the entire company to achieve corporate goals.

Rousers: energizing the organization

"THE MOST SERIOUS MISTAKES ARE NOT BEING MADE AS A RESULT OF WRONG ANSWERS. THE TRULY DANGEROUS THING IS ASKING THE WRONG QUESTION."

Peter Drucker

Rousers are pivotal to a company's success, as they're the ones who lead, motivate, inspire, rally and facilitate. Good leaders motivate people and gain their commitment to goals; they, in turn, promote these skills in others as these skills are required at all levels in an organization. Being calm and balanced and having huge reserves of energy and personal strength are necessary attributes. Such individuals challenge ideas and processes, encourage innovative thinking, empower others, shake things up, focus on the long-term, inspire everyone and draw people together.

Every strategy and ultimately, all operations, depend on people. Therefore, how leaders lead makes an incredible difference to a company's future. Ethics, openness, empathy and integrity figure prominently, since people will not follow someone they do not trust or a leader that does not care. If you passionately believe in your plans for the company, you are more likely to get others to share your enthusiasm. Essentially, you should be a good role model for others. In addition, people have to have confidence in the leader's ability to deliver.

Successful companies instill all these attributes into the organization's culture and are committed to developing people, improving processes and stretching everyone to achieve more. In particular, we will look at the differences between a transactional approach and a transformational approach to leadership, negotiation and motivation. Different situations call for different styles and can lead to very diverse outcomes. The advantage of a transformational approach is that the consequences are far reaching, improving the sense of working together toward shared aims, energizing and motivating people and improving performance.

A CORE SKILL OF A ROUSER IS THEIR ABILITY TO ENGAGE EMPLOYEES. THEY CREATE A POSITIVE BUSINESS ENVIRONMENT, WHERE PEOPLE ARE EMPOWERED AND WORK WELL TOGETHER, SUPPORTING EACH OTHER.

A core skill of a rouser is their ability to engage employees. This person creates a positive business environment where people are empowered and work well together, supporting each other. This is particularly important during periods of change or when difficulties arise. By bringing people along with them, rousers strengthen the company's ability to forge a successful future. In turbulent times with such rapidly changing markets, this is more important than ever.

Reputation: essential for strong brands and sustained success

Fortunes can rise or fall due to reputation so it is hardly surprising that reputation management is now a major part of strategic development and risk management. The business environment is constantly changing, often rapidly so, with opportunities and threats peppering the landscape. Also, the ubiquity of social networking sees news, including opinions of your products and company, spreading rapidly through markets and around the globe. This situation means that companies have to manage their reputations carefully – very carefully.

There are many aspects to managing reputation, as it is vulnerable from all sides. It can be enhanced or diminished by actions at every level, from corporate values and strategy through competitors and market changes to processes and trustworthiness. Leaders need to address issues across the board, in all activities, to ensure two things: that nothing damages reputation and that everything is leveraged to build it. Clearly, reputation can only be managed holistically, with reference to the whole company.

Any approach to managing reputation has to identify the key internal and external stakeholders, which can include everyone from consumers and suppliers to employees and the media. It is important not to have too narrow a focus as stakeholders come in all shapes and sizes and any oversights can have disastrous results. A company's reputation radar will undoubtedly have many stakeholders on its screen.

BRANDS, BRANDING AND REPUTATION MANAGEMENT

Obviously, brand and branding are core aspects of reputation management. Branding enables a company to distinguish itself in the market. It has a considerable impact on a wide range of business issues, including influencing purchasing decisions and levels of employee engagement. While branding can seem a rather intangible concept, it does, nonetheless, lead to very real, tangible assets: value, less exposure to uncertainty, higher revenues, consumer goodwill, erecting barriers to entry for competitors and expansion opportunities. Later in the book, we will look more closely at what makes a strong brand and what this means for companies.

In the past, the assessment of reputation was too often an afterthought in business planning. Today, many businesses have improved their reputation management but there is still room for considerable improvement. It is not enough to look to the bottom line and, when the profit for a particular product looks decent, pat ourselves on the back for a job well done, assuming we have done a good job on the reputation front. This turns the situation backward and it misses the complexity and subtleties involved. Reputation does not exist in isolation: it must be an integral part of strategy development and all operational and marketing decisions. As such, traversing this new reputation landscape requires us to be proactive, vigilant and analytical. Any factor that occupies such a pivotal space in strategy must be measurable. Quantifying such a broad, varied and intangible asset has always been difficult. Later we shall look at how to measure and manage reputation effectively.

Reputation underpins success and its effects are far reaching. Creating and protecting such a powerful aspect of the business requires us to use all six Rs to greatest effect – otherwise it will be: easy come, easy go. Holistic business is not a passing fad, it is here to stay and reputation management is a case in point: our six Rs come together to bolster reputation and reputation, in turn, supports them. Here it is wise to remember that reputations are earned: they are given to us by others. Everything the company does will ultimately have an impact on people's perception of our company. Today, people have unparalleled access to information and the opinions of others. So by way of warning, it is increasingly hard for any company to hide unpalatable facts, which makes being genuine in the pursuit of building a brand all the more important. In particular, brand values don't simply apply to a product, they apply to a whole company. This brings us to one last point: a reputation will only be strong and durable if it is genuinely true. This is why corporate values are the cornerstone of reputation – they have earned their place.

Building business relationships

Business is about people. This automatically puts managing relationships at the forefront of business activities. Moreover, the recent, seemingly exponential growth in the variety and number of points of contact with others has not only catapulted this task onto the business scene, it has made it more complicated and more important than ever before.

Success depends on the quality of all your relationships – both internal and external. The list of people and groups a company has to consider is exhaustive. From employees, distributors and suppliers to customers, opinion leaders and the media, businesses must manage a full range of relationships, each with different needs and nuances.

While other issues are similarly important, nothing matters more than employee relationships. Being able to attract and retain the best talent will directly affect your bottom line. As a result, the company's leaders need to work hard at developing relationships with their people, the relationships employees have with each other and how everyone relates to people outside the company – clearly, no small task.

Companies need to overcome any barriers that inhibit good working relationships. While competitiveness is an essential part of survival in the markets it can be counterproductive in internal relationships. Breaking down rivalries and getting people to open up and trust each other is an important first step. A significant way to do this is to make people feel connected to others and to the company. This connection is the key to building trust, confidence and teamwork. More significantly, it provides the camaraderie, strength and resolve that will carry a company through difficult times.

It is easy, in rapidly changing times to become out of step with developments and this also applies to relationship management. This is because the workforce and the workplace are not static. For example, globalization and technological and demographic changes have radically altered the dynamics of the working environment, and companies need to adapt their processes and thinking to keep pace with these changes. Moreover, the nature of the workplace is changing. It is flatter, and people often have different motivations and different ideas about how they would prefer to work. In Chapter 8 on relationships we look in detail at this new working environment; how companies can benefit and how productivity can be raised. You will gain commitment, attract the best candidates, improve retention, improve collaboration and release a large amount of potential that will drive innovation and profitability further by not being restrained by past conventions and by offering your people the right environment and incentives.

A VITAL SOURCE OF INFORMATION: CUSTOMERS

Too often, businesses focus excessively on internal information and ideas. This overlooks one of the most valuable sources of information: the customer. I say 'most valuable' not simply because the customer is ideally placed to assess what the company does but also because they are an extra source of innovative ideas and because of the bonus that is obtained by engaging directly with clients – namely, that customers feel valued and listened to and they spread the word, so to speak, to other potential customers. Let's stop for a moment to consider what this means. If customers feel valued and listened to, they are more likely to remain loyal customers. In part this is because they respond positively to having their opinions sought out and it is also because they feel their advice will be acted upon and, therefore, future products or services will be better suited to their needs. In addition, they provide a vast, unpaid source of product development! Moreover, by promoting an ongoing dialogue and relationship with customers, you will grow the company's relationship capital, which builds resilience for coping with future difficulties.

Trust lies at the heart of building relationships. It gives us confidence that promises and commitments can be relied upon, and this matters for both internal and external relationships. Externally, relationship marketing is an invaluable means of building trust in order to cultivate better relationships with customers (and other stakeholders), precisely because it focuses on retaining them as loyal customers over time rather than on selling one product in a one-off fashion. Now, community marketing is an exciting extension to this approach, with the capacity to generate a large population of people dedicated to your brand. To tap into this, it is essential to utilize networking to its full potential. Identify the key opinion leaders and engage them in order to influence others.

When it comes to building relationships, if there is one thing that companies need to consider it is this: we need to look beyond immediate transactions and develop an ongoing dialogue capable of forging relationships that matter. Competition is fierce and can easily blindside the unprepared and the unfit. Competitive advantage will be gained by those who have formed relationships strong enough to weather any storm – those with deep reserves of relationship capital.

Resilience – vital for adaptability, agility and reinvention

"YESTERDAY'S HOME RUNS DON'T WIN TODAY'S GAMES."

Babe Ruth

Resilience is now an essential part of business strategy and operations. Adaptability is a major consideration, as the world is an unpredictable and changeable place. Companies need to evaluate their capabilities and address any weaknesses. They need to prepare and be ready to take advantage of opportunities as well as to insulate themselves from shocks. The chapter on resilience will explore the importance of this and how to build resilient organizations.

Inertia is anathema to resilience. We have to constantly look for changes and signs of opportunities and threats, and respond accordingly. Being proactive, dynamic, alert and flexible are essential. We must even be prepared to completely change our business models. This requires a root and branch assessment and overhaul. Companies cannot afford weak spots: resilience is a company-wide occupation. Planning ahead and putting the right processes in place will enable your company to respond swiftly to changes or threats and put you in a position to lead change. In particular, the best source of resilience is your people. People matter for many reasons - for example, their engagement and energy drive the business forward - but they are an essential source of innovation.

Everyone should be on the same page and they should pull together. This is especially the case during difficulties. The turbulence of current markets brings many opportunities and risks, and companies need to call upon all their resources to navigate successfully through such uncharted waters.

Leaders need huge reserves of energy and determination, they need to be able to stay calm, focused, positive and goal oriented; they need to be challenging, forward thinking, open to new ideas and innovative – and they should encourage these attributes in others. The problems that companies face are way beyond the tasks of one individual to deal with, making teamwork and collaboration particularly important. Without question, experience is the best teacher. Anyone who has gone through difficulties can take this very steep learning curve and apply it to future situations. Given the magnitude of problems that you can be faced with, a key part of resilience is having confidence in your abilities.

Strong corporate values make a huge difference to a company's resilience, as they are the building blocks of rallying people to the same cause and drawing people together during times of change. Also, boldness and imagination are required attributes. Awareness of what is happening in the markets is essential, as action is often time sensitive – slow responders can be severely punished. However, it is also important to remember that resilience also includes the potential to make a comeback even when the odds are against you or when you have been slow on the uptake. This is when having a 'never say never' mindset is useful. If you are determined, it can be possible to turn situations around. As we shall see, as Archimedes intimated, it is all a question of leveraging the right things to obtain the desired result. And this leads us to the most basic realization: the main source of resilience is people. People are the reason companies succeed: get that right and you will weather any storm that comes your way.

The following chapters will look in detail at each of the six Rs in turn: Reason, Revenues, Rousers, Reputation, Relationships and Resilience, and highlight how they work together. When reading about each one of them, bear in mind how each of the six Rs supports the others. Working together, the six Rs are much stronger and can build an organization that grows success upon success.

The past few years have certainly been tumultuous and many companies have responded by cutting back and curtailing ambitions – and are also still nursing their wounds. Yet what sort of future is this approach likely to lead to? After all, it is often said that no one ever cut their way to growth. One thing is clear: what matters in good times and bad is a clear sense of purpose – a reason – and that is the focus for the next chapter.

Chapter Four

The Age of Reason

"When the mariner has been tossed for many days in thick weather, and on an unknown sea, he naturally avails himself of the first pause in the storm, the earliest glance of the sun, to take his latitude, and ascertain how far the elements have driven him from his true course. Let us imitate this prudence, and, before we float farther on the waves of this debate, refer to the point from which we departed."

DANIEL WEBSTER, UNITED STATES, SENATE, JANUARY, 1830

WITH GOOD REASON

Any attempt to build a business must start with the company's purpose – its reason for existence. Everything else springs from this. You cannot create value, if you are not clear about your corporate values and purpose. It may seem an obvious point but it is surprising how easy it is for a company to drift away from a stated mission or to lose sight of its purpose and values amid the many, many activities, pressures, considerations, demands, difficulties, operations, concerns, etc. Running a business is overwhelming, and it is precisely because it is that you should regularly stop for a reality check and ask yourself two questions: first, how does what we do and what we are planning to do, reflect on us as a company, and, second, are our products, actions and strategies aligned to what we stand for and what we want people to think of us? By articulating your higher goals for the company, what you want to achieve – the very essence of your company, and infusing those goals throughout the organization, you will have achieved the most important first step toward success:

getting everyone and all processes and strategies working toward the same goal.

This clarity is essential, as obscurity will just lead to confusion, conflicting efforts and uncertainty as to what should be done and, significantly, how things should be done. For example, knowing corporate values will affect the way employees relate to customers, since they will behave in a way that reflects those values. This is a critical point: everything the customer sees, hears or experiences (whether from interacting with your own people or listening to the opinions of others), will contribute to the success of your company. It is not enough to have lofty, elusive goals. It is necessary to align all aspects of your company and to rally all operations around your corporate values and purpose in order to (literally) deliver the goods!

CORPORATE VALUES AND MISSION STATEMENTS ARE NOT MERE WINDOW DRESSINGS. THEY PERMEATE ALL ACTIVITIES AND THEIR IMPACT IS FELT THROUGHOUT THE ORGANIZATION. TO BE EFFECTIVE, THEY SHOULD BE CLEARLY DEFINED AND COMMUNICATED TO EVERYONE AT ALL LEVELS IN THE COMPANY. EMPLOYEE COMMITMENT AND MOTIVATION, TO A LARGE EXTENT, SPRING FROM THE COMPANY'S VALUES AND MISSION. ULTIMATELY, CUSTOMERS AND OTHER STAKEHOLDERS WILL BE AFFECTED BY YOUR VALUES THROUGH ENTHUSIASTIC EMPLOYEES AND BECAUSE YOUR PRODUCTS, SERVICES, AND REPUTATION WILL REFLECT YOUR VALUES.

THE POINT IS THAT THE POINT MATTERS

All activities and strategies need to be guided by purpose to ensure that the company heads in the right direction – the direction that you intended when deciding what you really wanted to achieve. This is not a static, immovable view, however – it should never constrain you. Just as we need to respond to developments and change, we may also wish to update our mission statements and refocus our company's values from time to time – after all, events change and people change too. People are not static and isolated; they learn new things; they become aware of new situations and ideas; they, quite frankly, change their minds and acquire new goals and values. So tweaking and course corrections are not to be feared, rather, they need to be incorporated into your goals and values. It may require more effort to communicate any realignment and win people over but this should not deter you: if these new values are your point, what you think the company should now stand for, you should throw your weight behind it and make the point stick.

Keeping your company on the right track is not an easy task. Among the busy crossing lanes of the many business activities that leaders have to deal with, it can be hard to navigate a safe route. The reason behind what the company does, its purpose, is like a steadying hand at the rudder that keeps everything heading in the right direction. This doesn't just happen by chance. It requires resolve, energy, dedication, clarity of thought and focus. Ironically, to keep the business afloat and maintain the right heading, it is useful to step back from day-to-day business distractions and spend some time thinking about the company's higher goals. This will provide insight into how best to align activities and strategies and ensure all activities are focused on creating value and delivering growth.

Without question, reason is the foundation upon which the whole company is built. It dictates direction and controls our fortunes. As we have already seen, in Chapter 3, our motivations and

"BEFORE WE TRY TO DISCERN WHOM TO BELIEVE, LET US BE CERTAIN ABOUT WHAT WE BELIEVE. BEFORE DEMANDING ANYTHING OF OUR LEADERS, LET US FIRST DEMAND IT OF OURSELVES. LET US BE TRUE TO OURSELVES AND TO EVERYTHING THAT WE PROFESS TO HOLD DEAR."

Corazón Aquino, Ateneo de Manila University, Philippines

ambitions for our companies have an immediate and long-reaching impact on the level of success. In essence, rather than the traditional focus on maximizing profits, companies are seeking to maximize the impact of their reason for existence. We all wish to make a difference, and this is equally evident in the businesses we run. It is not that profit is not important – of course it is paramount – rather, it is that profit results from reason, not the other way around. Business is not backward. Get your priorities ahead of profits and profits will roll in as a consequence. If you still doubt the validity of this argument, remember the case study of Grameen Bank highlighted in Chapter 2.

To deliver value to customers, you have to have values. Your values should directly link to your customers. These values make an intimate connection with people, and, for customers and employees, they differentiate you from your competitors.

THE PEOPLE FACTOR

It is essential that your people share your values. Everyone has to pull in the same direction and all activities should be driven by the same force in order to avoid inconsistencies and conflict. Values and mission statements are very powerful means of gaining commitment and employee engagement. They can be highly inspirational and motivating, and they ensure everyone is committed to achieving company goals.

By encouraging greater participation and listening to the opinions and ideas of others, you will create an inclusive working environment that contributes much more to the company's development. Also, using other forms of motivation, including incentives and recognition, will bolster employee engagement. By defining your objectives and communicating these to employees you will help to achieve the result you are looking for. This will also require you to constantly re-evaluate and realign your peoples' and company's alignment to achieving these objectives.

Getting the offer right

Your values are reflected in the products you offer, influencing what customers, employees and other stakeholders think of your entire company. For this reason, it is important to make sure that your product and service offerings complement your values and mission statement. The quality of products should reflect your company's purpose, as should the segments you operate in. In other words, your products and services, everything your company does and stands for, speaks to your customers: make sure they say what you want customers to hear. By doing this, you will ensure that different aspects of your business work together and don't confuse your strategy, your customers, or your employees.

The meaning of work

Doing meaningful work is vital in generating individual potential. In this sense, both reason (the purpose of the work that is being completed) and rouser (the ability to engage and inspire people to achieve that purpose are closely connected. In fact, when an individual does meaningful work, they actually develop a sense of identity, worth and dignity. By achieving meaningful results, that person grows and moves toward their full potential. Somehow, they have an opportunity to become who they are and to contribute to the improvement of their life and of their community.

REASON IS THE FORCE THAT GIVES RISE TO EMPLOYEES THAT ARE ENGAGED; REASON DETERMINES HOW WE DIFFERENTIATE ONE EMPLOYER FROM ANOTHER. REASON IS AN ESSENTIAL, DEFINING COMPONENT OF AN EMPLOYER BRAND.

When one thinks of work, one often thinks of a job. But work is far more than a job. Although work certainly provides for basic subsistence needs and decent living conditions, this is not its only function. Work is, above all, an activity through which an individual fits into the world, creates new relations, uses their talents, learns, grows and develops their identity and a sense of belonging.

In the developed world in the 21st century, work has a strong emotional and social purpose. We use it to connect to our personal potential and also to contribute to our wider society. And yet how much space is there for this to happen in today's workplace? We have job descriptions, competencies and roles all created with good intent: to tell us what to do and to tell us how to do it, but where is the space to personalize our roles and shape how we deliver it? The danger is that we really are viewing people and individuals as 'human resources' – impersonal assets to be aggregated, rather than people to be managed and led. In truth, people increasingly need their work to have meaning – a vital benefit provided by our notion of reason.

Meaning, of course, is a highly personal and subjective notion. It differs among individuals and at different life stages. Writers in this area have identified a number of factors influencing how individuals derive meaning from work. These can be summarized as:

- The significance that work brings to our sense of identity;
- The orientation we have toward work; specifically how we achieve our personal values. These may range from autonomy to social advancement;
- The balance we are able to achieve between work and other important aspects of our lives, such as family and friends.

We might move through each of these areas of importance as our careers progress or simply be motivated by one. The key is understanding how work becomes meaningful to each individual. In their book *The Truth About Talent* writers Jacqueline Davies and Jeremy Kourdi highlight six factors that help work to become more meaningful:

Social purpose	Doing something that is useful to others or to society; something that contributes to society.
Moral correctness	Doing a job that is morally justifiable in terms of its processes and its results.

Achievement-related pleasure	Enjoying one's job, doing a job that stimulates the development of one's potential and that enables achieving one's goals.
Autonomy	Being able to use one's skills and judgment to solve problems and make decisions regarding one's job.
Recognition	Doing a job that corresponds to one's skills, whose results are recognized and whose salary is adequate
Positive relationships	Doing a job that enables making interesting contacts and good connections

It is interesting to reflect how simple these are and how universal. There has been much made of the need to be considerate of factors such as these for Generation Y, however, reason in general and these factors, in particular, are important wherever you are on the demographic timeline.

AMAZON

Amazon began life with one reason: to challenge the traditional publishing industry. With such an ambitious reason, that placed it on a collision course with an entire industry, never mind a few competitors. The challenges facing the company were immense from the outset.

Its founder, Jeff Bezos, is considered one of the founding fathers of e-commerce. With the goal of becoming the world's biggest bookstore, he clearly stated that he wanted Amazon to dominate the market. So, from the beginning, he sought to increase market share as quickly as possible at the expense of profits. This ambition soon grew and he set his sights on Amazon becoming the 'Earth's biggest anything store.' His vision is summed up in Amazon's aim to be the "world's most customer-centric company. The place where people come to find and discover anything they might want to buy online." Amazon's raison d'être is clearly evident in its focus on long-term, market-leadership considerations when making investment decisions, rather than on short-term profitability or short-term Wall Street reactions.

The innovative spirit, competitiveness and passion that sparked his reason for establishing the company in the first place, have permeated the entire organization. This is where the six Rs overlap, each supporting the other. As such, Amazon takes a holistic view of the organization, aware that everything affects success. Significantly, its operations, strategy, internal and external relationships, reputation, etc. are all pinned to Jeff Bezos' reasons for establishing and running the company. A constant innovator, he has instilled that innovative spirit into the company's DNA. This spirit and passion are fundamental to his personality and managerial style. As he says, "You don't choose your passions, your passions choose you."

Innovation, ambition and passion are the hallmarks of employee relationships at Amazon. The aim to create a "company of builders" is in perfect keeping with the innovative, challenging and bold purpose that infuses the company. Employees work in an inclusive, fast-paced and continually evolving environment, they have the freedom to innovate and are dedicated to quality and productivity.

One reason why Jeff Bezos started Amazon was that he saw how customer-unfriendly the traditional publishing industry could be. No surprise, then, that this reason is evident in his approach to customer relationships. Amazon seeks to be the most customer-centric company, where people can enjoy personalized shopping experiences and low prices across the entire product range. In essence, the company starts with the customer and works backward.

Today, it is an Internet Goliath that sells everything from books to laptops to gift baskets. Amazon earned its first full-year profit in 2003 and by 2008 the company's revenue had reached $4 billion. Net sales increased 28 percent year-on-year, reaching $24.51 billion in 2009. This was fifteen times higher than net sales ten years previously, when they reached $1.64 billion. By mid-2010, Kindle and e-book sales had reached $2.38 billion and Amazon's sales of e-books topped its sales of hardcover books. With e-book sales increasing by 200 percent per year, Jeff Bezos has predicted that e-books will overtake paperbacks and become the company's bestselling format within a year. Such a meteoric rise took the publishing industry by storm and is now impacting other industries – but this is hardly surprising for a company that was founded on such an ambitious mission that continues to shape the entire organization.

Interestingly, instead of selling the company once it was established and successful (which many dot-com entrepreneurs did) he stayed in control and manages the company to this day. His initial reason for starting Amazon has clearly had a long reach: the innovation, the challenge and the passion all continue to drive the company and Jeff Bezos, himself. This shows how powerful a company's reason for existence can be and why it is essential to infuse the whole company with it: fortunes depend on it.

THE BEST PLACE TO START BUILDING YOUR BUSINESS, BRAND AND CAREER

What is your guiding purpose or reason? Answering this question is the key to developing Reason and this is perhaps the most fundamental part of any organization. All the other Rs must come together in pursuit of Reason, and this R supports all the others in turn. It is clear to see why: Reason is the raison d'être, the very soul of a company, without which the company would be pointless and, most importantly, directionless. Everything springs from reason and intention – it sets the tone for the whole business. Reputation and Relationships are led by a company's Reason. Resilience is strengthened through strong corporate values and commitment to its purpose. Revenues increase when everyone is dedicated to the fulfillment of objectives and motivated by the company's mission statement and values. Inspiring people to follow you in pursuit of the company's mission is a key part of what a leader must do – especially during turbulent, insecure times.

Creating value for customers is complex. Many factors come into play; how you position your brand and how your company is portrayed through its policies – for example, toward corporate social responsibility – will have a defining impact. Corporate social responsibility is an extension of your values. It says a great deal about who you are and what you stand for. This matters because many issues relating to a company's reason are important to customers. They will be unimpressed by a company whose reputation pays scant regard to issues that are important to them and to the world. From the environment to human rights, if your company is not working with these considerations in mind, profits will suffer. If the goal of every company and chief executive is to maximize profits, then corporate social responsibility should be uppermost on the minds of every board member.

"TO BE SUCCESSFUL, YOU HAVE TO HAVE YOUR HEART IN YOUR BUSINESS, AND YOUR BUSINESS IN YOUR HEART."

Thomas Watson, Sr.

The truth of the matter is that your reason – like your values – has to be genuine. If you do not buy in to a particular viewpoint then it is unlikely that you will succeed in persuading others that your company is behind that cause. Customers and other stakeholders have an uncanny ability to see through the disingenuous. With news and opinions transmitted faster than ever before through modern media, including social networking, companies are held up to a ruthless and virtually-all-seeing lens. Pretenders will be routed out and the genuine will be rewarded.

"THE MAN WHO DOES NOT WORK FOR THE LOVE OF WORK BUT ONLY FOR MONEY IS NOT LIKELY TO NEITHER MAKE MONEY NOR FIND MUCH FUN IN LIFE."

Charles M. Schwab

If we remember the human element in business, if we stop for a moment and think as individuals rather than as faceless companies, we will be able to stay in touch with what really motivates us as individuals. This is where the true worth of a company lies: in the very real, very human sensibilities that drive us all. People – customers and employees – respond to what is honest and genuine, to those that empathize and show consideration, and they will respond positively to any company that reflects these qualities.

While reason may be the most significant intangible factor behind the success of our business and brand, revenues are the most significant tangible issue. This is the next R and it provides the focus for the next chapter, as everything is for nothing without the financial means to back up our plans.

Chapter Five

Revitalizing Revenues

"We expect all our businesses to have a positive impact on our top and bottom lines. Profitability is very important to us or we wouldn't be in this business."

JEFF BEZOS, FOUNDER OF AMAZON

The next building block of a successful business is revenues; specifically, how best to establish a robust business model that generates profitable income. Understanding why revenue is critical to success is not hard: quite simply, without it, everything else is for nothing. Generating and maintaining revenue and looking for new sources while being alert to threats to current revenue streams should be at the heart of what leaders do. Revenue leads to growth, helps drive profitability and ensures sustained longevity and success, and, as highlighted earlier, revenue depends on creating value that is both tangible and intangible.

KNOWING HOW TO GROW REVENUES REMAINS AT THE CORE OF STRATEGY AND IS OFTEN A MORE ELUSIVE TASK FOR LEADERS.

Any business or organization is a significant, long-term investment. Shaping and managing it requires the right strategy and the right structure. Keeping it fresh and vital requires a mix of entrepreneurial and innovative input. And each part of the business, including the tactics employed and the 'business model,' must support the organization's mission, underlying values, and, of course, its growth.

From the realm of revenue also comes the issue of generating, managing and maximizing resources. Does the organization fall into the category of B2B or B2C – business-to-business or business-to-consumer? Or is it a non-profit entity? No matter which, it needs resources to operate. Investors have their role but resources need to be generated in ways that are permanent, self-sustaining and profitable.

Those profitable returns can take various forms: tangible or intangible; financial or non-financial. Each offers the same thing at a fundamental level, whether it produces the ka-ching of a cash register or is qualitative or socially oriented in character. We saw in Chapter 2 how value creation is central to an organization's growth and sustainability. Since it wields such an influence, it is measurable, which leads us into the world of KPIs or Key Performance Indicators. These include well-known residents such as ROI – Return on Investment and ROE – Return on Equity as well as more recent arrivals such as ROB – Return on Brand and STV – Stakeholder Value. Whether financial or non-financial, these measures gauge the amount of value the entity delivers, which for our purpose we group under the heading of Revenue.

Increasing business revenue is a constant challenge – one that's made even tougher by competitive pressures, cash-flow challenges, other constraints (such as time) and a world of constant turbulence, unpredictability and change. Revenues matter because they allow you to invest in products, resources and processes that enable you to sell more. Crucially, the scarcity of one resource – such as customers for generating revenue, or capital for investing in enhanced sales systems – makes selling, and increasing revenue, difficult. One other question to consider is this: in your business, how might selling differ from increasing revenue? Let's say that selling means getting new customers or selling more to existing ones, whereas increasing revenues might mean increasing prices for items that are already 'sold,' perhaps by offering a new feature with your product or service. Selling and increasing revenue are, of course, very similar and frequently, but not always, they are the same.

CHANGE IS NOT JUST CHANGING, IT'S RACING

This chapter focuses on several essential elements of revenue generation, including the need for revenue-generation and change management to connect and relate to each other. Today, any discussion about value, revenue and profitability needs to address the issue of change. The connection between revenue and change is both obvious and obscure at the same time. It is obvious that things change: nothing new in that. Those changes will affect revenue generation. But as we highlighted in Chapter 1, what is significant is how the world is changing – and wreaking havoc on the unprepared. We just don't connect the two issues – change and revenue – often enough. Change is more comprehensive, extensive and rapid than it has ever been, and we all have to accept that business-as-usual is no longer an option.

The effects of this tidal wave of change can be seen everywhere, making a strategy that includes a policy towardup change essential. To fully appreciate the enormity of this, we shall look more closely at how such change impacts on an organization's ability to produce revenue both now and into the future.

Jerry Leamon at Deloitte sums up how overwhelming the changes that companies face are, and how important it is for them to put change at the heart of strategy development. "When we look far out on the business horizon, we see of vast portfolio of change brewing. Our Global Innovation Network (GIN) seeks to capture it before it hits and to turn it to Deloitte's advantage. This initiative, as the name denotes, drives and accelerates innovation. That creates value and potential streams of new revenue. We define our way forward. Then we work backward to align our plan to the strategic actions we need to take today."

So, how should leaders manage the connections between revenue and change? Several techniques and mindsets are useful.

Watching for the signs

Look around to detect any signs of change. As well as identifying smaller developments, ask yourself:

- What are the emerging megatrends, the seismic shifts shaping the strategic environment?
- Which have the highest probability and impact?

Organizations need to constantly watch for indicators and discuss what they could lead to, as this leads to a shared understanding, which then points the way to a likely scenario and desired endpoint. This approach is critical to success, as Deloitte has found. In 2010, their Global Innovation Network identified twenty megatrends:

1. Bio-mimicry (or learning from nature)
2. Cultural diversity
3. Digital lifestyle
4. Globalization 2.0
5. Individualization
6. Knowledge-based economy
7. Technology convergence
8. Ubiquitous intelligence
9. Increasing urbanization
10. Women on the rise
11. Business ecosystems
12. Energy and alternative resources
13. Climate change and sustainability
14. New patterns of mobility
15. Demographic change
16. Changes in work practices
17. Health
18. New consumption patterns
19. New political world order
20. Growing threats to international security

What does this mean for companies?

We need to capture an extended view of what's happening and to identify all the observable trends, because pinpointing and understanding them are important foundations for strategic business planning. By analyzing these further, we can unlock a series of impacts and, ultimately, a treasure chest of opportunities.

By identifying trends, companies can prepare to take advantage of opportunities and to create new ones, further building value, strength and profitability. Putting this all together is consultant Jerry Leamon from Deloitte: "The future is a matter of choice, not chance."

"THE FUTURE IS A MATTER OF CHOICE, NOT CHANCE."

Global Innovation Network, Deloitte

The K factor

Taking control and making the future more about choice, and less about chance, is pivotal. To achieve this, we need a strategy that assesses and reflects the changes taking place and even ones that are yet to occur. This results-oriented strategy capitalizes on the changes occurring in the world at large. The starting point for this is observing and gathering information. This information can then be used to fine-tune the path the organization is on. Much more than that, it will mobilize the whole company. By catching changes early, determining the impacts and integrating the findings into an actionable forward-looking business model, companies will build a stronger future.

To achieve this, you need to make connections between your existing knowledge and experience and the trends and changes taking place (both actual and potential) – what Tom Malnight and Tracey Keys from Global Trends calls the K Factor. He puts it very simply when he says that the key to navigating change is bridging the gap between what you knew, and what is new.

In particular, Tom Malnight and Tracey Keys explain that we should focus on three main areas of change:

- Resources
- Organizations and communities
- Shapers and influencers

Through detailed analysis, insight and application of the findings, we can gain competitive advantage and create value. The natural

A MINDSET THAT LOOKS FOR NEW SOURCES OF REVENUE STREAMS WHILE BEING ALERT TO THREATS TO CURRENT ONES IS BEST. THIS WILL HELP TO INFORM AND DIRECT STRATEGY.

endpoint of this approach is that companies start to lead change rather than simply react to it.

Thoughtfully applying this framework on both an industry and company basis will chart a course for the future. This exercise reveals the challenges the organization is likely to face. At the same time, it points to potential opportunities it can seize. By putting each trend through a series of lenses, more definitive options, choices and final decisions can be clearly defined and refined. The goal is to create, in Tom Malnight's words, an "early warning system to stay ahead of change."

IN PURSUIT OF OPPORTUNITIES, NEW MARKETS AND NEW MARKET SPACE

The techniques that worked in the past to set a company on a path to brisk and prolonged revenue growth, no longer hold true. This makes it essential to constantly revisit your strategic direction by recognizing and understanding the changes taking place, determining the consequences for your organization, and realizing the opportunities they present. Once all this information is gathered, it is imperative that you act on it.

As the title of this section suggests, we need to pursue opportunities, new markets and new market space. This was highlighted by W. Chan Kim and Renée Mauborgne in *Blue Ocean Strategy* (published by Harvard Business School, 2005). The book suggested that there are two kinds of market space: red oceans and blue oceans.

- **Red oceans** represent all of the industries existing today – the known market space. Here, industry boundaries are defined and accepted, and the competitive rules of the game are well understood. Companies try to outperform their rivals in order to garner a greater share of demand. As the space gets more crowded, prospects for profits and growth wane. Eventually, products become commodities, and the increasing competition turns the water bloody.

- **Blue oceans,** on the other hand, denote industries that do not yet exist – this is an unknown market space, devoid of competition. Here, demand is created rather than challenged. There is ample opportunity for growth that is both profitable and rapid. There are two ways to create blue oceans. In a few cases, companies conceive completely new industries, as eBay did with online auctions. More frequently, though, a blue ocean forms within a red ocean when a company alters the boundaries of an existing industry.

Red ocean or blue ocean? Finding the best route to long-lasting profitability

It is not hard to see the huge downside of red oceans. If you want to reap high rewards, an overcrowded sea of competitors is a very difficult place to be. The natural extension of this line of reasoning is that of a blue ocean, with its huge untapped potential, offering an abundance of opportunity for those able to see it and positioned to take advantage of it. With few competitors, these blue oceans of uncontested market space offer incredibly rich fishing. This potentially lucrative situation applies to the now and into the foreseeable future. And it holds true regardless of economic ups or downs.

This argument may seem self-evident: of course demand for something coupled with a lack of competitors would lead to an almost monopolistic advantage. But, if we look more deeply at the reason why this happens, it will also reveal something else that is significant. We have to ask ourselves: what is it about an uncontested marketplace that is really making the difference? The answer isn't simply about monopoly or first mover advantage, it is about value creation. Customers don't come to you because you are the only game in town; they come to you because your company has created something that they value – perhaps, something they never even knew they wanted.

The strategy your company takes will therefore depend on whether you are in an existing marketplace or moving into a new, relatively new or completely uncontested market. Each requires a different approach. Clearly, in an existing market, you will most likely be focusing on beating strong competition and constantly weighing costs against the value they generate, which keeps your company pursuing low costs and in blinkered service of existing demand. In an uncontested marketplace, the focus is significantly different: not only will the rules change; you will devise your own rules. Your strategy will assume you can eliminate the competition from the start by creating new and uncharted territories. You will generate demand that never existed and be positioned at the ready to exploit it. With such a privileged position, you will no longer be rigidly constrained by the need to balance costs against the value they generate. Eventually, the natural emphasis of strategy development becomes: how can we create even more uncontested, lucrative opportunities.

CUSTOMERS DON'T COME TO YOU BECAUSE YOU ARE THE ONLY GAME IN TOWN; THEY COME TO YOU BECAUSE YOUR COMPANY HAS CREATED SOMETHING THAT THEY VALUE ... THE STRATEGY YOUR COMPANY TAKES WILL THEREFORE DEPEND ON WHETHER YOU ARE IN AN EXISTING MARKETPLACE OR MOVING INTO A NEW, RELATIVELY OR COMPLETELY UNCONTESTED MARKET.

The importance of adjacencies and repeatables

In the December 2003 Harvard Business Review case study *Growth Outside the Core*, Chris Zook and James Allen explored the potential revenue-boosting strategy of expanding into new markets. Their research, involving 1,850 companies, revealed that there was only a 25 percent success rate. Significantly, their research also revealed a pattern. Success usually followed for companies that exploited 'adjacencies' and 'repeatables':

1. **Adjacencies** – when companies expand, success is often found in business activities that could be considered 'adjacent' to their usual activities. In fact, exceptional or sustained growth may come from moving in to adjacencies, and the best adjacency strategies leverage the core business. The drivers of successful adjacency moves include:

   - Building on strong, not weak platforms
   - Valuing closeness to the core
   - Seeking repeatable models
   - Following the customer

Finally, success is often found when companies repeat their success formula each time they expand into new areas.

2. **Repeatables** – by using tactics that have already been used successfully, companies are able to create and enter market spaces rapidly – long before competitors emerge or by taking new but existing companies by surprise. This 'repeatables' strategy can accelerate the flow of revenue, as it is swift. All the accrued skill and expertise is ready to deploy to take advantage of every opportunity. This approach has been termed 'the new math of profitable growth' for very good reason: the discipline, rigor, analysis and attention to detail are great and the potential rewards are even greater.

In fact, actions in six areas are crucial to expanding into new markets:

1. **Vision and Goals** – establish clear and highly motivating higher-level goals and principles.

2. **Where to Win** – focus on well-defined boundaries of target markets and segments. Also, choose the right method to prioritize (based on attractiveness and ability to succeed).

3. **How to Win** – this stage has three parts: building a clear, measurable, competitive and differentiated offer; developing the potential to achieve leadership in core activities, and using repeatable models to replicate and adapt successes.

4. **Required Capabilities** – this involves pre-emptive building of capacity and new world class skills.

5. **Strategic Imperatives and Initiatives** – understanding the right methods to receive feedback from customer and market with closed loops to decisions, and being able to implement with required speed and certainty.

6. **Aligned and Mobilized Organization** – translating strategy into clear goals, objectives and behaviors that are 'non-negotiable,' right down to the front line.

What does this mean for value creation?

While opening new markets is one revenue-enhancing strategy, changing an organization's structure and business model is another. This requires companies to address the issue of value creation from different angles. In *Creating New Market Space* (Harvard Business Review, January-February 1999, pp. 83-93), W. Chan Kim and Renée Mauborgne argue that a systematic approach to value innovation will enable companies to break free from their competitors. This is no small task for so many organizations, whose systems, operations and strategies are often defined and constrained by repetition, a focus on dealing with known competitors and by business-as-usual assumptions that all keep it rolling forward in the same way over and over.

REMEMBER THE PARADOX OF LEADERSHIP: THE STRONGER THE POSITION OF YOUR BUSINESS, THE MORE LIKELY IT IS OPERATING BELOW FULL POTENTIAL.

If there is one characteristic that typifies businesses trying to generate new value, it is that they seek to enhance revenue in ways that are unmet by prevailing market dynamics. Everything about these companies is different: they change their entire pattern of strategic thinking. Out goes the notion of competition based on incremental improvements in cost, quality or both. In comes extending the focus outside traditional boundaries to find (or create) unclaimed market space. When breakthroughs result, they will create value, and organizations will reap the rewards.

As Kim and Mauborgne identify, a systematic approach to value creation looks at six areas:

- Substitute industries
- Strategic groups within industries
- Chain of buyers
- Complementary product and service offerings
- Functional or emotional appeal to buyers
- Time

Each of these is summarized and compared to conventional competitive strategies in the table on "Shifting the Focus of Strategy."

Value networks

In addition, Xiaobo Wu and Wei Zhang see value creation and enhancing revenue as a function of the value network to achieve sustainable advantage. As they say, the value network has replaced the value chain to become the main focus of value creation. (*Business Model Innovations in China: From a Value Network Perspective*, Indiana University, Indianapolis and Bloomington, Indiana, April 15-17, 2009). While the value chain is a linear model, with suppliers at the front end and customers at the back, the value network, as the term implies, adds other players, layers and linkages. This network connects all relevant internal and external people through a system of value flows that ultimately creates more value for the company. The number of 'actors' can be many and varied, making managing, predicting and directing them difficult. Although this presents many challenges, by redefining our business models to include a close examination of the value network, companies will sift out many opportunities.

It is useful to examine the value network from five aspects, as Wu and Zhang suggest. By focusing business model innovation in the following five areas, businesses will reveal opportunities and strengthen their long-term future.

1. **Actor change.** Here, the actors include the main firm, affiliated companies, and all organizations and individuals that affect value creation activities. Applying the value network lens offers the potential to reel in additional customers and introduce them into the firm's value network. How do you bring new customers into the fold? By offering innovations that emanate from new areas of the market, such as the emerging or low end areas.

2. **Relation change.** Whereas actor change focuses on expanding the buying population, relation change offers new products and services to existing customers, providing further value. Examples of relation change include: mass-customization, total solution, and integrated innovation. These mechanisms provide more flexible and abundant products or service combinations through modularization and standardization.

3. **Network subdivision.** Network subdivision denotes splitting the network into small and new parts to derive greater value. This creates new functions and activities. An example of this is e-business outsourcing.

4. **Network extension.** The opposite of subdivision, network extension seeks to build up the network by locating opportunities within close reach of the main business. Essentially, by pushing out the existing borders, companies attract new actors into the value network.

5. **Network integration.** Integration is twofold. It offers the potential to expand the value network and to form one or more new networks. Identifying and connecting 'value islands' is the means to bringing in new actors and creating additional networks.

THE IMPACT OF INNOVATION ON REVENUE

Revenue is one of the most critical six Rs. So how should organizations ensure they lift revenue? The key to this goal is monitoring, measuring and innovation.

This starts with a focus on the changes and trends that are occurring now and are shaping the future. Companies face competitive threats, innovations and price cuts and they have to cope with change that is so rapid and extensive that markets may never return to the long accepted business-as-usual model. Change is part of the economic landscape and companies need to gear up accordingly, if they are to protect their revenue.

When faced with such change, management theory often suggests that businesses should perform a swift, wide and decisive analysis, to decide how to launch a counterattack. However, this approach is not always effective in today's world. Things are different: a shift is taking place ... a big shift. What companies need is a way of measuring the extent and impact of change. Deloitte created a new tool to do just that: the Shift Index.

The Shift Index

The Shift Index provides companies with a more-useful means of quantifying change. While so many business indicators are short-term in their scope, the Shift Index is able to measure long-term trends – trends that will significantly impact markets, even entire economies. This provides companies with invaluable data. The Shift Index consists of three indices rolled into one: The Foundation Index, Flow Index and Impact Index. Through the use of 25 metrics, it provides a reading of where we are on a performance scale in relation to the longer-term shifts occurring, as well as suggesting actionable clues. The measurements range from the well-known to some that are less familiar – starting with ROE for Return on Equity, ROA for Return on Assets, and ROIC for Return on Invested Capital.

Other metrics in the Shift Index include new ways of looking at cyclical change. One is of particular interest to the six R framework and larger premise of this book: employee passion.

Figure 5.1: Deloitte's Shift Index

Designed to make longer-term performance trends more relevant and actionable

Foundation Index	Flow Index	Impact Index
Technology Performance • Computing • Digital Storage • Bandwith **Infrastructure Performance** • Internet Users • Wireless Subscriptions **Public Polity** • Economic Freedom	**Virtual Flows** • Inter-firm Knowledge Flows • Wireless Activity • Internet Activity **Physical Flows** • Migration of People to Creative Cities • Travel Volume • Movement of Capital **Flows Amplifiers** • Worker Passion • Social Media Activity	**Markets** • Competitive Intensity • Labor Productivity • Stock Price Volatility **Firms** • Asset Profitability • ROA Performance Gap • Firm Topple Rate • Shareholder Value Gap **People** • Consumer Power • Brand Disloyalty • Retuns to Talent • Executive Turnover

Index	Category	Metrics
Impact Index	Markets	**Competitive Intensity:** Herfindahl-Hirschman Index **Labor Productivity:** Index of labor productivity as defined by the Bureau of Labor Statistics **Stock Price Volatility:** Average standard deviation of daily stock price returns over one year
	Firms	**Asset Profitability:** Total ROA for all US firms **ROA Performance Gap:** Gap in ROA between firms in the top and the bottom quartiles **Firm Topple Rate:** Annual rank shuffling amongst US firms **Shareholder Value Gap:** Gap in the TRS[1] between firm in the top and the bottom quartiles
	People	**Consumer Power:** Index of six consumer power measures **Brand Disloyalty:** Index of six disloyalty measures **Returns to Talent:** Compensation gap between more and less creative occupations grouping[s2] **Executive Turnover:** Number of Top Management terminated, retired or otherwise leaving companies
Flow Index	Virtual flows	**Inter-firm Knowledge Flows:** Extent to employee participation in knowledge flows across firms **Wireless Activity:** Total annual volume of mobile minutes and SMS messages **Internet activity:** Internet traffic between top 20 US Foreign Direct Investment inflows and outflows
	Physical flows	**Migration of People to Creative Cities:** Population gap between top and bottom creative cities[2] **Travel Volume:** Total volume of local commuter transit and passenger air transportation[3] **Movement of Capital:** Value of US Foreign Direct Investment inflows and outflows
	Amplifiers	**Worker Passion:** Percentage of employees most passionate about their jobs **Social Media Activity:** Time spent on Social Media as a percentage of total Internet time
Foundation Index	Technology performance	**Computing:** Computing power per unit of cost **Digital Storage:** Digital storage capacity per unit of cost **Bandwith:** Bandwith capacity per unit of cost
	Infrastructure penetration	**Internet Users:** Number of people actively using the Internet as compared to the US population **Wireless Subscription:** Percentage of active wireless subscriptions as compared to the US population
	Public policy	**Economic Freedom:** Index of 10 freedom components as defined by the Heritage Foundation

1 TRS - Total return to Shareholders
2 Creative occupations and cities defined by Richard Florida's "The rise of the Creative Class" 2004
3 Meaured by the Bureau of Transportation Statistics Transportation Services index
Source: Deloitte Analytics

Employee passion

By understanding what worker passion is and measuring its impact, we will see how it drives performance improvement. In John Hagel's view, "Passionate workers seek challenges; in a world of change, they see opportunity in the unexpected. We refer to this as a 'questing' disposition. They also have a 'connecting' disposition, which is a strong desire to collaborate, participate and take on challenges. Passionate employees are more likely to participate in knowledge flows and generate value for their companies."

"PASSIONATE EMPLOYEES ARE MORE LIKELY TO PARTICIPATE IN KNOWLEDGE FLOWS AND GENERATE VALUE FOR THEIR COMPANIES."

John Hagel, Deloitte

According to the Shift Index, for the years 2009 and 2010, only 20-25 percent of US workers were passionate about their jobs. The implication: most employees are disengaged. This cannot be a satisfactory state, and the lost opportunities that this implies must be costing firms huge sums. To reverse this trend, it is essential that organizations be much more proactive and innovative toward employee engagement. As Eric Openshaw at Deloitte argues, "the key for businesses is to create an environment conducive to retaining [passionate employees]. Management should identify those who are adept participants in knowledge flows, provide them with platforms and tools to pursue their passions, equip them with the proper guidance and governance and then celebrate their successes to inspire others."

Organizations seeking to achieve peak performance need to engage their employees. The results speak for themselves: companies with high engagement scores deliver better results than those with low scores, as the following statistics indicate:

- Over 160 percent – the earnings per share for organizations in the top quartile of employee engagement versus those with below-average engagement (Gallup Management Journal, June 14, 2007).

- Over 100 percent – the return on assets for organizations in the top quartile of employee engagement compared to those in the lowest quartile (JRA, November 2008).
- Over 150 percent – the revenue growth for organizations in the top quartile of employee engagement versus those in the lowest quartile (Business Wire, August 14, 2009).
- Over 40 percent – the profitability for Asian companies with high employee engagement scores compared to those with low scores (Hewitt Quarterly Asia Pacific, Vol. 5, Issue 2, July 2007).
- Over 78 percent – the productivity for Asian companies with high employee engagement scores versus those with low scores (Hewitt Quarterly Asia Pacific, Vol. 5, Issue 2, July 2007).

These statistics bring up an important fact of life. Companies seeking to ride the crest of the wave, in the Revenue and other R categories, must always track and measure. Metrics are essential. Return on Investment, Return on Brand, Return on Anything and Everything, these all establish benchmarks that direct strategies toward success. This quantitative approach sets expectations, creates budgets and generates feedback. It enables organizations to tweak, change, add, subtract – do whatever – to strengthen their potential to achieve sustained growth and profitability.

BEING ENTREPRENEURIAL

Prediction, structure and process

To maximize revenue, we also have to determine how to reconcile the inherent conflict between a big business structure and being entrepreneurial. In his paper *The Good, the Great and the Entrepreneurial*, Stuart Read at IMD business school grappled with this conflict. So often, big business and entrepreneurship remain at odds with each other because of the way businesses are structured and run. Stuart Read divides these into: Prediction, Structure and Process.

- **Prediction** – Companies often follow a policy of repeating activities that have been successful in the past. It is easy to see the flaw in this approach: it leaves other opportunities untapped.

- **Structure** – When companies grow, the extra layers of management and the complexity of operations often make the decision-making process much more rigid and hierarchical. This can block the way to further value creation.

- **Process** – Large organizations need to have specific procedures to cope with the many aspects of running a large operation and satisfying legal requirements. Unfortunately, these processes can also impede a firm's ability to look for new opportunities and innovations.

This situation, however, is being challenged. There are ways for large organizations to continue being entrepreneurial. The key is to remove the constraints placed on a company's structure, processes and strategy development. This will release its creativity and its ability to innovate and will enable it to look further over the economic landscape, seeing and creating new opportunities. As Stuart Read suggests, we have to enable employees to be more innovative by encouraging a more flexible mindset, providing planning tools that take a much broader view of markets and opportunities and, critically, by abandoning business-as-usual thinking. As Stuart Read notes, innovation thrives in uncertainty.

This may also involve some restructuring. For example, Stuart Read proposes dividing an organization into individual markets, as this creates a more entrepreneurial ethos. You will also need to ensure that employees have the latitude to pursue ideas. Flexibility lies at the core of creating value through developing new opportunities. By providing a flexible business environment that permeates everything from processes and structure to market analysis and strategy development, you will open up new avenues and greater revenues for your organization.

Finally, making organizations less hierarchical is also important when building a company that is truly capable of recognizing, capturing and harnessing new opportunities. In summary:

- Support an environment that generates new ideas within a large company
- Compartmentalize the organization into a portfolio of businesses
- Create channels of continuous exploration and development

DELIVERING OPERATIONAL SUCCESS

This R for Revenue chapter would not be complete without cutting to the core of how a business functions. To do that, we need to ask: what benchmark determines whether an organization hums or roars?

The Star Model

Jay R. Galbraith is an authority on global organizational design and development. His book *Designing Matrix Organizations that Actually Work: How IBM, Proctor & Gamble and Others Design for Success* (Jossey-Bass, 2008), provides a useful approach to pursuing operational excellence: The Star Model. This is a way for organizations to build a better engine for growth by ensuring the decision-making process is effective.

The model consists of five main design policies that, when represented graphically, form the image of a star. These five outer edges represent pulse or pressure points for an organization. They are:

Figure 5.2: IDEO's Innovative Culture Choices

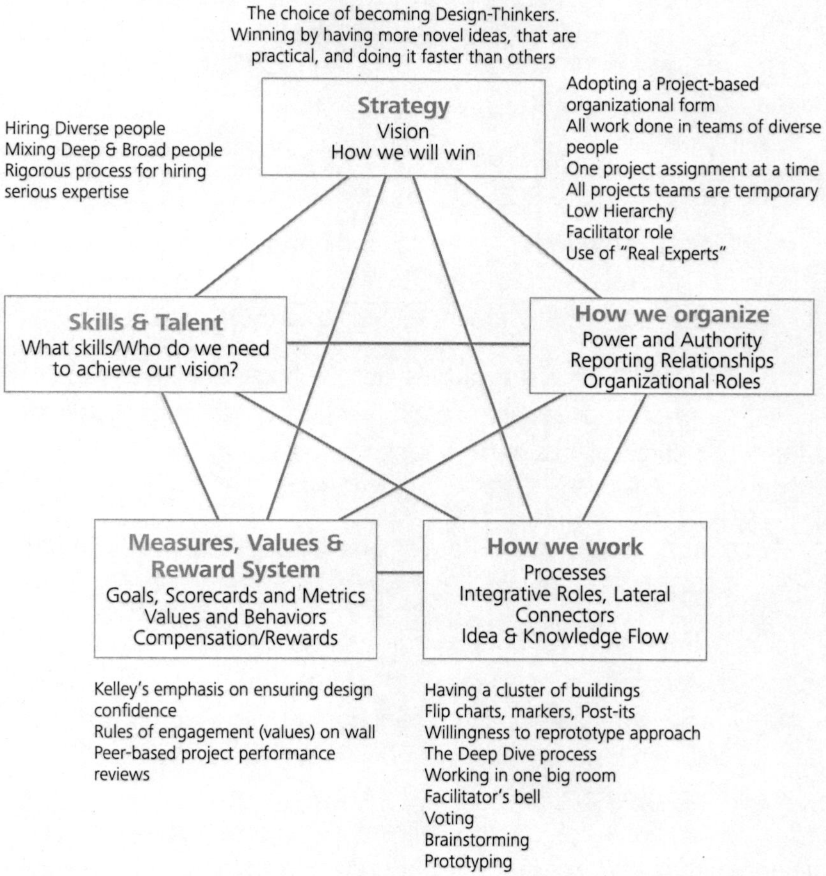

Source: Jay R. Galbraith, *Designing Organizations: An Executive Briefing on Strategy, Structure and Process* (San Francisco: Jossey-Bass, 1995), adapted by Bill Fishcher
© IMD

- **Strategy** – This sits at the top of the star because it signifies the leading concern for businesses, the blueprint for success. It includes goals, objectives, values, mission, products and services, markets, value propositions and competitive strengths, which organizations prioritize to determine their way forward.
- **Structure** – This denotes the position and placement of power, the hierarchy depicted in an organizational chart. Structure

consists of four segments: (1) specialization or the kind of jobs and numbers needed; (2) shape or number of human resources per department at each level; (3) distribution of power, that is, centralized or decentralized and lateral movements; (4) departmentalization or rules for forming departments and layers, including functions, products, workflow and markets.

- **Processes** – This reflects how the management structure functions on both the vertical and horizontal axes. The vertical axis addresses the allocation of various forms of resources, whereas the horizontal one revolves around workflow.
- **Rewards** – This sets out the policies and criteria that motivate people to drive an organization to achieve its goals, for example, salaries, promotions, bonuses, etc.
- **People** – This refers to the human element: the policies to recruit, select, rotate, train and develop resident talent in order to move the organization along its desired growth trajectory.

It is important to understand that structure is only one line item on an organization's watch list. With all of the changes taking place in the world, companies seeking to power up should focus on several dimensions. Take note of the points of intersection and their interplay in the Star Model, when designing policies. Shed the business-as-usual mindset. Instead, explore and exploit the changes that are occurring. Furthermore, to operate at high levels, impose balance, consistency and alignment in developing a business model. In essence, no corner of the star should outweigh any of the others. The most important part of using The Star Model is to think dynamically and form policies accordingly.

STARBUCKS

The international coffeehouse chain has seen it all: small beginnings, meteoric rise, shaky future and a spirited, remarkable recovery. While profit can only come from a balance between costs and revenue, as Starbucks has shown, if you don't generate revenue your costs can quickly get out of hand, threatening the entire future of your business.

Howard Schultz started with one small shop – a small coffeehouse on the waterfront in Seattle. He grew the business, generating huge revenues and, with it, the ability to reinvest and expand further until the name Starbucks became synonymous with coffee shop throughout the world. Of course, there are many reasons for Starbucks' success. However, there was one lesson that the company was about to learn the hard way: if you take your eye off your revenue stream, things can get ugly very quickly.

The economic downturn took many companies by surprise, and Starbucks was no exception. The impact on their revenue was crippling. When revenue dried up, stores had to be closed and people were laid off. This is only ever a short-term strategy, as a reduced operation usually means reduced revenue and, despite profits becoming a healthier percentage of income, profits are often smaller in absolute terms.

To address this situation, Howard Schultz looked to Starbucks' revenue stream. In his own words, Starbucks had allowed success to make them complacent. To steer the company back to success, he needed to generate revenue in order to secure the profitable growth the company needed for the future. Critically, to turn the situation around, Howard Schultz focused not only on getting customers back through the door but on increasing sales in other outlets: the overriding goal was to increase the stream of revenue as much as possible. Although having a great work environment and corporate culture matter, if you can't get customers through the door, it is all for nothing. As Starbucks discovered: revenues matter.

Once a company secures its operational foundation, what next?

You have ideas and hopes and you have built the organizational foundation to achieve them. To bridge the gap between these two positions, a gap where many fall down, you need to turn your attention to executing your plans. The goal is to lift revenue, and everything else you have done now relies on effective implementation.

In *Execution: The Discipline of Getting Things Done* (Crown Business, 2002), Larry Bossidy and Ram Charan emphasize the point that turning policies, programs and purposes into preferred performance is all about execution. As they put it, execution is "the missing link between aspirations and results." It does not refer simply to tactics, but rather to full-fledged discipline that permeates every aspect of the organization, from strategic thinking and behaviors to systems and procedures. It is the final part of building our R for Revenue: execution turbocharges a company's income stream.

Converting goals into gains sounds good, but how exactly do we achieve this? First, leadership plays a major role. Leaders must not only define the essence of execution, but also exhibit it. Essentially, you have to instill an execution-oriented environment throughout the organization. To start with, make sure that you know the business and the people and set clear goals and priorities. You should then follow through, checking, resolving conflicts, oiling the machine and ensuring that it functions well. It is important that everyone is realistic about the situation, and you must confront all aspects of performance, including mistakes. You must measure performance and reinforce results by rewarding accomplishments. Sharing knowledge and further developing your people through training and coaching is an important part of ensuring that effective execution will continue to deliver success. Also, to embed execution into the entire fabric of an organization, Larry Bossidy and Ram Charan recommend two actions. First, create the framework for cultural change by incorporating execution as a primary precept. Second, put the right people in the right positions by clarifying the roles and skills that will provide a competitive edge.

Finally, any aim to establish an execution-oriented strategy needs to link everything together: people, strategy and operations should not exist in separate silos. Connecting these functions forms a self-reinforcing system that drives operational performance even further.

Having considered the 'hard' and unforgiving issue of Revenue the next chapter explains the significance and impact of Rousers – those people who energize and drive performance, build relationships, provide resilience – from which revenue, reputation and ultimately success are derived.

Chapter Six

Rousers

"A leader leads by example, not by force."

SUN TZU, *THE ART OF WAR*

ROUSING LEADERSHIP

> "IF YOU CAN DREAM IT, YOU CAN DO IT."
>
> **Walt Disney**

Why are Rousers so important? They are the ones that put things in motion. They set off a chain reaction that propels the company forward, enabling it to grow beyond the ordinary to become truly great. To rouse people you need to lead them. This is not to imply that it only includes people at the top. Jobs do not come neatly packaged with a narrow range of required skills. No matter where someone is in an organization or what task they're doing, they can be hugely influential – motivating and inspiring others around them. And because leadership exists at every level of the organization, so too do Rousers. Leaders at the top need to motivate and inspire everyone and they need to encourage others to do so throughout the organization. Rousers are critical to growth, innovation, employee engagement, value creation and much, much more. In short, Rousers are the people who drive success.

What Rousers do

We've all experienced it: that moment when we hear something that inspires us so much we are instantly fired up and raring to achieve great things. It can be incredibly powerful. Now magnify that throughout an organization and for everyday: imagine how much progress that would lead to. All that buzz, excitement and enthusiasm results from a very special type of person: a Rouser. This person will:

- Put things into motion. They stir things up, agitate the status quo and not only create a sense of 'can do' but 'want to';
- Excite others through their lively thoughts and behavior. Their energy motivates and inspires people to excel;
- Pull others together and propel them in the same direction.

A Rouser leads. A Rouser inspires. A Rouser attracts and binds. A Rouser animates and compels. A Rouser sets off a chain reaction that leads to ideas, imagination, commitment, effort and achievement in many people, who pass this on to other people – and on it goes. This is the power of a Rouser. There is no doubting the impact these people have on their organizations.

LEADING PEOPLE THE RIGHT WAY

"OUTSTANDING LEADERS GO OUT OF THEIR WAY TO BOOST THE SELF-ESTEEM OF THEIR PERSONNEL. IF PEOPLE BELIEVE IN THEMSELVES, IT'S AMAZING WHAT THEY CAN ACCOMPLISH."

Sam Walton, Founder of Walmart

It is all in how you lead people. In today's increasingly complex world, the Rouser requires something of paramount importance: to get the results they are seeking, they need to lead in the right way. This point is made by Martha Maznevski at IMD business school, when she argues that leaders have to lead responsibly. Before anyone dismisses this as a truism, we should examine more closely what this really means.

Responsibility is not as straightforward as it seems – it is multifaceted. Although, there are two things that underpin everything else: a strong sense of ethics and integrity. Without these, everything else will be built on an unstable foundation, vulnerable to every knock and ultimately viewed by others as hollow and disingenuous.

Why are ethics and integrity so important? Of course, your people and customers will benefit from the many policies that are born of ethical considerations. Significantly, though, integrity has such power because of what it says about you. Quite simply, it shows you care, and this means people will trust you, and people who trust you will follow you because they will believe in the place you're taking them. This is not to imply any subterfuge. On the contrary, there is only one way to gain people's trust and inspire them to join you and that is to be genuine.

The relevance for leaders to rouse their people is clear: values matter. As George Kohlrieser, author of Hostage at the table, observes, "[Leaders] set high personal standards of behavior for themselves to act as a role model for others. Responsible leadership starts with the leader as a person – his or her integrity. This helps to create an organization characterized by respect, honesty, trust and caring beyond the leader's own self-interest."

Making it happen

A Rouser may have values, integrity and ethics, they may be energetic, dynamic and enthusiastic – but how do they stimulate others and generate followership? By infusing ethics into all aspects of the organization, from activities and procedures to achievements and earnings, the whole company will be drawn together, given purpose, become energized and thus enabled, move forward in one direction.

Importantly, exceptional leaders focus on the long-term. In essence, they create shareholder value, raising their companies from the short-term and leading their organizations to a profitable, strong and successful future. If Rousers are anything, they are tireless: they are constantly developing their people, devising better ways of doing things and pushing the boundaries of what is achievable. They are also honest: integrity requires that people know they can trust what you say – and that depends on accuracy, openness and reliability.

What else is needed?

"YOU MUST ROUSE INTO PEOPLE'S CONSCIOUSNESS THEIR OWN PRUDENCE AND STRENGTH IF YOU WANT TO RAISE THEIR CHARACTER."

Luc de Clapiers, Marquis de Vauvenargues, 1715-1747

Rousers would not be able to draw people to them if they did not have credibility. People may think you are decent, supportive and fair, but if they feel you are ordinary, less than impressive or even incapable, you will not have much influence. Basically, credentials matter.

As Jean-Pierre Lehmann of the Evian Group argues, leaders also need business acumen. They need to prove that they can build wealth, that they are part of the 'social group' and that they appreciate and rely on the knowledge of others around them.

ROUSERS AT WORK: ALIBABA, LEGO AND ZAPPOS.COM

Alibaba Group

A pioneer in the Chinese internet industry, Jack Ma founded the Alibaba Group, in 1999. His vision was to build an e-commerce ecosystem that allows consumers and businesses to do all aspects of business online, to create one million jobs, to change China's social and economic environment and to make China the largest internet market in the world. Ma says his goal is not to create "the most profitable company in China or the world, but to give China a global brand that will last, even if short-term profits must be sacrificed ... If Alibaba cannot become a Microsoft or Wal-Mart, I will regret it for the rest of my life." That is no small vision, and that is the point. A bold vision is inspirational and has the power to capture the imagination and gain commitment and loyalty.

His bold vision is matched by his approach to strategy. Asked about Alibaba's goals, Ma replied, "we win eBay, buy Yahoo! and stop Google. That is for fun. Competition is for fun." One thing stands out about this statement: how appealing it is. It attracts people to the cause and gets them on side. This is what Rousers do and why so many people get behind them – they rally, motivate and galvanize.

Vision and strategy are clearly powerful weapons in the Rouser's armory, but there is another important aspect: leadership style. Alibaba's success is in no small part down to Jack Ma's style of leadership. He is certainly charismatic. More than that, people follow him because he is credible and they trust him. He values communication and transparency, keeping in constant contact with employees and being approachable. Significantly, opinion-sharing is highly encouraged and there is a strong talent-centric culture. All of this sends one clear message: he values his people. Nothing gets people on side more readily than knowing that they are valued and that their voices will be heard.

Lego

Lego was founded in 1932 and its brand name has become one of the most iconic children's toys in the world. In 2004, however, the survival of this family-run company was at risk. For the first time in the company's history, Kjeld Kirk Kristiansen (grandson of the founder) handed over the reins to someone outside the family. Jørgen Vig Knudstorp took charge. When he became CEO, he was only 36 years-old and had only been with Lego for three years. A former McKinsey consultant, he set about devising a seven-year strategy known as the Shared Vision, with the aim of rebuilding the company and revitalizing the brand. Three things stand out about how he turned this vision into reality: leadership style, company structure and corporate culture.

For the first three years he had to focus on surviving, halting sales decline, reducing debt and managing cash flow, which required tight fiscal control and top-down management. During this period, the key to success depended on his making sure that he was approachable – as puts it, "managing at eye level." This makes a leader visible and promotes a sense of shared challenges – something not lost on employees. The camaraderie it instills inspires and generates trust and commitment.

As the tide turned, Lego focused on their core competencies and products. The management team decided to compete not by being the largest, but by being the best. This stage required a slightly different corporate structure to the one that was needed during the early turnaround period. The company structure was loosened and the top-down management style was relaxed to empower managers. This from-the-ground-up approach unlocked creativity and gave people the latitude to explore ideas.

Crucially, the corporate culture was also revolutionized at Lego. The emphasis shifted away from 'nurturing the child' to 'I am here to make money for the company' – managing to come back from the brink of disaster. The results speak for themselves. It is essential to get the culture right so that it works with your aims and not against them. Lego needed to make money – and make it fast. The softer, albeit commendable, mission to provide nurturing toys did not pay the bills! While Lego still produces high-quality, developmental toys, by re-orienting the employee mission statement to one of 'we are here to make money', both goals are satisfied. The case of Lego shows how important it is to ensure that corporate culture and goals support each other. Quite simply, by saying what you want, you will get what you want.

Returning to leadership style, for Knudstorp, the most fundamental aspects of leadership are to take responsibility and make things happen – "less talk and more action." The importance of this is clear: people feel you are worth following. For these to work, though, they have to have meaning and purpose, they have to be born of your answer to two questions Knudstorp asked himself, "Why does the company exist?" and "What makes the company unique?" The journey for any Rouser starts by looking inside.

Zappos.com

Being a Rouser is not just consequential for a company's internal operations; Rousers impact the marketplace by attracting consumers and building customer loyalty.

Tony Hsieh is CEO of Zappos.com, an online shoe, handbag and clothing store whose success springs from their aim to provide a superb customer experience – and building outstanding customer relationships lies at the heart of this vision. To achieve this, Tony Hsieh has not only infused his passion and vision throughout the organization, his enthusiasm and energy spreads directly to customers.

There is certainly a revolutionary and strong corporate culture, with the entire business revolving around the concept of happiness and the long-term growth of employees. There is a fun and loose work environment and, unusually, financial reward is very definitely not the driving force. Instead, the company is filled with genuine enthusiasm that is summed up in Tony Hsieh's approach to recruitment: "We hire for attitude. The rest (skills) can be trained."

Zappos pays below market salaries, focusing instead on employees' long-term growth. Employees are empowered and respected and the work environment is relaxed. It is all about having the right attitude. As Tony Hsieh says, "If you can get the employee to stay and be happy, inspired and motivated working for the company, then the long-term benefits are huge." He leads from the front, taking an astonishingly low salary for a CEO ($37,000!) and his office is a simple cubicle. This is someone who leads by example, a key attribute of Rousers.

Customers respond enthusiastically to the unconventional and innovative approach. The reason the company constantly exceeds expectations and has such an emotional resonance with its customers is because the company is not focused on money., Instead, it is focused on the customer experience – similar to how the company treats its employees. This is not some subjective point, the reason it works is because Tony Hsieh genuinely believes it. Not only does his view permeate the company, this same vision inspires his customers to be drawn to the products and the brand. This reflects an overriding feature of Rousers: they are genuine and people both inside and outside the company respond positively to that.

It wouldn't be too much of a stretch to say that the entire business revolves around happiness. Before anyone dismisses this as too idealistic an attitude to survive in the tough world of retailing, sidelining monetary reward and raising employee and customer happiness, far from being at the expense of profit, has provided a healthy return on investment precisely because people value, trust and get behind that enthusiasm and those ideals.

Business today is global. No one can escape it; what happens on the global stage affects us all. This raises an interesting question: are the principal dimensions of successful leadership universally applicable, or do different regions or countries display alternative approaches?

In *Transformational leadership: an examination of cross-national differences and similarities* (in Leadership & Organization Development Journal, Vol. 24 Iss: 1, pp.5 - 15), Karen Boehnke, Nick Bontis, Joseph J. DiStefano and Andrea C. DiStefano reveal two major leadership styles:

- **Transactional leadership** – defined as "a series of exchanges and bargains between leaders and followers";
- **Transformational leadership** –"goes beyond exchanging inducements for desired performance by developing, intellectually stimulating and inspiring followers to transcend their own self-interests for a higher collective purpose."

This reflects the work of James MacGregor Burns, who, in his book, *Leadership* (HarperCollins, 1978), described these two styles and concluded that the simple essence of leadership is a relationship between two or more people. How these relationships play out makes a great deal of difference – and while both leadership styles are needed, they are needed in different situations and with different people.

There are distinct differences between transactional leaders that view relationships as a series of exchanges – I'll give you this, if you give me that – and transformational leaders that seek to change the playing field by moving beyond the usual approach, appreciating the subtleties involved – the inherent untapped potential, to generate new ways of working and new incentives.

Rousers instinctively deploy each approach, as appropriate. Yet there is no denying that transformational leadership has the potential to raise everyone's game. The simple reason for this is that it taps directly into our instinctive need for fair play and social cohesion. When we feel we belong and are valued and when we feel we can trust is the person leading us, we will be motivated, we will be energized and we will follow. This is no small achievement: we only follow who we trust and trust is not easy to gain. For a leader, no matter at what level within an organization, to gain the trust and loyalty of those around them, matters – the long-term success of the organization depends on it.

Ben Bryant, professor at IMD business school, believes that there are certain core features (behaviors and personal characteristics) that define transformational leadership. He groups these into the following clusters:

Feature	Behavior
Opportunity seeker	Solves problems, has insights, finds the right idea or right solution
Intellectual	Takes sensible risks (both personal and organizational), recognizes constraints
Creative	Goes against status quo, doesn't always do the expected and can behave unconventionally
Moral	Behaves based on values, beliefs and sense of moral purpose, acts trustworthy

Confident	Displays assuredness, optimism, self-efficacy and internal control
Inspirational and/or visionary	Articulates new ideas or goals, uses artful communication, dramatic metaphors and exciting presentations to control followers' attention and to inspire them
Empathetic	Shows sensitivity to followers' needs and desires, cares for others, encourages emotions and expression, doesn't abuse power

"THE GREAT LEADERS ALWAYS STAGE-MANAGE THEIR EFFORTS ... WHILE THE REAL LEADERS ARE DOWN IN THE RANKS, QUIETLY CHANGING THE WORLD."

Charles de Gaulle

Returning to the question of whether there is a pattern of leadership styles across geographies, transformational leadership is widely recognized as a trigger for exceptional operational performance on a global basis. According to the research team led by Karen Boehnke, despite needing to adapt to national differences, transformational leadership greatly improves performance.

At this point it is useful to highlight several points:

- **Leadership is not just for formal leaders.** It applies to leadership in its broadest sense. As already mentioned, leadership happens at every level within an organization.
- **Transactional and transformational leadership styles are not mutually exclusive.** It is not a case of one and only one – good leaders are a hybrid, possibly with one side more dominant than the other. Such leaders are adept at knowing which style to apply and when.

- Interestingly, **transactional and transformational styles can be leveraged.** Leaders can transition in and out of one or the other, as required.

To be a Rouser, as Kim Cameron and Arran Caza argue, in *Developing Strategies for Responsible Leadership* (University of Michigan, May 2005), employee empowerment is fundamental. By adopting the following techniques, they suggest that leaders can greatly enhance the potential of their people.

- **Promote a positive climate.** Negativity creates more problems than it solves. This is achieved by emphasizing people's strengths and dealing appropriately with weaknesses by resolving issues. Ensuring that this positive approach permeates the organization will boost morale and energize your people – also, by dealing effectively with any mistakes, you will ensure that problems do not become endemic.

- **Promote positive connections.** By developing close, trusting working relationships, you will bring people with you who will, in turn, bring the support of others.

- **Promote positive communications.** Being positive is not a soft option: it motivates and energizes people and has a direct impact on the bottom line. By emphasizing people's strengths, they will respond positively, deal with issues and improve their performance. Blame is counterproductive; problems are best resolved from a positive, 'let's make this work' position.

- **Promote employee engagement.** If employees don't find their jobs interesting or useful, then your customers will eventually feel similarly disenchanted. Ensure that your people find their jobs interesting and meaningful by enriching the work environment by involving and motivating them and offering opportunities for creativity, advancement, achievement, recognition and personal fulfillment.

In light of recent shake-ups in the top ranks of major companies, responsible leadership is no simple matter. So what does the future hold? In *Handbook on Responsible Leadership and Governance in Global Business* (Oxford University Press, 2005), Jonathan P. Doh and Stephen A. Stumpf point to the need for an integrated approach to responsible leadership. They argue that there is a missing link: while "individual commitments to leadership, ethics and social responsibility are evident in most corporations, many companies appear to fall short in combining these duties into an integrated set of policies and culture that guides behavior and decisions."

Here, integration is the key. By linking a wide range of internal elements, including social responsibility, integration establishes a framework that functions as a system of checks and balances. Having the proper foundation in place will support your aims and will help to address the many situations you will face. When a fully integrated approach is executed appropriately, it keeps the long-range interests of stakeholders at the front of the leader's thinking

Rousers are charismatic, ethical, accountable and caring. They exude passion and enlist allegiance toward a shared goal. They motivate and communicate in a way that engages and encourages excellence in everyone. Significantly, they take a long and wide view, integrating and transforming purpose into action. Most importantly, they do not go it alone: they bring people with them.

The future that companies face is uncertain and will be difficult. The impact *Rousers* can make throughout a company is immense: they ignite an organization and its people to achieve greatness. In the next chapter we highlight the next foundation for successful businesses, brands and careers: the challenge of building and maintaining *Reputation.*

Chapter Seven

Reputation

"A good reputation is more valuable than money."

PUBLILIUS SYRUS (FIRST CENTURY BC), MAXIMS

If you have any doubt about just how critical reputation is, think for a moment about the horrendous mistakes made by Enron, Lehman Brothers and WorldComm and what these did to the reputations of these giant firms. When awareness of their wrongdoings reached critical mass it sent their reputations tumbling. Don't look for these names among stable, progressive businesses – they're gone. These companies demonstrate how the six Rs intersect and affect each other – with the certainty of dominoes falling: once one is set off, it is not long before the others follow. This is particularly evident with our next R: Reputation. Its impact is formidable: a company's fortune can rise meteorically or be obliterated. This may

"REPUTATION IS STILL A PRECIOUS COMMODITY IN BANKING. ALTHOUGH PROFITABILITY MAY BE THE BEST FOUNDATION OF A BANK'S NAME, ITS NAME IS ALSO THE BEST FOUNDATION OF ITS LONG-TERM PROFITABILITY."

***The Economist*, February 23, 2008**

sound extreme but these scenarios always remain possibilities for any company that takes its eye off the ball. It is understandable how this situation can happen. Day-to-day, reputation management is one activity among many, and it can be easy to overlook just how much reputation is contributing to your organization and how what you do, each moment, every day, affects your company's image, brand and share price. This is never more important than in these first decades of the 21st century, when news of your company can travel worldwide in a matter of moments. Consequently, all business activities should be conducted with reputation in mind and this starts with the company's values, mission statement and vision. These are the building blocks that frame the critical R for Reputation.

INSTANT, VITAL, ALL-ENCOMPASSING: THE ESSENCE OF REPUTATION

In recent years, the concept of reputation has become a major issue in business and management. Business leaders, the world over, no longer regard traditional financial indices as the only indicator of a company's progress. As a measure of success, corporate reputation has equaled, if not surpassed, the importance of stock market performance and earnings or the recovery of investments.

Interest in reputation has soared; its ascent has boosted its status from hot potato to main course. In his book *New Strategies for Reputation Management* (Kogan Page Publishers, 2008) Andrew Griffin reflects on this reputation revolution. "Everybody's talking about it. It seems that organizations of all shapes and sizes and in all sectors are fully conversant in the language of reputation. Of course, it is talked about in some countries and some companies more than others ... It is now commonplace to hear terms such as 'reputation protection,' 'reputation risk management,' and 'reputation strategy' at the very top of a company."

It is likely that many of us think we have a pretty good idea of what reputation is. Yet, it is also likely that when we try to identify it, the picture soon looks much more complicated than we first thought. It permeates an organization from the top echelons to the bottom line.

If we can't precisely define reputation, how can we expect everyone in an organization to know how to manage it successfully? In *Refocusing Reputation Management* (Corporate Executive Board, 2005) the Communications Executive Council addresses this issue. In this group's view, reputation "represents a loosely defined intangible concept that can vary across groups. Simply exhorting [a] company to 'improve our reputation' provides little concrete guidance and is likely to leave managers and staff wondering what this means and what they are supposed to do differently."

Stakeholders

Reputation has to be viewed in relation to stakeholders. What stakeholders think is critical. What stakeholders think can be influenced by what companies want them to think. In other words, a company should be concerned by the perceptions of key stakeholders and not by the perceptions of groups of no relevance. Yet that raises an interesting question: which stakeholders are among those of primary interest to a firm? Consumers, clients, investors, suppliers, journalists, politicians, interest groups, lobbyists – each is only one of many stakeholders that should be prominent on an organization's reputation radar screen. We have to be careful not to have too narrow a focus when determining our stakeholders, as reputation can be seriously damaged by overlooking anyone or anything. Nonetheless, the mention of consumers leads us to the next key aspect of reputation: branding.

"A BUSINESS BASED ON BRAND IS, VERY SIMPLY, A BUSINESS PRIMED FOR SUCCESS."

David F. D'Alessandro

Brands and branding

Brands and branding have exploded both in meaning and use. Everything and everyone seems to be a brand or branded. Products and people, enterprises and entities are often regarded as brands. In every sense of the word, whatever a business offers and delivers is inextricably linked to its overall brand, which is a main underpinning of its reputation.

Clearly, then, branding lies at the heart of reputation management. A brand not only influences buying decisions but also internal business decisions and behavior. Brand and reputation are joined – better yet, they are fused; two sides of the same coin giving rise to new synergies and opportunities. For example, Alan Bergstrom, Executive Director of The Institute for Brand Leadership, makes the point that, "To us, a brand is the sum total of all perceived functional and emotional aspects of a product or service." He goes on to say, "Branding is about adding a higher level of meaning to a product or service, thereby increasing its value to customers and other stakeholders. A brand's value is positively related, then, to the extent of stakeholders' emotional attachment to it."

Drawing on this definition, a brand is how an organization distinguishes itself and its products and services in the market. To uncover just how important branding is we will look at the real life situation of buying a car. Most of us will engage in this activity several times over the years. Commonly regarded as the second largest expenditure we make, it is also a complicated buying decision for customers. There is much at stake and just as much, if not more, to consider.

The start of the process. The process of buying a car starts when we begin to look, set a budget, research and come up with a working list of cars that interest us. Then, for argument's sake, we narrow the choices to four, as shown below (of course, the data is for illustrative purposes only).

Figure 7.1: Complex decision making: Buying a car ...

	MODEL A	MODEL B	MODEL C	MODEL D
Price (£)	30880	31225	28300	29170
Engine	2798cc 24-Valve Six-cylinder Variable valve timing	2997cc 24-Valve Six-cylinder Variable valve timing	2967cc 24-Valve Six-cylinder Variable valve timing	2959cc 24-Valve Six-cylinder Variable valve timing
Power	198bhp at 5500 rpm	218 bhp at 5800 rpm	240 bhp at 6900 rpm	226 bhp at 6200 rpm
Torque	207 lb ft at 3500 mm	219 lb ft at 3800 rpm	221 lb ft at 4500 rpm	202 lb ft at 5000 rpm
Transmission	Five-speed manual Rear-wheel drive	Five-speed manual Rear-wheel drive	Five-speed manual Rear-wheel drive	Five-speed manual Rear-wheel drive
Front Suspension	MacPherson struts Coil springs Anti-roll bar & control arms	Double wishbones Coil springs Anti-roll bar & control arms	Double wishbones Coil springs Anti-roll bar & control arms	Double wishbones Coil springs Anti-roll bar & control arms
Rear Suspension	Double transverse links Coil springs Toe links Anti-roll bar	Double wishbones Coil springs Toe links Anti-roll bar	Double wishbones Coil springs Toe links Anti-roll bar	Double wishbones Coil springs Toe links Anti-roll bar
Weight	1440 kg	1720 kg	1628 kg	1510 kg
Max speed	147 mph	143 mph	146 mph	150 mph
0-60 mph	7.3 secs	7.3 secs	7.3 secs	7.3 secs
Fuel economy	28.5 mpg	24.8 mpg	27.7 mpg	22.6 mpg

Source: Foro Empresa, Gobierno de Aragón

The contenders. Model A, Model B, Model C or Model D: which will it be? First, look at all of that comparative information. Is there something that could help cut through the morass of overwhelming and confusing features and statistics?

The solution. Admittedly, it may seem odd to add another variable to this already-long list of variables. How could adding a factor clarify rather than lead to more confusion? If we redo the table, inserting this extra feature along the top, we should see the difference that this extra information makes.

Figure 7.2: Is it easier now?

	MODEL A	MODEL B	MODEL C	MODEL D
Price (£)	30880	31225	28300	29170
Engine	2798cc 24-Valve Six-cylinder Variable valve timing	2997cc 24-Valve Six-cylinder Variable valve timing	2967cc 24-Valve Six-cylinder Variable valve timing	2959cc 24-Valve Six-cylinder Variable valve timing
Power	198bhp at 5500 rpm	218 bhp at 5800 rpm	240 bhp at 6900 rpm	226 bhp at 6200 rpm
Torque	207 lb ft at 3500 mm	219 lb ft at 3800 rpm	221 lb ft at 4500 rpm	202 lb ft at 5000 rpm
Transmission	Five-speed manual Rear-wheel drive	Five-speed manual Rear-wheel drive	Five-speed manual Rear-wheel drive	Five-speed manual Rear-wheel drive
Front Suspension	MacPherson struts Coil springs Anti-roll bar & control arms	Double wishbones Coil springs Anti-roll bar & control arms	Double wishbones Coil springs Anti-roll bar & control arms	Double wishbones Coil springs Anti-roll bar & control arms
Rear Suspension	Double transverse links Coil springs Toe links Anti-roll bar	Double wishbones Coil springs Toe links Anti-roll bar	Double wishbones Coil springs Toe links Anti-roll bar	Double wishbones Coil springs Toe links Anti-roll bar
Weight	1440 kg	1720 kg	1628 kg	1510 kg
Max speed	147 mph	143 mph	146 mph	150 mph
0-60 mph	7.3 secs	7.3 secs	7.3 secs	7.3 secs
Fuel economy	28.5 mpg	24.8 mpg	27.7 mpg	22.6 mpg

Source: Foro Empresa, Gobierno de Aragón

Now, our task has suddenly become much simpler: that's the power of brand. Brand cuts through the details, removes the need to sift through a lot of data. It gives the customer an easy way of seeing your product as different – even when the technical differences between products are not great, as in the case

"TODAY BRANDS ARE EVERYTHING, AND ALL KINDS OF PRODUCTS AND SERVICES – FROM ACCOUNTING FIRMS TO SNEAKER MAKERS TO RESTAURANTS – ARE FIGURING OUT HOW TO TRANSCEND THE NARROW BOUNDARIES OF THEIR CATEGORIES."

Tom Peters,
The Brand Called You
Fast Company Magazine

> "BRAND VALUE IS VERY MUCH LIKE AN ONION. IT HAS LAYERS AND A CORE. THE CORE IS THE USER WHO WILL STICK WITH YOU UNTIL THE VERY END."
>
> **Edwin Artzt, former chairman and CEO, Procter & Gamble**

of our four cars. With a list of seemingly similar options from which to choose, brand plays a key role. Quite simply, brand can sway the vote. Do you want to be behind the wheel of the "ultimate driving machine," as BMW's tagline assures? Do you fantasize about "your chance to own an Alfa Romeo," as that company's message suggests? Are you apt to act on the impulse Jaguar wishes to create through its "Don't dream it. Drive it" brand statement?

A brand refers to something intangible. Yet, out of the intangible, something tangible is created: real value. A strong brand is a force that exerts an impression, a feeling, a promise. Strong brands magnify the impact of great products and services: they accelerate and enhance cash flows; they reduce uncertainties.

Figure 7.3: Strong brands magnify the impact of great products and accelerate growth

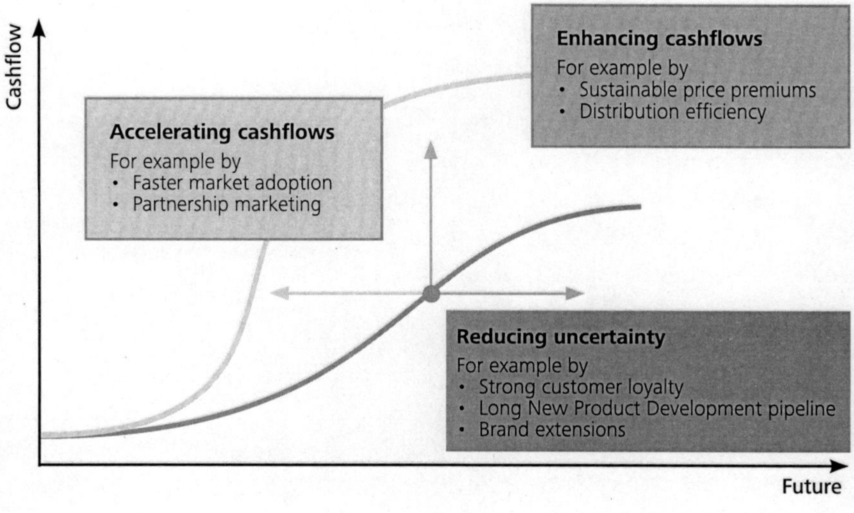

Are there hard and fast proofs that support this view? The evidence indicates that:

- Brand creates value;
- The stronger the brand, the more value it creates;
- Brand, as a pathway to value, drives distinctive, sustained profitable growth.

It is undeniable that strong brands enhance financial success. As such, they are key assets that need to be carefully managed.

According to research conducted by Millward Brown, strong brands help build strong business by enabling the following:

- Achieving price premiums over competitors
- Attracting customers
- Creating barriers to entry for new competitors, as customers remain loyal
- Providing 'insurance' during economic downturns, as loyal customers still prefer their favorite brands
- Providing reservoirs of consumer goodwill that help a company cope with a knock to the product or the company
- Enable a business to capitalize on opportunities to expand into new markets

Exactly what is a strong brand?

"A COMPANY'S BRAND IS THE PRIMARY SOURCE OF ITS COMPETITIVE ADVANTAGE AND A VALUABLE STRATEGIC ASSET."

David Aaker

David Aaker is one of the world's leading experts on brand management. He argues that because brands create inherent value, they become part of an organization's total assets. He explores the issue of brand success in *Why Are Strong Brands Strong?* (Marketing News, August 30, 2010).

Strong brands, according to Aaker, "not only deliver on their value proposition, as they have done for many years, but also they are visible in the marketplace and are a part of people's routines.

People like the familiar." This observation sits at the top of a list of items that defines the nature of a strong brand:

- Highly valued by customers
- Familiar and highly visible
- Trusted quality
- Indicates success
- Brand vision that inspires
- Infused with energy

Some of these attributes are fairly obvious. Of course, a brand is strengthened when it is valued by customers. And it is not hard to see why success works, as the product is clearly tried, tested and proven. It may also tap into people's desire to be part of something successful. Others are less obvious. For example, what does having energy mean? The most successful brands really do have energy, and one way they get this is through innovation. In fact, most leading brands remain dynamic and successful because of four elements:

- Visionary thinking or demonstrating future orientation, articulating a clear view of the future allowing for changes in the market.
- Aligned strategic thinking, with distinct plans and objectives aligned with the overall business strategy.
- Differentiating your business and brand using market, competitor and brand knowledge.
- Driving change and innovation, successfully developing and implementing new ideas and initiatives.

A company's vision is an interesting case. By offering a certain vision to customers, we can associate a product very closely to them, so that it becomes integral to their lifestyles – for example, a product has the power to create a new interest or way of living, which will then become the default brand in people's thinking. Whether the attribute is obvious or not, the devil, they say, is in the details: it is not always easy to acquire these virtues when building a strong brand.

Clearly, 'strong' is the most sought-after slot in branding. So: how do we get it? What drives the power of brand? What creates that invisible, yet magnetic field that has the potential to draw us in? In other words, how do you create a strong brand?

The answer is not one, but a series of tangible and intangible items and categories that magically seem to distinguish a brand. And this requires us to put Reputation at the core of business strategy and operations. Essentially, branding is about everything a company does, both internally (within the company) and externally, and it runs like a single thread to the outside world. We can see this when looking at the key aspects of building a brand: identity, values and beliefs, behaviors, authenticity and image and perception.

Figure 7.4: Brand essence

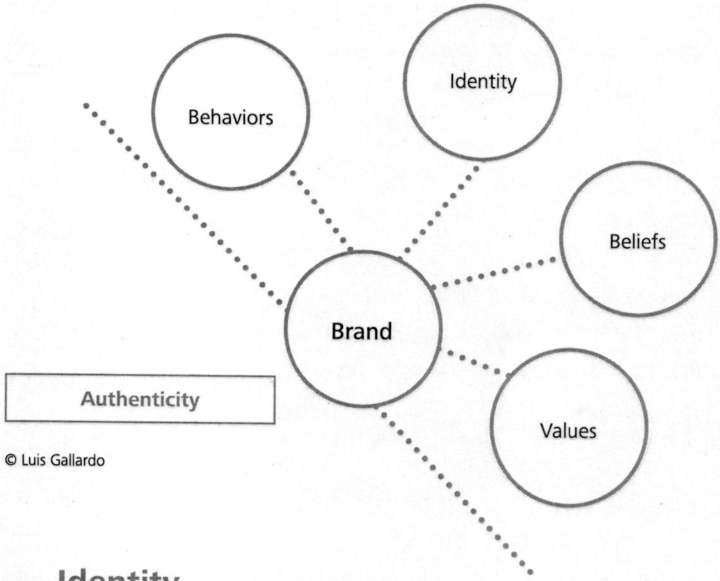

© Luis Gallardo

Identity

The importance of instantly recognizable or eye-catching symbols was highlighted at a dinner party. A woman, sitting next to Raymond Loewy (creator of the Exxon name and logo), asked him why he put two Xs in Exxon. "Why ask?" he replied. To which the woman said it was because she couldn't help noticing. "Well," he responded, "that's the answer." (From *The Art of Looking Sideways* by Alan Fletcher)

We would all agree that logo, color and typography establish a brand's visual identity, along with photography, illustration and advertising styles. These key design principles and executions create the look of a brand. Importantly, though, identity is not just about these elements. Brand name and brand concept, even the tone the brand sets, also inform its identity. Identity is the overall effect, the total package that results from consistently applying all parts of the branding system. Identity seeks to create intent. How it is communicated in the marketplace will reflect the brand's personality to everyone – existing and potential customers and stakeholders.

"IN THE CONTEXT OF LIVING THE BRAND, PURPOSES AND VALUES ARE NOT CREATED, THEY EXIST – THE ISSUE IS HOW WELL THEY ARE ARTICULATED AND EMBEDDED."

Nicholas Ind, *Living the Brand*

Values and beliefs

What does a brand stand for? What does it want to be known for? These are a brand's values and beliefs. Values give customers a quick way of knowing the essence of a brand. These are the attributes, attitudes and qualities associated with it; they are meaningful characteristics that define the brand. Beliefs signify the principles that guide the brand. These help explain what the brand is, what it does and why. Values and beliefs inspire and intrigue. Put together, they create a promise intended to resonate.

We should also remember that the values and beliefs associated with a brand are not simply the result of a carefully orchestrated plan; all business activities ultimately have an impact on a brand's intended values, as people will integrate other information they discover about a company with its intended brand values for the product. This means we have to be thorough, careful and vigilant, and we have to be consistent in the values we communicate to all stakeholders.

Behaviors

The brand's behaviors take its values and beliefs to the next level. Essentially, brand behavior is all about knowing how the brand delivers on the promises it makes to its stakeholders. All that a brand does, says and follows through on are its behaviors, and we need to manage this complex and subtle aspect of branding carefully. We need to look beyond the immediate offering of the product: it's the whole brand experience, the totality of actions, played out, both within an organization and in the marketplace. As Robert Haas, from Levi Strauss, argues, "Companies have to wake up to the fact that they are more than a product on a shelf. They're behavior as well."

"AUTHENTICITY IS THE BENCHMARK AGAINST WHICH ALL BRANDS ARE NOW JUDGED."

John Grant, *The New Marketing Manifesto: The 12 Rules for Building Successful Brands in the 21st Century*

Authenticity

A brand can aspire to be something – anything, for that matter. But it won't be around for too long if it doesn't follow through on its claims. In this way, authenticity is a litmus test for sustainable brand success. Trust and integrity – the hallmarks of brand authenticity – go back to our earlier comments on values. Business is not just about making a profit, but rather, doing things well, being true, creating something meaningful for an organization's legions of stakeholders. Do you want your brand to achieve credibility? Then you must connect with your customers honestly and earn their trust. Authenticity is earned and must be worked at continually. You must align it with the strategy of the company and manage it accordingly, keeping it up to date and focused on the needs of stakeholders. The need to be authentic springs from accountability: in other words, you are accountable for the consequences. If your brand offering is not reliable and trusted, the consequences can be damaging.

Image and perceptions

Image is a complex, symbolic construct that evolves from a brand's identity, attributes, messages, behaviors and personality. The mechanics of creating an image involve taking all of these aspects, adding other information as it becomes available, and then applying this image consistently across multiple channels. It is this process that will make a brand special and set it apart from others. We're not done, though, as this is just half the story. Image flows from a bundle of thoughts, emotions and sensory stimulants. It is short term. Image is what pours the foundation and paves the way for perception.

Perception is about reaction. It is the result of brand image. It is what stakeholders think about everything the brand does, says and delivers – it judges whether the brand promise matches reality. To make this task harder for organizations, perception is subjective – it varies according to each stakeholder's perspective.

Ideally, image creates a halo effect. In brand marketing, this occurs when perception of a desirable trait, or feature associated with one product extends to another or even to the entire line, brand or organization. This mechanism resides at the root of sponsorship or celebrity marketing, which ultimately and definitively strives to transfer emotions or traits associated with an event or spokesperson to the brand. As Walter Landor, at Landor Associates puts it, "Products are made in the factory, but brands are created in the mind."

Figure 7.5: Brand perception

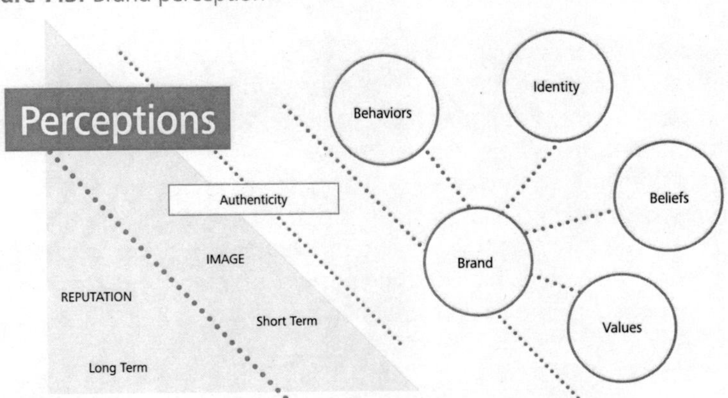

© Luis Gallardo

BRILLIANT BRAND BUILDING

Babolat

Based in Lyons, France, Babolat provides specialist tennis equipment. It is the oldest tennis equipment company in the world and is still a family-run business. In 1998, Eric Babolat became the CEO and aimed to take their quality brand and expand into the highly competitive U.S. market that was dominated by the Big Three: Wilson, Head and Prince. This was no small challenge, many would have said near-impossible, yet, despite the formidable barriers to entry, they were phenomenally successful – achieving a 34.3 percent market share in specialist tennis stores in the U.S. in 2010. In taking on the Big Three, the key to their success was establishing and promoting their Reputation.

How do you tackle an almost-impenetrable market? What Babolat realized was that reputation must drive strategy. They focused their strategy to emphasize the professional-level, high quality standard of their tennis equipment. This sprung from Eric Babolat's own vision of the company: he knew they were the best; tennis, quite simply, was what they did, it was everything they did. His task was making sure that everyone else shared his belief: when people think about the highest standards for equipment in tennis, they think Babolat.

Becoming a brand leader and obtaining the loyalty of retailers and suppliers was what it was all about – and that hinged on establishing, managing and leveraging reputation. As Eric Babolat states, "Our brand is first, and every decision goes around that."

They implemented a carefully planned distribution strategy, designed around reputation, which focused on its premier brand and avoiding the discount market – they targeted specialized stores and shops for professional tennis players. To quickly establish their brand's credibility , Babolat used endorsements from professional players (such as Rafael Nadal, Andy Roddick and Kim Clijsters) and then leveraged their reputation into other areas. They extended the high quality reputation of their tennis equipment to other product lines, including clothing and shoes.

Their alliance with the top tennis players boosted their reputation. It must be noted, though, that this reputation is deserved. Branding and reputation rely on having a trusted product –many professional tennis players would not put their names to a product they did not value. Product quality and reliability have to match their PR campaigns; otherwise any disingenuous claims would soon be apparent to customers.

The story of Babolat shows how interrelated the six Rs are. You cannot separate them: they are all in service of each other. Reputation is meaningless without the others and the others are meaningless without Reputation. A holistic approach to business is no transient business fad; today, it is an inescapable fact of business life. The world is too complex, fickle and ruthless for any other approach. If companies want to be successful, they have to incorporate all of the six Rs into their strategy – and Reputation is what binds them all, fueling every aspect of a company's progress.

Brand positioning

The concept of positioning relates to how a product is perceived by customers relative to its competitors. The concept originated in the advertising industry as a way of identifying the product attributes that needed to be inserted into the buyer's consciousness: for example, it may be cheap, innovative, cool or high quality. Positioning helps to provide a clear focus. It is essentially about influencing attitudes and perceptions about a product or company brand, rather than changing the product itself. Positioning improves performance by increasing awareness of a company's or product's capabilities and by refreshing or reinforcing an existing brand.

The following techniques are useful for achieving distinction or for effectively staking a claim in a specific market segment:

- **Understand the market.** This involves finding a niche or part of the market where there is space to establish and maintain a profitable position. Not only does this require an understanding of the market, but also the key trends and factors influencing the market. This may require the recognition that in certain markets, at certain times, there are simply no attainable positions left.

- **Focus on the customer.** When planning or considering the position of the product or business, it is important to remain externally focused and consider how the customer will perceive and react/respond to the message or offer. To put it another way, what message will have the greatest impact on the customer in the way that was intended?

- **Manage timing.** Positioning is often easiest when you are the first in a new market: the value of first-mover advantage. From this position, it is possible to get to know the customer and to market in detail and then build a strong customer base and rapport with customers. Often, as a first-mover, the brand image appears responsive and innovative. For brands that are not first-movers, it is important to choose the right moment to launch, ideally when the market leader is weak or quiet or both.

- **Avoid head-on confrontation with the market leader.** The brand with the most to lose is the market leader; they will therefore react very powerfully against newcomers, using all the resources at their disposal – wealth, fame and customers. The brand that is attacking the market leader, therefore, needs some valuable, attention-grabbing, distinguishing feature and they must strongly convey this in their message.

- **Consistency is essential.** Once a position has been taken, it needs to be consistently and unfailingly defended. More than that, it has to be actively developed or the potential benefits of occupying that position will erode.

- **Choose a powerful and simple message.** To be effective, the message needs to be clear, simple and consistent (such as: Volkswagen launching the Beetle in the U.S. with the slogan Small is Beautiful; Mars Bars' claim to help you Work, Rest and Play; everything that the Ford Motor Company did was Driven by You, while Coca-Cola remains The Real Thing). The message should strike a chord with the recipient. Often the best way to establish a position is to 'go with the flow' and associate with an idea, issue or concern that may already be in people's minds.

What does all this tell us about branding? Primarily: so much hinges on perception. We can see this, if we take a brief look at what makes a brand iconic. Brand is not just one-dimensional or an idea: it is BIG and Alive. It resonates in the marketplace; it engages imagination and trust; it transforms products and services into something relevant, unique and true. As John Kay from the Financial Times describes, our perception of a brand allows us to share its values. "'I am irresistible,' I say, as I put on my designer fragrance. 'I am a merchant banker,' I say, as I climb out of my BMW. 'I am a juvenile lout,' I say, as I pour an extra strong lager. 'I am handsome,' I say, as I put on my Levi jeans."

Branding is all about perception, and perception drives our R for Reputation. We've come full circle. As we've just seen, brands are built. This leads to the inevitable question: Does that apply to reputation too?

CREATING REPUTATION

Organizations have always been concerned with reputation. However, the emphasis when managing reputation was usually after the event: that is, a company would assess its reputation according to particular measurements such as profitability or one of many operational indicators. In essence, if all the lines were going up then everyone was happy. The problem was that this simplistic approach did not account for just how complex managing reputation is. It is no longer a simple correlation between a successful bottom line and products. If organizations wish to establish, maintain and grow their reputations then they need a completely different approach. Instead of being treated as an afterthought, reputation should be placed at the center of strategy development, operational decisions, marketing activities and management of all stakeholders – it should inform and drive all business activities. Reputation does not operate in isolation so it has to be a major part of strategy. This inevitably follows from our point that all six Rs support each other.

Putting reputation at the core

"IDEAS SUCH AS ORGANIZATIONAL IDENTITY, REPUTATION AND CORPORATE BRANDING HAVE BEEN AROUND FOR A LONG TIME. BUT NEVER BEFORE HAVE THE INTERESTS THAT PROMOTE THESE IDEAS WITHIN BUSINESS – THE FUNCTIONS OF HRM [HUMAN RESOURCE MANAGEMENT], COMMUNICATION, MARKETING, STRATEGY AND ACCOUNTING – BEEN IN GREATER NEED OF ONE ANOTHER'S SUPPORT."

Majken Schultz, Mary Jo Hatch, and Mogens Holten Larsen, *The Expressive Organization*

To create and maintain its reputation, an organization must accept the first rule: everything affects reputation. This means that we have to see all business activities from the point of view of reputation. This being the case, creating and managing reputation necessarily requires a multidisciplinary approach. For that to happen, organizations must place reputation at its core. That is, they should consider reputation a main component of strategy and link it to other key functions, both internal and external. Then mobilize and integrate all of these threads to shape and manage reputation. Only by doing this will we be able to achieve the desired result.

HOW REPUTATION AND STRATEGY STRENGTHEN BUSINESSES

Patagonia

Headquartered in Ventura, in the U.S., Patagonia is a privately owned, international company that designs and sells outdoor clothing, outdoor gear, footwear and luggage. The founder and owner is Yvon Chouinard, and his approach and strategy have been shaped by one aim: to behave as if the company would still exist 100 years from now. Furthermore, the company's mission statement is, "Build the best product, cause no unnecessary harm and use business to inspire and implement solutions to the environmental crisis." With such aims, reputation becomes an integral part of all business activities.

Describing himself as 'a reluctant businessman,' Yvon Chouinard's goals and beliefs put reputation front and center at Patagonia. The company is a trend setter, with product innovation, marketing activities and support for environmental and social causes leading the industry. Products are of the highest quality standards, and, with a reputation for developing innovative products, it receives considerable press coverage. The company enjoys a loyal customer base and by using brand ambassadors from different athletic backgrounds (who serve as gear testers and endorse the brand as suitable for serious athletes) has augmented its reputation with customers.

There is a forward thinking and passionate belief in giving employees a flexible work environment. At the same time, the company demands hard work, creativity, collaboration and results. "We wanted to blur the distinctions between work and play and between work and family ... I don't care when you work. All I care about is that the job gets done and the work is excellent. If you come in at 7 p.m. at night because you want to go surfing at 2 p.m., that is fine with me. But it can't impact your fellow workers." This corporate culture means it has a reputation for being a great place to work and, as such, it attracts talented people – receiving an average of 900 resumes for every job opening.

Having a good reputation isn't just for customers and employees; it also affects relationships with suppliers and vendors. Being debt-free has allowed Patagonia to extend credit to its wholesalers that are being affected by the financial crisis. This has strengthened its reputation with vendors, increasing long-term loyalty toward Patagonia.

As one would expect of a company infused by environmental ideals, Patagonia has always been a champion of corporate social responsibility and has made sizeable donations to grassroots environmental organizations. Interestingly, in 1986, Patagonia committed to donate 10 percent of their profits each year to non-profit groups, which they later upped to 1 percent of sales, or 10 percent of profits, whichever was greater. How many companies would redesign the way donations are calculated in order to give more to charities – even though their already-high donations more than secured a good reputation? With the belief that the company should be run as if it would exist in 100 years time, reputation is evidently important, but it isn't chased forit's own sake: it thrives because it reflects the people at Patagonia. In essence, it springs from rather than leads their values, approach and strategy.

The fact that Patagonia has thrived during the recent economic crisis, recording its best two years in 2008 and 2009 in terms of both revenue and net income, shows that reputation affects all the other Rs and goes some way to proving that reputations count. Patagonia's entire corporate identity is built on philanthropy and environmental consciousness, and its reputation reflects how much these are valued by customers and employees. And that is the point: at Patagonia, reputation isn't just some carefully managed add-on to strategy; it is also what genuinely matters to them. That is the biggest lesson of all: a reputation grows because it is deserved; if it is not deserved, it will easily unravel.

Building reputation

Reputation follows from what the stakeholders think of you and your products. So any attempt to build reputation has to start with this premise: cover all the bases.

The first port of call should be your employees. Employees count – big time. Recall the opening of this chapter about a company's visions and values? These cornerstones of corporate culture matter when building reputation, because they affect your employees – who are the ones who relate directly and indirectly with your customers. They are your company's ambassadors. As such, they have an active role that provides a two-way channel between the organization and its stakeholders. An employee who values the company and its products will be a better and more committed ambassador – and their enthusiasm will be infectious and positively affect your customers. Key to this is creating such an upbeat environment that the employees will create extra value by their attitude of always seeking to provide service that goes beyond what a customer expects. It is also likely that employees will think of ways that the company can improve.

THE PROCESS OF INTEGRATING REPUTATION INTO ALL BUSINESS ACTIVITIES IS SUMMED UP IN THREE AIMS: CONFRONT, COLLABORATE AND CONTROL.

Clearly, employees play a crucial role in fostering and safeguarding corporate reputation, which places great emphasis on getting internal communications right. In this regard, we now realize that even seemingly innocuous communications to employees have the potential to affect a company's reputation.

How to achieve this can be seen by looking at the communication programs of companies with high reputations. Research conducted by Dortok shows that communication policies need to focus on communication and be end-to-end in scope. That is: you should draw up a communication plan that aligns employees with strategy, including steps for applying the plan, regularly measuring results and evaluating the findings, to improve the process for the future.

"THE MOMENT YOU BEGIN TO DRAW YOUR ATTENTION TO THE INTANGIBLE DIMENSION OF YOUR COMPANY, TO THE REPUTATIONAL DIMENSION OF BUSINESS, YOU ACHIEVE A HIGHER LEVEL OF AWARENESS. YOU START TO REALIZE THAT THERE IS A VAST EXPANSE OF WEALTH BEYOND PHYSICAL ASSETS. YOU SEE THAT THE THINGS THAT MATTER MOST TO YOUR BUSINESS, THAT ENABLE IT TO WORK, TO BE PRODUCTIVE – TRUST, INTEGRITY, FAIR DEALING – EXIST BEYOND CONVENTIONAL MEASUREMENTS OF THE FIRM'S VALUE."

Kevin T. Jackson, *Building Reputational Capital*

By bringing employees into your plans and strategy, you will gain their trust and allegiance and, more importantly, their enthusiasm – can you imagine a better ambassador for your business?

There are other stakeholders to consider, from customers to the media, and a reputation strategy must consider all of their relationships with internal and external interest groups. This is where one R meets another: R for Reputation; R for Relationships. This emphasizes the interplay among the six Rs and the strength they derive from each other to drive profit and growth.

This leads us to some interesting questions. Do all stakeholders factor equally into an organization's reputation? Can reputation be all things to all groups and does it want to be?

The answers to these questions underscore the benefit of situating reputation at the heart of strategy. To begin with, we have to identify the groups we think will really matter – the opinion of the people in these groups is critical to establishing a good reputation.

There's no escaping it: strategy is reputation

Positioning reputation within the strategy function has even more significance: in particular, refocusing. There is a new trend in reputation management to view reputation as a means rather than an end. In other words, companies are putting reputation through the strategy lens, repositioning it to become an integral part of both strategy development and its execution. Upmost in their thinking is determining those aspects of reputation that top tier stakeholders deem to be of the highest value.

The new reputation landscape

How should you traverse this new reputation landscape? First, you have to be proactive. You also need to link the organization's reputation to its strategic goals. To do this you should quantify the positive and negative consequences of the factors of your reputation that will affect the brand. In this regard, you should identify the elements that either underpin success or harm reputation and then plan your strategy accordingly. Finally, you need to identify and align your reputation strategy with the wants and needs of the most important stakeholders

This sort of analysis requires measurements and assessment. There is a range of tools to determine, measure, and protect reputation, including diagnostics, such as a SWOT analysis (Strengths, Weaknesses, Opportunities and Threats) and an issues management process, as well as playbooks, protocols and public relations.

Dr. Charles Fombrun, chairman and founder of the Reputation Institute, drove the stake in the ground that sprouted into the full-fledged field of corporate reputation by providing valuable insight into how companies can measure reputation. He proposed using a company's stated book value and market value to place a value on reputation. He referred to the difference between the two as a company's intangible assets. It was not, in his opinion, an unreasonable assumption to interpret intangible assets as reputational capital.

Here Reputational capital is what gives organizations a competitive edge, as it attracts the best employees, makes shares attractive to investors, facilitates premium pricing and secures market dominance. A reputational audit will help you determine your company's reputational capital and highlight what you need to do to realize its potential or how to make improvements. This will identify your strengths and weaknesses, which you can use to make any necessary course corrections and to develop your future strategy.

Although reputation may vary in content, context, and touch-points from industry to industry, one aspect holds true for all. That is, the ever-growing need to gauge and protect a firm's reputation online. That undertaking is fast becoming as vast as the worldwide web itself.

Let's face it: we live in the age of new media, where public conversations bring together people from all over the globe. Thanks to the Internet, anyone anywhere can create a buzz that ushers in new heroes or ruins an organization's reputation in a matter of moments.

Governments, corporations and individuals can be exposed in online chats by more than one billion Internet users. That's downright impressive. It is one of the most powerful shapers of public perception. Crowd-sourcing or open sourcing, social networking and Web 2.0 prove that information can become more valuable as more people use it. It is a force to be reckoned with; it is a force that all business strategies need to engage with.

There are a few To Dos to help us navigate online reputation, including:

- Embrace the online channel to build reputations and brand
- Appoint full-time professionals to think about, monitor and act on digital activities, in real time
- Communicate, communicate, communicate to proactively manage reputation
- Advocate, support, observe, and engage in multiple streams to deliver strategy
- Stay ahead of online trends and conversations by incorporating this medium at the core level

Managing reputation in the 21st century: How we got here and where are we going

Interest in reputation has soared; its ascent has boosted its status from hot potato to main course within an organization's strategy sector. In *New Strategies for Reputation Management* (Kogan Page, 2008) Andrew Griffin reflects on this reputation revolution: "Everybody's talking about it. It seems that organizations of all shapes and sizes and in all sectors are fully conversant in the language of reputation. Of course, it is talked about in some countries and some companies more than others.... It is now commonplace to hear terms such as 'reputation protection', 'reputation risk management,' and 'reputation strategy' at the very top of a company." It permeates an organization from the top echelons to the bottom line. Moreover, we have to consider the international angle, as policies and strategies that work well on our home turf may or may not translate to other countries. A strong brand goes a long way to overcoming any cross-border barriers, as the reputation of a strong brand travels. As companies become more connected and international, creating a first-class reputation across borders is critical. For some companies, this can be the difference between success and failure.

Reputation is the cornerstone of any business: without it, everything else will count for nothing. Everywhere we look in a company we see mission statements, corporate values, vision, etc. Yet, having been forged within the company's offices, it is easy to view them largely for internal consumption and to overlook how important these all are and how they reverberate throughout the world's markets. Reputations spread far and wide and they can travel very rapidly; they can be hard to earn and easily lost. It is imperative that we fully understand that everything that happens inside a company has the potential to impact on its reputation. Therefore, to ensure that building and maintaining reputation is successful, we need to start by looking inside the organization – making sure that our values and qualities are shared by those within the company so that these then feed through to the marketplace and customers in the way we want.

Whether it's online or off, reputation transcends time and place, as well as the individual indicators of traditional performance and profitability. The final word should go to the American poet, essayist, critic, and diplomat James Russell Lowell, who had a reputation as a trouble maker while at Harvard University – accordingly, securing his own brand and reputation:

"Reputation is only a candle, of wavering and uncertain flame, and easily blown out, but it is the light by which the world looks for and finds merit."

As we have seen, Reputation, and in particular, brands, are the result of everything that happens both internally and externally. They connect with the outside world and need to be managed carefully, constantly and assiduously. The same is true of the next R, Relationships, and this is the focus for the next chapter.

Chapter Eight

Building Strong Relationships

"Developing strong relationships offers a stream of benefits and opportunities. When we bond with others, we create trust, we are more effective in what we do, and we form ties that transcend boundaries such as geography, culture, and personal differences. These linkages forge loyalty, commitment, and high performance. They create value and protect us, which is especially helpful in times of crisis."

BEN BRYANT, LEADERSHIP PROFESSOR, IMD

WHY FOCUS ON RELATIONSHIPS?

"*GUANXI* DESCRIBES THE BASIC DYNAMIC IN PERSONALIZED NETWORKS OF INFLUENCE AND IS A CENTRAL IDEA IN CHINESE SOCIETY."

Winter Nie, Professor, IMD; author, *In the Shadow of the Dragon*

Welcome to the new era of relationships in business. Perhaps you remember the hoopla created by the concept of 'six degrees of separation' in the 1990s, with its assertion that we are only six connections away from any person on the planet. Today, that probably seems very old-fashioned as we are used to the highly connected world of the early 21st century. The global business networking site LinkedIn calculates that a subscriber with 250 first line contacts is linked to over five million other professionals. Fascinating – but what is the point of this? Why are we so obsessed with connections and relating to people? The short answer is because people are essentially social creatures, but more specifically the great variety and number of points of contact with other people means that developing and managing relationships has never been so important – or so complicated. People can also understand each other's views much more easily now than ever before and this is especially true in business. In essence: relationships rule.

Organizations have much to consider about relationships since they generate opportunities as well as challenges and they profoundly shape almost everything that organizations are trying to accomplish: from selling to teamworking, customer service to innovation, engagement and energy to customer loyalty and competitiveness.

This situation applies to internal relationships, including employees and other stakeholders, as well as to external relationships including those with customers, distributors, the media, opinion leaders and vendors. It is important to develop strong relationships with all stakeholders, as success depends on the quality of those relationships.

Understanding internal relationships

It is easy to see why internal relationships (meaning those between colleagues and suppliers) matter, since a company relies heavily upon its employees. It is less easy to know how to ensure that these happen. An organization poised to be the best at any and all points over time needs to attract and retain the best talent. An acknowledged expert on internal business relationships, Ben Bryant, leadership professor with the Swiss business school IMD, argues that many barriers exist that get in the way of good working relationships. These include competitiveness and rivalry, guarded behavior, an unwillingness to open up and the tendency to see others more in terms of their job title than as people. This way of working is symptomatic of a lack of any real connection between people and can lead to limited, potentially damaging relationships. Where there is a poor level of connection, it is likely that people's motives and behaviors will not be understood and conflict may result. To avoid this, organizations should promote ways of working that help people feel connected.

This may sound like just another of those touchy-feely fads that does its rounds in business thinking. It may sound like it – but it absolutely isn't. Feeling connected with our colleagues is the foundation upon which strong relationships grow. Everything springs from it: trust, certainty, confidence, comradeship, ability to make decisions. The benefits to the business are clear; as Ben Bryant says, "We are more effective in what we do and we form ties that transcend boundaries, such as geography, culture, and personal differences. These linkages forge loyalty, commitment, and high performance. They create value and protect us, which is especially helpful in times of crisis."

Even when we have this facet of internal relationships under control, there is more to be done. Organizations must ensure that their relationship practices and policies are in step with the times. After all, the tectonic plates in the business world are always shifting, and we have to move with them. Globalization, technology, demographics, and other major trends have altered the dynamics of work. What's more, the number, pace, and extent of these developments shows no sign of stopping; in fact, the opposite appears to be true – the rate of change is accelerating.

"THE LADDER IS SPLINTERING INTO THE CORPORATE LATTICE."

Cathleen Benko and Molly Anderson, *The Corporate Lattice: Achieving High Performance in the Changing World of Work*

If the workforce has changed then the workplace has too. Accordingly, businesses need to revise their thinking in the realm of relationships. In particular, the previously accepted, linear mode and mindset toward employee advancement has been challenged. The one-size-fits-all approach that focused on offering a bigger office, bigger paycheck and greater power and prestige now needs reexamining. Today, if we were to look for the corporate ladder we'd be in for a surprise: it's gone. It has been replaced by what Cathleen Benko and Molly Anderson refer to as the corporate lattice, which, they say, has developed because, "Globalization and technology are creating organizations with fewer rungs and more options for how, when, and where work gets done. And these are only two of many major shifts that have occurred."

Using the corporate lattice

"FROM THIS OPENNESS AND COLLABORATION COME CAMARADERIE AMONG COLLEAGUES, MOTIVATED TEAMS, AND INNOVATIONS."

Cathleen Benko and Molly Anderson, *The Corporate Lattice: Achieving High Performance in the Changing World of Work*

A major advantage of the corporate lattice is that it enables people to work more flexibly and productively. It is better able to tap into each individual's motivation and offer the working conditions and opportunities that they are looking for. With less hierarchy and better connections between people, organizations are realizing that lattices release large amounts of 'potential,' greatly improving productivity and employee retention.

This way of working has profound implications for relationships in the workplace. No longer constrained by the hierarchical structure of the past, every aspect of relationships improves – from better collaboration to the flow of internal communications. The advantages don't stop there, as the authors observe, "From this openness and collaboration come camaraderie among colleagues, motivated teams, and innovations."

They suggest that organizations should look at several important issues, notably how to:

- Engage the workforce – for example, use an intranet to facilitate communications, including blogs and remember to include past employees and those retired from the company.
- Help our people grow and develop – use mentoring, coaching, a company 'university' and a training allowance.

- Provide flexibility – consider using virtual working to ensure that employees are better able to maintain a healthy and productive work/life balance.
- Recognize and reward – these can include 'spot' rewards, performance-related pay, contests and recognition in a company-wide newsletter.
- Build trust – surveys and town-hall style meetings can be useful here, as they make people know that they are valued and that they are being listened to and can contribute.

Organizations should encourage and facilitate relationship-building activities with their internal stakeholders. But this is only half the story: building relationships with external stakeholders is the other half.

Developing external relationships

Too often, business thinking and analysis assesses an issue from the organization's perspective using internally generated metrics, measures and conclusions. Yet some of these conclusions miss one obvious source of information: the clients themselves. This oversight leaves an important gap in a company's knowledge – one we will seek to overcome here. If a company wants to be successful in the marketplace, it must improve its relationships with external stakeholders. To do this, it must directly and regularly engage with customers – and its communications must be meaningful.

MOMENTS THAT MATTER

Deloitte

Proving the central significance of external relationships is Ralph Classon, one of Deloitte's long-time clients, who believes that, "Business success is all about people. It's about continuity, regular meetings, in between communication, following a client's business, and caring. I define outstanding service … as a variation on a familiar acronym, CPA = Client-centric, Proactive, Accountable." Recognizing the importance of relationship building,

Deloitte has initiated a program to put this principle into play – they call it the Moments That Matter lab.

Bill Freda of Deloitte says that the aim to generate breakaway growth basically relies on the tried and trusted method of "drawing attention to the client experience. The emphasis is on relationships." Of course, Deloitte has always focused on developing and maintaining strong client relationships; what this new approach has done is to intensify the focus, deal with complexity, clarify the situation and reveal solutions in a directly relevant way that strengthens relationships with customers. Crucially, the Moments That Matters lab provides a means for people to immerse themselves in what's important, away from the bustle of everyday activities, and zoom in on the best ways to invest in relationships.

BUILDING SUSTAINABLE RELATIONSHIPS

Relationship capital is the gold standard for building relationships with external stakeholders. Quite simply, it is what drives a business. By investing in relationships, capital and goodwill accumulate over time, providing companies with a valuable cushion against future difficulties. In this way, the Relationship R is closely related to the Resilience R. Although it's an intangible asset, those who create it (service providers, in this case) and those who receive it (clients) come to rely on it.

BUILDING BRAND RELATIONSHIPS – BRICK BY BRICK

Lego

Founded in 1932, Lego is one of the most iconic children's toys in the world. In 2004, the company hit financial difficulties and, for the first time in the company's history, someone from outside the family was appointed CEO. Jørgen Vig Knudstorp took charge and set about rebuilding the company and revitalizing the brand. To do this, he devised a seven-year strategy known as the Shared Vision. Central to his plans was the need to build strong relationships with customers and employees.

His relationship with employees grew out of this shared vision and his leadership style. In the early years, the focus was on ensuring the company's survival and turning the situation around. This demanded a top-down style of management – which is often frowned upon in business literature. However, the financial situation left little room for maneuver and the fact that it succeeded was due to Knudstorp building the right conditions for good relationships to develop. He gave people a shared vision so that everyone was on the same page, working together toward the same goals. In short, the certainty and purpose of this shared vision was the glue for good working relationships. After all, any relationship requires knowing why there is a relationship there in the first place: it must have a purpose.

The mission statement was a call to arms: 'we are here to make money'. This was about more than simply communicating the company's aims: it was about building the right relationship with employees. When there are clear goals and a sense of purpose, relationships are more collegial. By creating a bond between everyone, people work better with each other. Everything leaders do and say has an impact on relationships in the workplace.

Also, he made sure he was visible and approachable – as puts it, "managing at eye level." It seems an obvious thing to say but it is often overlooked: it is easier to have a relationship with someone that is there, someone you can approach and have a conversation with. Being visible and approachable and promoting a sense of shared challenges built camaraderie, trust and commitment. Once the financial tide was turned, Lego could move toward a looser, ground-up corporate structure that empowered managers and unlocked creativity and ideas.

Forming strong relationships hinges on what the people at Lego think of Knudstorp. Quite simply, employees will make a judgment on whether a leader is worth following. At Lego, people trust Knudstorp because he takes responsibility and makes things happen. Interestingly, Knudstorp's own belief that leadership should have "less talk and more action" also sets the tone for other relationships in the company. The emphasis is on each person taking responsibility and delivering results, and because everyone knows this, it creates an environment where people work well together to get things done.

One of the key issues that led Lego to its crisis was its lack of attention to customer relationships. In the main, it ignored its customers. Instead of learning directly from them, discovering what they really wanted, Lego relied on information provided by retailers. And that was not enough. With sales falling dramatically, Lego needed to learn more about its customers if it was to turn the situation around – and relationship marketing and community marketing were to help them do just that.

As part of the turnaround, Lego developed the notion of a 'creative platform' that engages in two-way conversations with customers. The company now has direct contact with consumers through its own sales channels, clubs and collaboration programs. The backbone of the customer communications exercise is the Lego Club, which has almost three million members. The Lego community is certainly one of the company's core assets. It actively encourages fans to interact with the company, including sharing their ideas for new products. While they have only 120 staff designers, they can potentially access 120,000 volunteer designers outside the company to help them develop new products. This creates an added advantage – Lego knows what its customers are looking for and that removes the uncertainty of 'will customers buy it'? that surrounds all product development. Moreover, this two-way communication really does get customers to psychologically invest in the company. When people feel part of something and feel that they are contributing to it, they want to stay with the group. By listening to customers, acting on their suggestions and encouraging them to share their ideas and thoughts with each other, Lego has built a loyal customer base. Building such a two-way relationship not only gave Lego the information it wanted, customers felt valued and they felt part of a community. Lego was turning 'customers' into 'loyal customers.' The result was swift, sales increased and customer preservation grew. The company went from making a $327 million net loss in 2004 to a

$232 million net profit just four years later. That is the difference that developing strong customer relationships makes – Lego had learned to put all the pieces together.

The benefits of sustainable relationships also follow a two-way directional path. For example, through deep reserves of relationship capital, service providers gain greater credibility and access to customers. Clients receive more service than expected, such as personal advice and strategic insight.

Figure 8.1: Building sustainable relationships

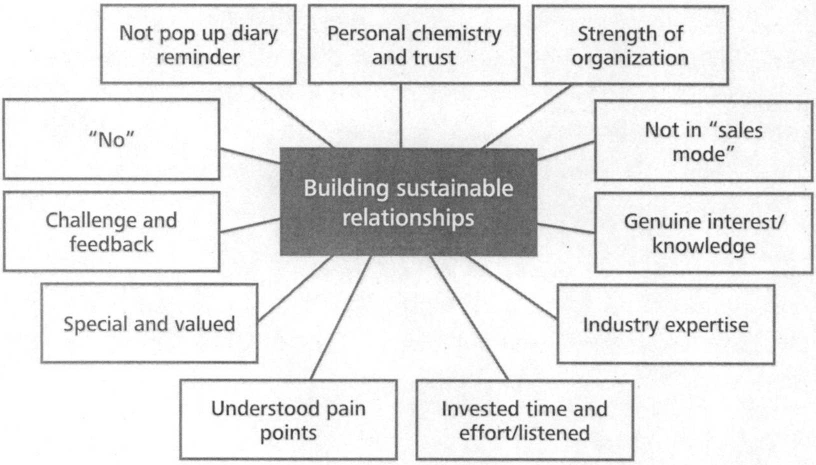

Relationships with clients – especially high-paying ones, with equally high expectations – are not always easy to get right. A common challenge faced across industries is how to deal with those high-stakes exchanges and opportunities. How you deal with these situations ranges from 'great' to 'oh-no' – and this is where relationship capital comes in. When teams create outstanding value for clients, the organization's reserves of relationship capital surge. Conversely, a company that does not deliver what the client is expecting very quickly draws down on their reserves, and the account runs the risk of being permanently depleted. The question, of course, is: What can a business do to gain and maintain traction?

The solution? This is where the Moments that Matter lab approach comes in very useful: it helps to get the right solution and suggest a productive way forward. Here, you should leave all theoretical notions, PowerPoint slides and lectures behind, and simply discuss what's working and what is not. This involves exploring real-life situations and issues from the point of view of strengthening and sustaining client relationships. This information should be brainstormed and the resulting ideas should be put through the prism of two types of moments: those you respond to and those you create. From this, a plan will emerge that will capitalize on these Moments That Matter that will create profound value for the organization.

> "RELATIONSHIPS AND TRUST. THIS IS THE BEDROCK OF LIFE."
>
> **Mukesh Ambani, Chairman & Managing Director, Reliance Industries**

If there is one aspect that will always emerge from any discussion on relationship capital and Moments that Matter, and one that underscores another element of the R for Relationship factor, it is trust.

A question of trust

Why is trust such an interesting concept? Perhaps the answer lies with the fact that it spans both the logical and emotional aspects of human thinking and behavior. Trust flows from experience and knowledge, as well as from consistency. Nevertheless, trust is also a sense of confidence, a feeling about someone or something's ability to deliver on a promise. Any way you look at it, while we may use information and data, trust requires judgment and a leap of faith.

For success in business and other relationships, trust is imperative. With this in mind, how do we generate trust? If there is one overriding rule, it is this: trust has to be earned.

Earning trust

Andrew Sobel studies how to manage trusted client relationships. In his book, 'Clients for Life,' written with Jagdish Sheth, he offers a model built upon seven attributes. These principles are applicable to all professionals who serve clients in all fields and industries. To be trusted, effective leaders must have:

- Empathy – specifically, ask great questions and listen
- Selfless independence – balance dedication with detachment and objectivity
- Depth as well as breadth of knowledge
- Synthesis – combining ideas as well as analysing them
- Judgment that incorporates their own and their clients' values and beliefs with their clients' organizational capabilities
- Conviction to communicate recommendations with belief and energy
- Integrity and competence – built through mutual familiarity with the client

A common trait of trusted advisor relationships is that the advisor places a higher value on maintaining and preserving the relationship itself than on the outcome of the current transaction. The advisor makes a substantial investment in the client, without guarantee of return, before the relationship generates any income, let alone any profit.

David H. Maister, Charles H. Green and Robert M. Galford address the subject of trust in their book, *The Trusted Advisor* (Free Press, 2001). Their research has highlighted the following key points:

- It is essential to focus on the client's needs rather than on your own. In this regard, it is also important to relate to the client as an individual rather than as a job title.
- A focus on problem definition and resolution is more important than technical or content mastery.
- A strong competitive drive should not be aimed at competitors; instead, it should be aimed at constantly finding new ways to be of greater service to the client.
- The focus should be on doing the right thing rather than on achieving specific outcomes. In other words, the means are as important as the end result.
- You should do the right thing for the client rather than be led by your own organization's rewards and dynamics.
- View methodologies, models, techniques and business processes as a means to an end – if they prove effective for a client, keep them, but discard them if they don't.
- Always value the quality of contact with clients – successful client relationships depend on the accumulation of high-quality contacts.
- Dedication to helping clients with their issues lies at the core of a good relationship – the client will know if this is genuine and they will value it when it is.

DEVELOPING RELATIONSHIPS WITH CURRENT AND POTENTIAL CUSTOMERS

Starbucks

Starbucks began life with one, small outlet in Seattle. It was hugely popular and it soon became an internationally successful coffeehouse chain. When revenues fell during an economic downturn, the founder, Howard Schultz, admitted that past success had made them complacent. Customers had drifted away in part, because they no longer felt that connection with Starbucks; the close relationship with customers that the company had always valued and worked at had disappeared – and, along with it, customers were disappearing too. Starbucks set about reversing this situation, aiming to win customers back. Getting customers through the door was the priority, and that would only happen by successfully rebuilding all relationships both with customers and employees.

Everything rests on building relationships. This simple truth is summed up by Howard Schultz's belief, "The best way to deliver the greatest customer experience is to deliver the best employee experience." In light of this, before we look at how Starbucks builds excellent customer relationships, we will look at the employee experience.

The inclusive, connected approach is evident from the outset – employees are known as partners. They are not just called partners, they really are considered partners. It is an attitude that promotes good relationships, where people feel equal and that their opinions matter. This atmosphere means that people are more confident, they will value what they do and will work well with colleagues, which ultimately results in an excellent customer experience. Also, a number of policies (from corporate healthcare to staff stock options) make the clear statement that partners are valued. The small-company atmosphere is highly conducive to partners being able to connect with each other and work well together – promoting trust, responsibility and dependability. Staff training is very high on the company's agenda; not only training them in basic skills and product knowledge but also encouraging genuine enthusiasm for coffee and customers. Relationship building doesn't stop there. Starbucks further builds trust through its responsible, we-all-share-the-planet approach to doing business and with community-minded and environmentally responsible policies. This attitude of a shared planet is reflected in its sense of shared community in the workplace. This matters: for relationships to grow, there has to be a point of connection; people need shared experiences. Of course, this attitude also helps to build strong relationships with customers.

If one idea dominates Starbucks' approach it is being totally customer-centric. Starbucks was conceived as a place for conversation that has a sense of community. It was designed to be a third place – not home, not work – where people could go to relax and enjoy a different, special experience during their day. From the outset, building great customer relationships was central to their approach. The space isn't just a place to have a cup of coffee; it is a place where you share a portion of your day with Starbucks. Having an easy, relaxed space, establishing rapport and gaining trust means customers enjoy a connection to Starbucks. As soon as customers walk through the door, and most likely the reason they walked through that door, is that they will feel they belong and that they are sharing the space with like-minded people. Being able to develop such a close relationship with their customers is a key reason for Starbuck's success. This connection helped the company rebuild its stock of relationship capital that it had previously depleted. As Starbucks found out: you should never let the coffee cup run dry.

Relationship marketing

Relationship marketing is a technique for building loyalty and business by enhancing customers' levels of satisfaction, understanding and trust. It focuses on managing and cultivating a company's clients and stakeholders. It relies on two-way communication to identify and meet current clients' preferences and needs. In this way, relationship marketing approaches customers from the perspective of retaining them, rather than directly selling to them. The idea is that happy customers will stay longer with a particular product, service or brand. Sales, and in particular, continued sales, will then flow not just for the short term, but over the long haul.

Community marketing takes this concept further by engaging customers at the point where their interest already is, or has the potential to become, a community. Meaningful communication is critical in building relationships and building connections around a product or service to form a community infuses relationships with meaning. For example, businesses using LinkedIn to find specific contacts is still a valuable way of connecting with people and a great example of the value of networking – an issue we'll discuss later.

Forrester Research advocates this customer-centric strategy, especially for the business-to-business (B2B) market. In fact, it considers community marketing mandatory, "marketers must abandon time-worn broadcasting and adopt community-focused marketing. Community marketing replaces traditional offer-response strategies with communications that foster dialogue; embrace community issues and values; and position brands, vendor experts, and products as valuable community resources."

How do you form a community? There are various tools available. Web 2.0 offers a range of interactive means that promote community marketing, such as blogs, Internet forums, RSS feeds, social networks and wikis. Further, organizations have their own arsenal of items. These include podcasts and webcasts made for community members that provide value and elicit further dialogue with and among customers. Also, face-to-face approaches matter. Advisory boards fall into this category. An important aspect of building a community is forming partnerships with stakeholders.

A critical success factor when building a community – or building any relationship – that is often neglected is networking.

Networking

The question we all want to know the answer to is: are savvy networkers hard-wired or can these skills be grown? The answer is that they can be developed, according to N. Anand and Jay Conger in *Capabilities of the Consummate Networker* (Organizational Dynamics, 2007, Vol. 36, No. 1, pp.13-17). The secret lies in four capabilities:

- **Understanding** and being able to identify the most important factor that will assure a successful result.
- **Knowing** which people to connect, in order to facilitate any plans – that is, match-making.
- **Managing** and improving your network, constantly.
- **Building** – always working to build good relationships with others.

Enhancing networking skills is not easy; it requires sustained effort. As Anand and Conger note, "Without fail, the managers who are most effective at networking that we researched told us they worked hard at developing their networking skills. It required a serious investment of time and focus on their part.... It is not a birthright of the chosen few."

MOVING BEYOND TRANSACTIONS

There's a common thread that runs throughout this chapter. For a business to generate sustainable earnings and profit it needs to move relationships with stakeholders beyond transactions. They must move the needle from deals/sales/service to experiences. Relevance, interest and personalization are all significant – these elements expand Moments that Matter into Relationships that Matter.

In our global, decentralized sphere of business operation, we still thrive on the personal touch. This applies to all relationships. The potential loss of personalization received public attention with the publication of John Naisbitt's book, *Megatrends* (Warner Books, 1982). "High tech/high touch" is how the author described the need for balance, "The more high technology around us, the more need for the human touch." Interestingly, high tech has changed the nature of personal touch and has facilitated it to an unprecedented degree, through, for example, blogs, tweets and other social media.

Those businesses that convert interactions with stakeholders into experiences and value are on the road to success. Social media has and continues to help.

Social media, for business and other uses, has grown so rapidly and garnered so much influence that it has spawned "Twitaholic.com." At the moment, those people with well over a million followers are: Britney Spears, Ashton Kutcher, Ellen DeGeneres, Lady Gaga, President Barack Obama and others. Is this the new form of high tech/high touch?

For businesses that use these tools to connect with people – keeping them informed, asking for their support, giving them special insights or things of value – the benefits in terms of relationships are very powerful. In fact, the more ways that a company can capitalize on this R, the better positioned it is to secure its place on the road to sustained growth and profit. If you are seeking to turbocharge your business, as AT&T and Bell System suggest, "Reach out and touch someone." When building strong business relationships this advice certainly rings true.

Figure 8.2: From digital to social business

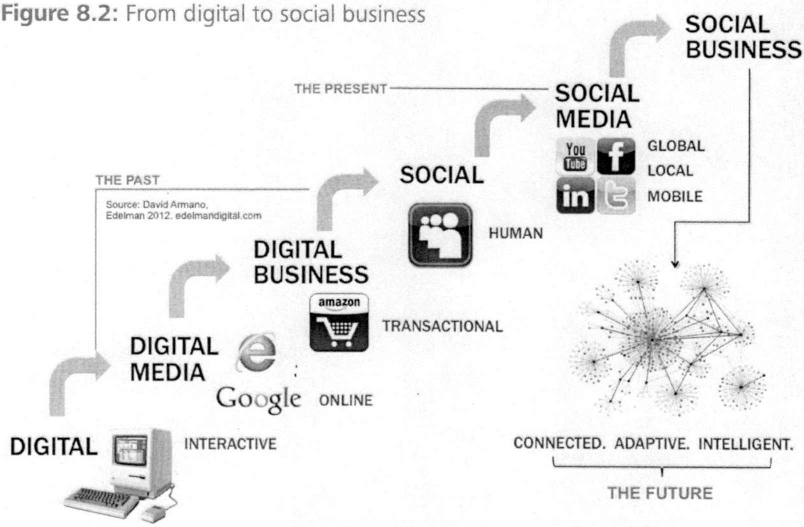

One final point to note about relationships is that even the most successful can hit a rough patch – after all, no one is perfect and all relationships, even the most successful, have their moments of tension or difficulty. What matters is how these challenges or concerns are addressed and, more generally, how readily companies learn about the best way to improve the relationship. This requires that companies evaluate their capabilities and address any weaknesses – the skill of Resilience, which is the focus for the next chapter.

Chapter Nine

Developing Resilience

"I have missed more than 9,000 shots in my career. I have lost almost 300 games. On 26 occasions I have been entrusted to take the game winning shot ... and I missed. I have failed over and over and over again in my life. And that's precisely why I succeed."

MICHAEL JORDAN, FORMER PROFESSIONAL BASKETBALL PLAYER

In a world defined by rapid change and volatility, resilience has taken on a whole new meaning. It is no longer simply a case of being able to fend off the occasional knock here and there – the capacity to quickly adapt, recover and return reinvigorated is a constant requirement. Consequently, resilience is now a critical part of any business strategy, and being flexible and ready to act should be the cornerstone of your business thinking. It is into this unpredictable world that we now enter, and resilience needs to be one of our closest companions.

"THE ONLY THING YOU'LL REGRET ABOUT A HARD DECISION IS THAT YOU DIDN'T DO IT SOONER."

Cathie Black, President, Hearst Magazines, remembering advice from a colleague

RESILIENCE: WHAT IT MEANS AND WHY IT MATTERS

Resilience requires companies to evaluate their capabilities and address any weaknesses. The business world is unfortunately full of examples of once-successful firms that have hit hard times. Why is it that some companies are able to weather change, while others struggle? Blundering on regardless, companies often ignored the signs that things weren't right. Given the difficult time of the current recession, companies and shareholders are increasingly looking to dependable, stable investments. This is not a climate where any company can afford to take their eye off the ball – they must constantly review internal capabilities and scan the business landscape to identify opportunities and threats. Drifting along, comfortable with the status quo, is not an option, as inertia is often a precursor to decline. Companies need to be proactive, dynamic, alert and flexible. Ideally, they must even be ready to completely change their business models before the need to change is forced upon them.

Building resilience requires a root and branch assessment and an overhaul of the organization. Every aspect needs to be addressed, from structures, procedures and strategy to the quality of leaders, individuals' resilience and how teams work. Evaluate the level of cooperation between people and teams – there should be a high level of trust and a shared purpose. Do people go on with their jobs and take objective, realistic approaches? You need to assess the whole organization's ability to respond swiftly and effectively to events and put systems and procedures in place and develop the necessary skills and resilience in your people. By planning ahead of time and having the right processes in place, your company will be better placed to cope with changes when they occur. However, you must also make sure that any rules and procedures that you put in place allow people the necessary space to innovate and be flexible, as these are essential to equipping the organization to develop new ideas and to react quickly. People are the most important part of an organization and everything depends on them. It is here that we will start our journey to create resilient companies.

DEVELOPING RESILIENCE: THE RIGHT PEOPLE, THE RIGHT TEAMS

> "CULTURE IS THE GLUE, THE UNDERLYING NETWORK THAT HOLDS US ALL TOGETHER ... THERE IS NO MORE IMPORTANT TASK FOR SENIOR MANAGEMENT THAN TO NURTURE AND REFRESH THE CULTURE AND VALUES."
>
> **Stephen Green, former Chairman, HSBC**

Companies need to actively pursue a policy of building resilience – not only in terms of the organization but also for individuals and how teams work. The problems and volatile markets that companies face require everyone to be on the same page and pull together. Turbulence brings opportunities and risks in equal measure. As individuals, we should take responsibility and call on, or acquire, the necessary personal qualities to help us cope with change. Also, teams have to work well, and the organization as a whole should be strengthened. Leaders should ensure they have the necessary capabilities and they should develop these skills in others.

RESILIENCE: THE KEY TO LONGEVITY AND SUCCESS

HSBC

Currently headquartered in London, HSBC bank was originally founded in Hong Kong in 1856 and, since then, it has expanded its operations around the world to become one of the largest banks in the industry. It has always had a sharp focus on customers, flexed with changing markets and been driven by a measured, entrepreneurial spirit. This has stood them in good stead over the years, and never more so than during the recent financial crisis, when some of the largest names in the industry either fell by the wayside or went hat in hand to governments for bailout money. Of course, the reasons for such a disaster in the banking industry are many but one thing does stand out: many banks were not resilient enough. And this is what made the difference: HSBC was better placed than most to weather the storm, by making sure the company was already better insulated against potential shocks.

Since the recent, global meltdown, the focus is now on setting stronger liquidity and capital reserve levels for banks. HSBC was already ahead of the curve in this regard, since several years before the financial crisis it had its own view about capital requirements and what it considered to be sensible levels of liquidity. As a result, it took a short-term hit by paying off its exposure in the subprime market and putting aside greater reserves than was then formally required (a higher Tier 1 capital ratio than many competitors). This cushioned HSBC against the worst effects of the crisis that felled many of its rivals. Of particular significance was the fact that it had faced up to its own exposure in the subprime mortgage lending crisis long before other banks were prepared to acknowledge there was a real problem. In other words, resilience was, and is, an important factor in its strategy, operations, culture and values, which keeps them alert to changes and ready to react quickly.

In addition to the vagaries of the market, HSBC deals with many countries, all with a raft of legislation and compliance issues – and all with different attitudes and beliefs. The bank possesses an extensive and proactive capability for handling this. While it has not been immune to falling afoul of legislation, its efforts and vigilance have protected it from the harsher fates of other companies – whose fines have been significantly greater.

Stephen Green, former Chairman of HSBC, believes that the market itself is a tough adjudicator of resilience; a company will stand or fall on the response of the market to its offering and actions. This is where reason and resilience interlink. As Stephen Green argues, resilience is diminished when a company loses sight of the customer and when it forgets the reason it is in business in the first place. Today, customers and markets expect more from companies and banks, and this brings us to how another of our six Rs, relationships, is connected to resilience. At HSBC, there is a sharp focus on building relationships with customers. And this includes both direct contact and the many indirect routes to influencing relationships, such as how all HSBC's actions affect how it is perceived – in other words, its reputation.

This move, toward greater responsibility and managing reputation in business, can be seen in the World Economic Forums, which now extend beyond pure economic issues to include discussions on values and ethics. It is hardly surprising that corporate values are crucial to HSBC building resilience. Stephen Green remarks that "some of the good old-fashioned principles by which we have always sought to run this company for the last hundred years – strong capital, strong liquidity, diversified business – have counted for quite a lot." Stephen Green (*The Focus*, Volume XIV/1 www.ezsfocus.com Egon Zehnder International).

Accordingly, building resilience into the culture is an integral part of HSBC's approach. In Stephen Green's view, "Culture is the glue, the underlying network that holds us all together ... There is no more important task for senior management than to nurture and refresh the culture and values." (Reported in *The Focus*, Volume XIV/1 www.ezsfocus.com Egon Zehnder International.) At HSBC, to achieve sustainable profits in the long-term, the focus is on taking a long-term view of customer relationships, employee engagement and development, business investments and corporate social responsibility. This last point is increasingly important to building resilience because, as we have seen, both the reason why you are in business and your reputation are key aspects of resilience. Corporate social responsibility reflects who you are and what you stand for, and this is not lost on customers, employees, investors, the media, etc. The values that HSBC espouses as a company promote trust between the bank and its existing and potential customers (and its employees) and enhance its reputation in the market. This matters because customer retention and the acquisition of new customers are paramount, as is having an engaged, enthusiastic workforce. A key role of HSBC's leadership is to make sure that its culture and values are firmly embedded throughout the organization and are renewed to keep the bank aligned with current needs and future opportunities. Moreover, whenever an acquisition is made, HSBC works hard to transfer its culture and values to the new company.

Every year, the board at HSBC meets to discuss corporate values and to assess whether they are achieving those values in practice. The bank also carries out yearly surveys to gauge the level of employee engagement. This reveals the bank's strengths and weaknesses and where things could be improved. Interestingly, these surveys have revealed that the bank's approach to corporate social responsibility is highly valued by employees. Stephen Green notes: "These kinds of things matter, and they are part of what it takes to ensure that there's cohesiveness, and an enthusiasm for doing a good job. For the vast majority of people it is not enough simply to say, here's a job and we'll pay you for it. They actually want a sense of reward that is not monetary out of doing their job." (*The Focus*, Volume XIV/1 www.ezsfocus.com Egon Zehnder International.) And, as we saw in Chapter 8 on relationships, enthusiastic, engaged employees lead to excellent customer service.

In such a volatile world, companies cannot afford to be complacent. Self-awareness and self-criticism are key factors for HSBC in order to avoid complacency and to improve. To do this, HSBC instills reflection, self-criticism and improvement into its culture. This is not to say that the bank avoids risk; rather, it is about having the right safeguards in place so that risks are managed carefully to maintain overall resilience within the bank, should anything go wrong. Stephen Green recognizes the importance of being, "honest with yourself; to recognize when things have gone wrong; to recognize when it's your fault, but also to recognize that you always have the chance of renewal and a fresh start." (*The Focus*, Volume XIV/1 www.ezsfocus.com Egon Zehnder International.) Not wasting time berating yourself but, instead, learning from all your experiences and mistakes and moving on is essential – otherwise, the atmosphere runs the risk of becoming overly negative, counter-productive and even toxic.

A significant policy at HSBC that contributes to employee motivation and retention is to recruit senior people from within the company. Consequently, the people in senior roles or at board level have been with the company for a long time. The advantage is that these people know the bank very well, have a demonstrated commitment to the company, are a good fit and share the values and culture. Similarly, recruitment is focused on looking for people who fit with HSBC's values and culture. The bank's International

Management Program for graduates takes people with the right fit, ability, and motivation and develops them for a lifelong career in a high-powered, exciting, global environment. This level of commitment and training from the company is how they attract and retain the best candidates. HSBC's policy toward recruitment, development and promotion provides consistency and that undoubtedly contributes to the bank's resilience.

The world economy has changed, with the weakening of traditional power blocs and the rise of others. To navigate this new landscape, HSBC repositions and realigns itself in order to take advantage of opportunities, avert threats, overcome vulnerabilities and minimize risk. Resilience is a conscious and constant activity that should reach every part of the organization. There is no place for complacency – the markets can be fickle and volatile, and you have to be prepared for any eventuality. Even though HSBC did not suffer as badly as other banks during the financial crisis, its leaders are not resting on their laurels. They have reviewed, planned and initiated an extensive, root and branch overhaul of systems and procedures to avert the possibility of future problems. This is not just in response to the demands from regulators, governments, investors and customers; it is because HSBC's leaders know the value of resilience – it has always been a cornerstone of the bank's approach. HSBC knows that without resilience, the fate that befell other giants of the banking industry, such as Lehman Brothers, will be waiting, ready to strike..

Resilience rule #1: look after your people

Avoiding or minimizing stress is a key issue in today's frantic, uncertain world. People under stress are often not alert to what is happening around them, as, understandably, they can be almost entirely internally focused. They may also have poor attention skills or be prone to oversights and mistakes. It is useful to establish a network of mutual support so that people do not feel isolated and they will know how to obtain help should they need it. In addition, you should develop your people so that they have personal flexibility and the ability and readiness to adapt to changing situations. Brittle people do not react well to stress or change. Interestingly, this applies to businesses as well as people. A brittle, unbending business is likely to snap when faced with change. Enduring businesses, like successful people, are both strong and flexible.

Resilience rule #2: develop confidence in yourself and others

People need inner strength and the ability to remain calm, focused and confident when handling crises. They will need energy, drive, determination and conviction. If these qualities are part of the organization's culture and values, you are more likely to build a workforce and leaders that are more resilient. Experience is a good teacher, in this regard, as it exposes us to pressures and challenges, and we will take this learning to other situations. Being positive, having clear goals and being open to new ideas and possibilities are ideal attributes, as are being innovative, asking questions and being able to think ahead.

Confidence is particularly important. It will make a significant difference knowing that you can control situations and direct your own responses and the future of the company. Be good at planning and be organized and reliable and always be aware of what you want the future to look like, maintaining the flexibility to make any changes –or even to completely overhaul the organization's direction if you think that is necessary.

Resilience rule #3: provide support and challenge

Spend some time reassessing the way things are done. Ask yourself: is there a better way of approaching an issue or completing tasks? Seek the opinions of others and, together, improve the systems and procedures to make them more resilient. Ensure that your people will be able to respond to changes, including sudden crises, quickly, efficiently and successfully. This will also require you to make the necessary resources and support available to enable people to respond.

Leaders need to be strong and resilient. In particular, people in senior roles need the necessary experience, skills and behaviors to steer the company and its people through difficult or turbulent times and to maintain everyone's morale, commitment and enthusiasm. Do this by identifying individuals with resilience and using them to keep others motivated. They will need outstanding people skills and influencing skills, to be calm and measured, able to take control of situations, be proactive and have enormous reserves of energy and drive. An often overlooked aspect of how easy it is for a company to become vulnerable to the inevitability of decline is the erosion of hope. During difficult times, it is essential that leaders handle situations and people properly and that they maintain morale.

"YOU GET PEOPLE TO HELP YOU BY TELLING THE TRUTH."

Randy Pausch, former professor of computer science, Carnegie Mellon University

Resilience rule #4: look for original – and possibly unconventional – insights

Senior people should possess excellent critical, strategic and lateral thinking skills, and have the ability to be objective, realistic and factual, innovative and creative. In addition, they should possess market awareness and be able to get 'the big picture view' and understand the details, avoiding inertia. All of these qualities figure prominently in the list of skills required for improving resilience.

Resilience rule #5: value learning and experience

Expose people to experiences that will equip them for dealing with crises and difficult situations. Experience is certainly a great teacher; if individuals are used to dealing with difficult situations, they will be more comfortable with, and confident in, their ability to handle any event, be less likely to panic, able to remain in control and retain the ability to think both logically and creatively in times of crisis. In particular, experience keeps people alert to signs in the business environment of any potential problems that are looming. It is not just about experiencing difficulties it is also about learning how to handle them positively and well. Make sure that people are supported and guided and have positive experiences and successes and that they learn valuable lessons to take into future situations. This is not to say that you have to hold someone's hand, since this would hardly test an individual's mettle in coping with challenges. Rather, it is about providing support where necessary, to ensure that learning experiences do not erode confidence to the point where an individual can no longer function effectively in the present and consequently, become unlikely to perform well in future crises.

Resilience rule #6: put the right people in the right roles

There are many assessment tests that are available to help find the right candidate for a particular role or task. While these can be useful, there is no substitute for a person's actual record of achievement – in particular, the challenges they faced, the mistakes they made, how they tackled the issue and what they have learned from the experience.

Evaluate your recruitment criteria and make sure you are not looking backwards. There is often a tendency to recruit people according to certain characteristics and skills based on what worked well in the company's past. However, the past has gone. Remember that you are not just hiring for today, you are hiring to prepare your company for tomorrow, which will undoubtedly have new challenges and may require new approaches.

Resilience needs to be part of all succession planning decisions. It needs to be handled well, as the consequences of failure can be extremely serious and costly. The person selected should be ideally suited to the demands of the job and have the necessary experience to help them cope with any eventuality. They need to be strong and they also need to be open and flexible.

While internal recruitment can be a great source of resilience, as in the case of HSBC, it does run the risk of inertia and can entail overlooking even better candidates with experience more suited to new challenges and changes in the market. At the highest levels, finding the right candidate from outside the organization can be extremely difficult; that's why companies often take the easier route of recruiting from within – although, it has to be said, there are also perfectly valid reasons for appointing a well-qualified, internal candidate. That said, it is always advisable to look further afield, as you may realize that there are skill gaps in internal candidates' abilities – gaps you may not even be aware of if you are always looking internally. Moreover, succession planning is exactly that: it is a planning process. As such, it should be viewed as a continual activity. By staying alert to both internal and external people, how they are developing, their record and experience, you will be in a better position when you next need to go shopping for a new candidate.

> "YOU NEED PEOPLE WHO HAVE COURAGE AND DETERMINATION AND WHO ARE WILLING TO TAKE A RISK AND PUT IN A LOT OF HARD WORK."
>
> **Cathie Black, President, Hearst Magazines**

Furthermore, any succession planning decision starts with a clear description of what skills and experience the candidate should possess. This will only be of use if the criteria have been arrived at following consultation with key people and groups and by considering the demands of the job in light of current and future strategy and issues that are in line with the company's culture.

Resilience rule #7: develop teamwork – the vital component for resilience

The challenges facing companies and the sheer scale of the tasks involved require teamwork all the way to the top. The variety and complexity of issues demand the resources and abilities of many different people, with different areas of expertise and various skills. Consequently, effective teamworking is crucial, and is the only way to achieve goals. It is essential that everyone in the team is clear about the problems that need to be faced and what has to be done. Also, it is useful to plan ahead of time exactly who will be responsible for making sure that each task is completed. Assigning tasks to the best-suited person or team will promote a successful outcome – in other words, play to people's strengths. This will make everything run smoothly and minimize panic. Teams should work well together. Trust, dependability, and openness are essential, as is strong leadership qualities and a realistic attitude. By working closely together, supporting each other, sharing ideas and spreading the workload, facing an overwhelming challenge will be less daunting, much easier to tackle and more successfully resolved.

Teams need to be seen holistically. By this I mean that effective teams result from all the people within them and, most importantly, how they work together. They also need to be able to look beyond the organizational walls and be aware of external factors and stakeholders. Teams work within the whole organization and, as such, need to relate well to others. Essentially, the whole organization is a team and the individuals and teams within it still have to work together, moving in the same direction and supporting each other toward one aim: the success of the company.

RESILIENCE AT WORK

Hearst Magazines

Hearst Magazines is part of the Hearst Corporation and it publishes some of the most popular magazines in over 100 countries around the world, including Marie Claire, Cosmopolitan and Good Housekeeping. It currently enjoys a healthy portfolio and revenue stream but it has not always been a straightforward journey. A few bumps led to the derailment of some projects, and, like many in publishing, it has faced a very difficult time. But, with Cathie Black as president, the company has shown remarkable resilience and is now one of the most successful magazine publishing houses in the world. A key aspect of surviving difficult times, at the Hearst Corporation, has been to remember what the company stands for – and stick to their convictions. Innovation and diversification have always been part of the company's approach. In the past, when threats appeared, the Hearst Corporation diversified into other areas, including television, to build resilience. In the magazine division, new projects are constantly being reviewed and it uses technology to add value to the business.

At Hearst Magazines it is also important to look for synergies, to plug the gaps in the product offering and to be bold. While the company produced magazines that included some articles on food, it did not have a magazine focused solely on food. So, even during the grips of a recession, the company launched a new and fairly risky publication called Food Network Magazine in a joint venture with Scripps, who ran the popular cable TV channel called the Food Network (which, at the time, had almost 100 million subscribers and aired in other countries). In a highly competitive market that is already awash with cookery journals, this was not without risk. This challenge did not faze the leadership, however, who trusted in the organization's ability to leverage skills, experience and reputation. This required confidence and boldness.

Key to making such a bold investment decision was breaking the typical mold in the publication industry that dictates that a return on a new publication can take five years. During a recession, a new mindset was needed. They scaled back the usual costs and scope involved in launching a new publication and set new, challenging parameters. Two things made a significant difference. First, they launched the magazine when it was good enough to go onto the market, accepting that further changes could be made later – previously, they underwent a costly and protracted development period. Second, they massively reduced the number of people working on the magazine and that slashed costs. Basically, the company did more with less. The results vindicated the decision: within one year of launch, the magazine enjoyed a circulation of 1.3 million, and in 2009, there were 300 million subscribers. It now occupies the coveted number one slot in the U.S. for food magazines at newsstands. Undoubtedly, the synergy with the Food Network channel has boosted sales.

Critically, the leaders at Hearst Magazines responded innovatively to changes in the market. The economic downturn meant that advertisers were no longer willing (or able) to pay as much. So they tried a different approach by not charging for test advertising. Previously, the industry would charge a low initial rate for advertising in a newly launched test magazine, which would then be increased should the magazine sell more copies than expected. This situation was never popular with advertisers, since they had no idea what the final bill would be – hardly a satisfactory state of affairs, especially during a recession, since this prevented advertisers from managing their costs. Not charging for advertising may sound like a recipe for disaster for a product that usually doesn't break even for five years (it broke even in much less time) but this was a calculated and measured tactic. The people at Hearst Magazines felt that test advertising would not make a huge, immediate difference to revenue but that getting the right sorts of advertisers in the beginning, and showing them the difference that advertising in the magazine could make would matter for future revenue. Also, this offer meant that they had more control over which companies advertised and that enabled them to create the right look and feel in order to make the magazine more appealing to customers.

Having the right team around is essential. As Cathie Black says, you need "people who have courage and determination and who are willing to take a risk and put in a lot of hard work." (*The Focus*, Volume XIV/1 www.ezsfocus.com Egon Zehnder International) She believes in treating her people well and being open to their ideas. The company rewards people for their contributions and hard work, which keeps morale high and employees engaged – particularly important in such a high-pressured environment. Also, Hearst Magazines regularly conducts sessions with people from different parts of the company to explore what kind of future people would like for the company. This inclusive approach certainly makes people know they are valued but, significantly, it leads to the development of many ideas and viewpoints. All of this information better informs strategic and operational decisions and it fosters a sense of shared direction and purpose.

Leading from the front and inspiring others is paramount to Cathie Black's leadership style. This matters, if you want the commitment and dedication of your people, since employees are less likely to follow someone that doesn't set a good example. Similarly, she believes that the leadership team should show unanimity. Obviously, disunity can leave people throughout the organization feeling unsettled, nervous, directionless and demotivated. In addition, when handling difficult situations, being honest with people is particularly important for gaining trust, support and commitment to plans.

A fundamental aspect of resilience at Hearst Magazines is that leaders take control of issues and situations, rather than allowing themselves to be led in directions they did not choose. A case in point is how they reacted to the general negativity of the dwindling impact and arena of newspaper publications. Rather than wait for this negative attitude to spread to magazines, Cathie Black, along with other key figures in the industry, took control, stuck to her strong conviction that magazines are an effective medium and commissioned an advertising campaign to put forward the case for the vibrancy and effectiveness of magazines based on facts rather than incorrect speculation. She is proactive and brings people along with her – including external parties. Contrary to popular belief, despite the downturn, magazines have enjoyed increasing sales and in particular, their readership is drawn heavily from the most prized demographic – the 18-34 year-old segment. As their advertising campaign has demonstrated, this makes magazines a particularly effective medium for advertisers.

Resilience, as the old adage 'forewarned is forearmed' suggests, relies on the ability to scan the environment and be aware of changing circumstances. Significantly, the people at Hearst Magazines keep alert to signs of impending problems. For example, when they received fewer replies to the subscription card inserts from the magazine Talk, they suspected that trouble was brewing. Sure enough, circulation figures soon fell precipitously.

Experiencing difficulties has certainly taught the people at Hearst Magazines. In 2001, the magazine Talk was pulled in its third year of publication. It had been the product of a joint venture. Unfortunately, most of the editorial decisions and business plans had been made before Hearst Magazines joined, and those involved did not fully appreciate the ramifications of this. This mistake was avoided in the joint venture with the Food Network channel. Similarly, when Cathie Black helped set up *USA Today* earlier in her career, she faced immense challenges that equipped her for the future. "I think that experience [at *USA Today*] prepared me for any eventuality, from dealing with Wall Street to giving speeches and presentations to exercising editorial involvement and figuring out our strategies."

Building and running a resilient company involves making many difficult choices. You need inner strength to cope with the pressure and the energy and commitment to carry your policies through. It is not for the faint of heart but Cathie Black remembers some advice given to her by a previous employee at Hearst Magazines, "the only thing you'll regret about a hard decision is that you didn't do it sooner."

SUSTAINABILITY

By integrating sustainability into your strategy and operations you will build stronger, more resilient organizations. To do this, make sure that you get the right team and leader to manage sustainability so that your company is better placed to operate successfully. A sustainability program needs a leader who can manage change, influence others and win support. Without the ability to persuade others, especially key influencers within the organization, progress is likely to be slow and ineffectual. It is essential to educate everyone in the organization about the merits of sustainability so that they fully appreciate the risks and opportunities involved, and to gain their commitment. You need to make the case for sustainability, point out the advantages and win people over.

"THE PAST CANNOT BE OVERCOME. IT IS THE PAST. BUT ITS TRACES AND, ABOVE ALL, THE LESSONS TO BE LEARNED FROM IT EXTEND TO THE PRESENT."

Gerhard Schröder, Chancellor of Germany 1998-2005

There is a compelling case to be made for the commercial advantages of a program of sustainability. It circumvents or minimizes risk and provides considerable competitive advantage. By making departments responsible for achieving specific goals, you will ensure participation and commitment.

Realigning a company in order to achieve sustainability targets is not easy. It requires purposeful dedication, clarity of objectives and the ability to handle a myriad of issues. Compliance also figures prominently and actions must always be measured against any regulatory requirements. Nonetheless, sustainability goes beyond compliance and should also focus on commercial benefits – from limiting risks and reducing costs to enhancing reputation and appealing to customers.

A key aspect of any sustainability program is to remain open to new ideas and to be ready to flex, as new information or challenges come to light. Fundamentally, sustainability has to be a part of all strategic and operational developments, to ensure that the company does not stray into areas that will be ultimately harmful to long-term profitable growth. The role of sustainability in building resilient organizations cannot be overstated. Far from being a soft issue and 'I have to comply with regulations' chore, it should be a core value of the organization – a powerful means of reducing risk, sourcing new opportunities and moving the company onto a path of sustainable growth.

Sustainability is much more than concern for environmental issues. Today, it goes beyond the traditional view of sustainability to include other aspects that ensure the long-term, sustainable growth of the company.

Avoiding inertia and having foresight are essential to exposing weaknesses, exploiting opportunities and building long-term resilience. For example, Ford's CEO, Alan Mulally, took advantage of low interest rates to borrow substantial sums of money to restructure the company, improve manufacturing processes and overhaul their product offerings. He was widely criticized for this tactic, since borrowing so much money seemed all out of proportion for a company that was facing an immediate and serious threat. However, as Alan Mulally foresaw, this upgrade prepared the company for the future. And this is the point: at its best, resilience is about adapting before a potential problem becomes a real problem. While we can all be caught off guard from time to time or need to immediately react to events, ideally, resilience should be proactive rather than reactive.

Interestingly, Jim Collins identifies several stages where companies repeatedly ignore signs and inevitably decline. Initially, companies can be overconfident and overstretch themselves into areas that do not necessarily fit with the rest of the company. Then they will ignore signs that indicate that things aren't going well – or even deny that a problem exists at all. When the problems can no longer be avoided, it is often so late that these companies go into desperation mode and fail to turn the situation around.

Complacency, lack of objectivity and forgetting what the company's purpose is and what the company stands for are significant factors that lead to this situation. Here, it is important to keep an eye on two of our six Rs: reason and in particular, revenue. Any plan has to be funded; without generating the appropriate level of revenue to implement and sustain those plans, the business is likely to run into trouble. This, however, is not an inevitable situation: if you take control and are prepared to do whatever it takes, including completely restructuring or realigning the business, you can turn a company around.

An idea of the extent of the changes that you may have to implement is highlighted by the example of the Finnish company, Nokia. Starting as a paper mill in the 19th century, it has faced many challenges and market changes and has diversified, realigned its company and offered different products, accordingly – from generating electricity to making car tires. When the company faced difficulties in the 1980s it was completely restructured and is now a major telecommunications company. This flexibility and adaptability enhanced its ability to survive many market upheavals and take advantage of opportunities. The company did not worry about what it was producing; it was focused on the overall success and survival of the business. After all, a company is about making money, first and foremost – nothing else can be achieved without revenue.

Although it is possible to rescue a company, it is obviously better to build resilience before problems occur – either to avoid difficulties or to equip you to handle challenges more effectively. The examples of HSBC and Hearst Magazines show how companies put resilience front and center in all their strategic, operational and people issues, and reveal exactly how important it is to instill resilience throughout an organization.

HOW DO YOU DEVELOP RESILIENCE?

There are several techniques, capabilities and ways of thinking that will help you ensure success.

- Align the company's culture and its goals
- Know your organization and your people – their strengths and weaknesses
- Evaluate available options
- Imagine solutions and see likely or different possible futures
- Be flexible
- Inspire and lead others
- Be open to new ideas and to change
- Possess the drive needed to handle demanding situations, stress and pressure
- Learn from experience
- Expose yourself and your people to new, challenging experiences
- Cultivate inner strength
- Nurture creativity and innovation
- Surround yourself with the right people
- Avoid inertia
- Develop insight and foresight
- Build a culture of resilience

VALUES, SKILLS AND RESILIENCE ARE INDIVIDUAL

Strong corporate values matter. They provide a sense of shared purpose and keep people working together for the same goals. These values are the very foundation that everything else is built upon and are especially important when dealing with change and uncertain times. Boldness and imagination are other key aspects for surviving crises and growing a business, as is awareness of the environment around you. It is certainly the case that we are often unaware of opportunities or problems until it is so late that it becomes much harder to react successfully or to resolve issues. However, the key word here is 'harder.' This is not the same thing as impossible. With the right attitude and approach, by figuring out how to change the situation, it can be possible to turn even the direst of situations around. After all, as Archimedes said, "Give me a place to stand, and I will change the world."

What matters, however, is that each individual comes to their own belief that these issues – values, purpose, boldness, imagination and others – are important and interprets them in their own personal, individual way. In fact, the most significant lesson for any business leader is to know that, while structures, procedures, processes and systems can all be improved, the true source of resilience is people. Everything rests with them: they are the reason a company succeeds. This leads us to the next part of the book: people need to think holistically, as a team and with the six Rs clearly in mind, but they also need to take personal responsibility for making this happen. This is a challenge we describe as Thinking Holistically, Acting Personally, and it provides the focus for the next chapter.

Chapter Ten

The Holistic Way to Build a World-Class Business

This book is based on one simple belief: that to succeed in today's volatile, challenging and competitive climate and be ready for tomorrow's opportunities and risks, leaders need to Think Holistically and Act Personally. It is this balance between strategy and tactics, big picture and detail, planning and action, corporate direction and personal responsibility, which helps to ensure progress and resilience for the organization. In practice, as we have seen, this means succeeding in six broad areas: leading with a purpose and reason, generating and maximizing revenues, rousing and engaging people and their talents, building relationships, developing a clear reputation and being resilient. These six Rs don't

'BUSINESS-AS-USUAL' AND CERTAINTY HAVE LONG GONE, AND WE MUST NOW REALIGN OUR COMPANIES TO DEAL EFFECTIVELY WITH THE CHALLENGES AND OPPORTUNITIES OF TODAY'S COMPLEX, VOLATILE BUSINESS WORLD. COMPANIES AND THEIR PEOPLE NEED A FRESH MINDSET AND APPROACH.

operate in isolation: they overlap and support each other, and failure in one area will undermine the others. So now we turn to building a framework where our six Rs work together so that they result in a strong, high-performing organization. First, however, the foundation for the framework lies in a clear understanding of the present challenges and the recognition that many companies are standing on a burning platform.

IN CASE WE FORGET ...

The world is certainly a volatile, fickle place. Markets are more competitive and unpredictable; the pace of change is unprecedented and new challenges are constantly emerging. Financial meltdowns, market turmoil, technological advances and new opportunities have left many reeling and others enjoying meteoric success. Certainty is a thing of the past. Today, organizations face an array of problems and a wealth of opportunities, making flexibility and energy the watchwords of the day. We need to build robust companies that can weather any storm – and this is not easy. If there is one thing that the six Rs have taught us it is to take a total approach in our businesses. Clearly, this is no small task, but then the rewards are correspondingly immense. It is now time to put everything we have learned to work, and implement the THAP framework: Think Holistic, Act Personal.

Business-as-usual and certainty have long gone and we must now realign our companies to deal effectively with the challenges and opportunities of today's complex, volatile business world. Companies need the right mindset and approach and they need the best systems in place to ensure profitable growth. The overwhelming number of changes and burgeoning competition is truly daunting, and it would be impossible to account for every eventuality. Instead, we should aim to strengthen our businesses, make them robust enough for any challenge. It is like the old adage: give a person a fish and they will eat for one day; teach them to fish and they will eat for a lifetime. We need to do the same with our companies: rather than being reactive and constantly firefighting, we need to be proactive and form them to deal with any eventuality. Only by doing this will we be battle ready and ensure the long-term survival of our companies.

To insulate our companies from risks, while being ready to exploit opportunities, we need to stay tuned to the environment and be able to respond to it swiftly and appropriately. This point can't be emphasized enough – in a world of hyper-discontinuity, success depends on knowing what to do with information. The battle line will inevitably be fought over this very point, as it is this that gives us the ability to adapt and dominate.

This leaves us with the unavoidable truth: to ensure long-term survival, we have to put the right processes, culture and leadership in place. This may involve radical changes to your company but if you want to succeed, that is exactly what you will have to do – there is no easy way around it. As we said in the opening chapter, this may be a harsh wake-up call but we have to adjust to the new reality that the past is no longer relevant and the future is up for grabs. The future belongs to companies that are battle ready.

CRITICAL, STRATEGIC, LATERAL THINKING HELPS US APPROACH ISSUES AND SITUATIONS ACCURATELY, LOGICALLY AND CREATIVELY AND THIS ENABLES US TO CHALLENGE EXISTING BELIEFS OR PLANS AND TO IMAGINE NEW POSSIBILITIES.

There are four key areas businesses need to address: how to Think effectively, take a Holistic approach, Act in the right way at the right time, and take Personal responsibility for making progress. All of these four areas then need to be integrated so that they work together. Being good in one or two areas is not enough; companies need to cover all the bases if they want to hit a home run.

THINKING BETTER

Thinking is a complex activity and getting it right is critical to every aspect of running a business. It is a multidimensional process that involves identifying, analyzing and synthesizing information from many different sources. If incisive, insightful decision making is one of the high standards demanded in today's business environment, we need to make sure that our thinking skills are up to the task. Easy, you may think, but it is surprisingly difficult to make the right decision at the right time in a way that leads to success (for example, by involving others so they are fully engaged). No one wants to make a stupid decision and some of the biggest corporate failures – from Enron to Lehman Brothers and Bear Stearns – were run by smart people. The chapter on thinking will reveal how poorly understood thinking skills can be and how we could all do with a refresher course.

Critical thinking enables us to assess situations logically, rationally, without bias and with an open mind. We are constantly bombarded with an array of information and we have to pick our way through all of it, deciding what is relevant, what can be discarded, what is subjective, what is factual, how past experiences are influencing our thoughts and assessing if our own uncertainty (or that of others) is clouding an issue, or possible solutions, in some way. Arriving at an accurate and effective conclusion from this mass of information is difficult. Critical thinking will help us steer our way through by highlighting the facts and what's involved. It assesses everything in terms of accuracy, scope, relevance, reliability and significance. It is about seeing a situation in the cold light of day.

Critical thinking

Reading this book, you may already be in a leadership role in your company and you will undoubtedly have had a mixture of successes and failures en route – we all do. By acquiring or improving critical thinking skills you will be even better placed to take your company further, strengthening it not just for today but for the business world of tomorrow. The payoff: sustained profit and growth.

Why is critical thinking so important? It removes emotions. It steers us away from thinking traps. It circumvents preconceived notions. It deals with facts but, more than that, it lifts our sights from the muddle of information and blind alleys so that the economic landscape is laid bare before us. Only by seeing what is really out there can we hope to see the best solutions, develop effective strategies and take the right actions.

No matter what level you are operating at in your company, critical thinking is essential. No part of an organization operates alone. Everyone, at every level, contributes to the bottom line. Being tuned to what is around you, being able to notice flaws and opportunities, evaluating the facts accurately and suggesting improvements and actions will add to the overall success of the company.

Strategic thinking

Strategic thinking is a vital skill: it is goal oriented, it takes in the whole landscape and it is all about securing competitive advantage. Business acumen and insights lie at the core of this skill. We need to know where to allocate resources for the greatest effect, and we need to know which actions will lead to the best outcome. It is a mode of thinking that focuses our attention away from outdated ideas and onto what matters now.

While there is definitely a broad-sweep aspect to this method, this is not to suggest a lack of rigor or detail. On the contrary, it is an inclusive, extensive and highly detailed approach that evaluates all perspectives. This is fundamental, as any strategy ultimately relies on your ability to identify and evaluate all the trends, relationships and patterns that exist (as well as ones that do not yet exist).

Strategic thinking means taking the whole organization into account and you need to see it in different time frames – past, present and future. Strategic thinking is where everything comes together. It combines critical and creative thinking to develop and test hypotheses and to devise the best solutions. It sees the world for what it is and what it could be. Being able to recognize new realities or imagine a new reality of your choosing and then acting on your insight and making it happen is the domain of strategic thinking. This is not a one-off exercise; it is a constant requirement. We must always remain open to new information and be ready to act.

Why is strategic thinking so important? It makes us flexible, responsive, resilient, determined and focused. Seeing the big picture makes the path in front clear – it gives us an awareness of the scale of what needs to be done, where and how we need to act; it makes us bolder and it enables us to maneuver our companies through risks and opportunities to secure long-term, sustainable growth.

THE ROLE OF STRATEGIC THINKING CANNOT BE OVERSTATED. IT ENABLES US TO MANAGE CHANGE AND UNCERTAINTY AND IT IS THE ROUTE TO CREATING VALUE.

Although strategic thinking is certainly demanding and is not for the faint of heart, just like critical thinking, it can be learned. It takes you away from business-as-usual thinking to see new possibilities. It will help you to understand your goals better and reveal how to achieve them. It is both reflective and proactive, generating ideas, limiting risks and pointing the way to the right course of action. Significantly, it is about knowing your opponent and outwitting them while also knowing where alliances and cooperation will be mutually beneficial. Knowing that your plans are based on such a thorough foundation will build confidence not just for yourself but for everyone in the organization, improving their commitment to the execution of your strategy. Today, an important part of strategic thinking is engaging and aligning resources in order to generate the support you will need to achieve your goals.

Lateral thinking

Why does lateral thinking matter? Because the world is changing rapidly and, as a result, it is unlikely that firms will survive such a shifting landscape without the ability to stretch their thinking in innovative, challenging and creative ways.

A changing environment demands agility. Strategy can no longer rely on boosting performance through the brute force of economies of scale. Now, the ability to think laterally ensures that we remain agile, ready to react quickly and innovatively. With its broad, challenging and creative perspective, lateral thinking provides invaluable insight. In particular, it views situations from a unique position and can reveal new opportunities that may be overlooked by other approaches.

Lateral thinking views a problem from many angles, including the unconventional, in order to challenge the existing situation and develop new ideas. It is all about challenging both our preconceptions and our instinctive perception of any given situation. We therefore need to escape from a traditional, logical way of thinking and focus our sights on the less obvious ways of doing things. After all, value is dictated by offering a product or service that is needed, wanted and has an element of scarcity. Here, it is essential to make a conscious effort to challenge our preconceptions and avoid the black and white world of 'yes' or 'no' – things are not black or white in the lateral thinking world, there is a range of possibilities that all need to be examined, along with all of the subtle gaps in between. In other words, we need to think completely outside the box and see things that others can't see. Do that and you will open up a world of possibilities and, consequently, gain incisive competitive advantage, break from the herd and become a market leader.

This is not to suggest that lateral thinking lacks rigor and detail. Rather, it is a place of logical imagination. Its value lies in taking us out of our comfort zone to develop new possibilities. Tomorrow's world will not be conquered by sticking rigidly to past approaches no matter how successful they may have been; tomorrow's world belongs to those who can imagine what others cannot and who take us into unchartered territory – this is the place where exciting opportunities reside.

When you need to move your company in a radically new direction, lateral thinking comes into its own. Because the whole field seems to revolve around creativity and thinking outside the box, if you don't naturally think that way, it can leave you feeling that this approach would be out of your reach. By now, I'm sure that you will know my response to such fears: if you want to do it, you can; there is nothing magical or elusive; it is simply a matter of learning the tricks of the trade, so to speak.

In this regard, the techniques Edward de Bono has developed will equip you with the necessary skills. His approach will help you use lateral thinking sessions to take you through several stages: to enable you to focus on issues, assess the current state of play, devise a wish list of hoped for solutions, generate ideas to achieve those solutions and then assess the viability of proposals. At each stage, you have to challenge assumptions and subject your ideas to critical assessment by repeatedly asking 'why?' and 'what if?' This eliminates the out of date or the ineffectual and identifies new opportunities. Thinking should not be constrained; it is all about thinking boldly, even outrageously, to spark ideas and reveal new options.

Conventional thinking is fine for conventional problems but the world is no longer a conventional place. It is a place of shifting vistas and rapid change, where the company that can offer what no one else has thought of, or that can adapt quickly, reigns.

TAKING A HOLISTIC VIEW

There is no getting away from the fact that a company is a whole, integrated entity: nothing and no one acts in isolation. Moreover, companies do not operate independently of their environment but instead are part of a whole world of activity and possibilities. Welcome to the age of holism.

What does taking a holistic approach achieve, and why is it fast becoming the main route to success? The short answer is sustained profitability and growth. The longer answer is that success hinges on seeing the whole landscape, both internally and externally, to identify where opportunities lie and to know how to best fit all the parts together. This then enables the company to create something that is much greater than the sum of its parts. Only by doing this will we create value, build resilience and drive profitability.

All business activities are ultimately connected – even if they do not, at first sight, appear to be. If you doubt the reality of this, think of how a small problem in a seemingly mundane part of the business can wreak untolled havoc on a business's reputation, with consequent ramifications elsewhere in the business. Think also of how a strong corporate mission statement can inspire and motivate everyone who works in the organization, and how that then feeds through to customers and stakeholders. We all know how damaging it can be to be out of step with new trends or changes in tastes, which makes it more difficult to attract investment or to pursue other ventures. Think of the competitive advantage to be gained from utilizing all the creative potential within the organization by creating a flexible, open, inclusive working environment. The aim of every business leader should be to make sure that all aspects of their company work together well, with the result that the company is much more than the sum of its parts.

Thinking big

It is the nature of business today that makes this approach indispensable. Many companies are complex international operations in terms of customers, suppliers, competitors and market changes. All the departments and divisions, each with an array of functions, people, issues and lines of business, often in different locations, leave an organization vulnerable. This is especially the case if it isn't able to keep everything in focus and understand how the distinct elements operate as a whole and part of the wider world. A holistic approach will reveal where things can be improved and better prepare us to take advantage of opportunities or even create new ones. It will engage employees and utilize their skills to the fullest. It will point the way to enhancing the customer experience. Today, more than ever, businesses need to be fluid; they need to be flexible and ready to adapt. There is no option for allowing any part of your organization to stand in the way of this goal; only by knowing how every part of your business works and how it works with the rest of the organization, external players and markets, will you be able to achieve this. In other words, you have to Think Big.

With its emphasis on treating an organization as an integrated whole – with interconnected, individual, yet inseparable parts – systems theory gives us a means of assessing a company holistically. To do this, you need to take multiple perspectives and a cross-functional approach to identify the patterns, subtleties and interrelationships involved and the information necessary to develop effective strategies. Most importantly, you need to appreciate that whatever you find, it will not stay the same: businesses are dynamic; they need to adapt to changes.

Holism gives us a valuable approach to strategic development, operational issues, company realignment and problem solving. It challenges and tests our existing thinking. By generating a flow of information and being open to new ideas, it provides an inclusive, engaging working environment; one that is capable of innovation and improvement. In particular, it enables us to turn our companies into learning organizations, capable of flexing, growing and pushing our potential further and further.

Little things make a big difference: systems maps

A major advantage of a holistic approach is that it uses systems maps to help us identify where changes, even small changes, can make a big difference. These maps plot the different parts and processes of an organization to reveal how they interact with each other and how they fit into the entire company. By constructing these maps, you will be able to fine tune your approach and better position the organization.

This is certainly not an easy task: the number of internal and external players and influences are vast, and any analysis is necessarily complex and subtle. However, it is essential that we operate in this mode: a broad, multidisciplinary approach informs strategy and enables us to offer customers greater value. Quite simply, holism opens up a world of possibilities.

TIME TO ACT

Inevitably, the time comes when the talk and analysis need to be put into play. You have to move from what can be the reassuring, safe zone of discussion and planning and take action.

Clearly, all actions will only be as effective as the quality of the thinking on which they are based. A key issue to address is knowing how and when to act. This is where testing helps: it enables us to know when to push forward or hold back, when something is good to go or when revisions need to be made.

Beta testing

In this regard, a highly effective tool is beta testing. This is where companies gather data from expert customers through real world tests in order to assess the quality, features, suitability and likely demand of products before launch. By doing this, products can be perfected, market success better evaluated and risk minimized. It will also give companies a sense of when to act. Significantly, this has another important attribute: it enables companies to win over expert customers that are key influencers in the marketplace.

Tipping points

Knowing when and how to act and being ready to respond quickly are particularly important in relation to tipping points. These are the moments when something takes hold and becomes firmly rooted. It is the point where change occurs on a large scale and turns a product into a 'must have.' Central to developing and exploiting tipping points are:

- Making demand for your product spread like a virus, by …
- Targeting key influencers and …
- Making products 'sticky' as well as …
- Watching for events that could be used to create new trends and …
- Looking to create or exploit connections.

A fundamental aspect of tipping points is interdependence. The reason why a product can suddenly become popular is that people are connected to and influenced by everything around them, which means the demand for a product can grow rapidly when people are exposed to the right prompts and influences. Accordingly, an effective means of initiating a tipping point is by creating a community around your potential customers, where they can enjoy using the product or service and share their ideas with other like-minded people, and where they are in a position to be influenced by the key influencers in the industry and spread news of the product to others. This creates the necessary buzz that a product needs for it to go viral.

Whether you are creating a new trend or quickly following an existing one, it is essential to constantly scan the environment at large and ready your organization to take swift and effective action. Engineering your own tipping point has the potential of securing market dominance, becoming the 'must have' brand and generating almost monopoly profits in the short-term, and customer loyalty in the longer-term.

Understanding psychology and behavior

Of course, knowing how and when to act is underpinned by an understanding of psychology and behavior. For example, behavioral economics offers useful insight into buying behavior. It looks at the roles of social, cognitive and emotional factors, and it examines how we make decisions.

The traditional view that customers make rational decisions has come under fire; it appears that irrationality is more embedded into our buying behaviors than we might care to admit. However, the good news for businesses is that while this behavior may be rather illogical, it is also remarkably predictable. This situation arises because we tend to follow thinking traps and consequently, repeat certain decisions over and over.

These thinking and behavioral traps lead to some interesting possibilities, such as the use of decoy products to enable customers to have a point of comparison for your main product. Moreover, when setting prices, we should always bear in mind how hard it is to shift perception away from past prices, which can severely restrict the ability to change prices in the future. And we all know how important it is to get the right people (and many people) using our products, as people follow people, in the belief that the product must be good or is desirable in some way. A major challenge for companies is to know how to break people from attitudes and actions that led to previous buying decisions – we are creatures of habit, even in the face of superior or better value products. For each customer, many things come into play that affect the decision to buy, and companies need to figure out how to manipulate these causes and how best to overcome objections or concerns.

Innovation, a creative mindset and the joy of crowdsourcing

The key to taking the right action at the right time is to instill a culture of innovation throughout the organization. This will lead to companies that are flexible and mutually supportive, that engender trust and cooperation that encourage innovation and that motivate, engage and inspire employees. In a volatile, unpredictable world these decentralized, flatter, open organizations are better positioned to react. Being able to adapt is no longer an option: it is essential.

Gathering the right information is critical. To this end, crowdsourcing is the new kid on the block. This method reveals an invaluable insight by aggregating and averaging all of the individual responses to arrive at one overriding answer. It is based on the belief that, as a whole, the crowd comes to a better answer more often than even a smart individual will when they are operating in isolation. By seeking the opinion of the crowd, companies gain access to data that may otherwise have remained hidden, which enables products to be perfected before launch. Basically, this enables a company to greatly and cost-effectively expand its talent pool. The resulting increase in the pace of innovation and problem solving can make the difference between being a market leader or an also ran – or even oblivion. No wonder that R&D is morphing into C&D – Connect and Develop.

As an extra bonus, by engaging the opinions of others outside the organization, companies are also gaining access to potential customers and are in a position to lead them in a particular direction, build their brand's and product's reputation and even to tap into the ability of influential individuals to promote products to others.

Networks matter – both real and virtual

Critical to informing action is establishing an effective networking strategy, both internally and externally, that is capable of driving innovation and generating and growing demand. Networking extends the company's sphere of influence. When deployed and used correctly, networks will build awareness, interest and credibility. Here, the reach and power of social media comes into its own. By engaging all stakeholders, you will be able to plan and execute your strategy to its full potential.

Despite the power of the internet, it is wise not to overlook the importance of face time. Not only do customers value this, employees do too. For example, many companies operate across borders, which can leave people feeling cut off or ignored and this can result in vast untapped reserves of potential in other operations going to waste. To counter this, some companies make a concerted effort to have a physical presence in other countries and to invite employees to visit their sites elsewhere. Although costly, the cost of not having in-person contact can be greater. This also applies to customers and even if your company is based entirely online, it can be advantageous to organize events where customers can meet people from the company. This can enhance your brand's image and build closer customer relationships and loyalty.

Taking action is a permanent state of affairs. We need to:

- Stay alert to the external environment
- Keep our businesses ready to respond and adapt
- Be open to new ideas and always look to improve.

IF THERE IS ONE APPROACH THAT LIES AT THE HEART OF ALL SUCCESSFUL ACTIONS IT IS ASKING 'WHAT IF?' AND THEN BEING OPEN TO THE POSSIBILITIES.

This is the point where you bring everything together and put your ideas into play. Get it right and long-term, sustained growth will be yours. Remember, if there is one approach that lies at the heart of all successful actions it is asking 'what if?' and then being open to the possibilities.

GET PERSONAL. BE RESPONSIBLE

Develop self-awareness

If we don't understand people, including ourselves, we cannot hope to run a successful business. Being self-aware and understanding how best to interact with others underpins everything. To put it more brutally: all your efforts can be completely undermined if you do not relate to others correctly. It is certainly the case that there are things we can do that will greatly enhance performance, release the full potential of everyone in the company and build the company's reputation and ability to win customers. Significantly, by identifying and acting on patterns in behavior, we will be able to manage relationships effectively in order to get the results we are looking for.

One tool to help us understand human dynamics is transactional analysis. This gives us a way of determining someone's personality type so that we will know how to relate to them and manage the relationship successfully. By understanding the way different people will behave in different situations, we can respond appropriately. To determine someone's personality type (and your own), you have to be knowledgeable and observant. Watch out for clues that indicate both the main and secondary aspects of a person's personality – including body language, tone of voice, eye contact (or lack of), facial expressions, choice of words, etc.

> IF THERE IS ONE APPROACH THAT LIES AT THE HEART OF ALL SUCCESSFUL ACTIONS IT IS ASKING 'WHAT IF?' AND THEN BEING OPEN TO THE POSSIBILITIES.

It is hardly surprising that this is important in business since it equips us to influence relationships and steer others to our viewpoints. It can help us to avert problems and, significantly, it engages clients. That, in turn, secures long-term revenue. When facing changes such as company restructuring or realignment, knowing how to handle relationships is crucial.

Today, the ubiquitous Myers-Briggs test is part of many company's development programs. It improves our own self-awareness, enabling us to know our strengths and weaknesses and determine how to manage our behavior when we are in different situations. It also helps us to identify the personality types of others, and that enables us to know how best to relate to them.

By understanding your own preferences, behaviors and the way you work and communicate, you will be able to play to your strengths, mitigate any shortcomings and enhance your skills. This knowledge can help a company in teambuilding, conflict resolution, leadership and for shaping corporate culture.

Another aspect of understanding human dynamics is appreciating how we work on an instinctive, biological level. How we behave is affected by the chemicals in our brains. While we can learn to deal with their impact we are unavoidably subject to them. Of particular interest here, is the way that neurochemicals shape our personality types, specifically: dopamine (and norepinephrine), oxytocin, serotonin, estrogen and testosterone. The presence of these chemicals leads different people to respond very differently to situations and to exhibit markedly different behaviors – from analytical or creative, bold or cautious to conventional or adventurous. Again, knowing this information prepares us for getting the best out of relationships and knowing people's strengths and weaknesses, which, for example, is useful for knowing who to assign to each task for the greatest effect.

In addition, knowing your own personality type and having a sense of clients' characteristics provides valuable information for building strong, productive relationships with customers. In other words, we can use this insight to create positive client chemistry. Of course, people are rarely one thing or another; individuals possess a combination of traits, maybe with some more dominant than others. This is why it is necessary to consider the whole range of temperaments in a person, and certainly to weigh each one, but it is also important that we are ready to flex our style should someone move into another, less prominent trait.

The benefits of applying this approach to client relationships are significant. For example, if a client is very driven, detailed and decisive, they are less likely to be impressed by someone who acts largely by intuition rather than by using facts. Of course, while we can't put our clients through a battery of tests to determine their personality types, we can observe them. In addition to body language, mentioned earlier, look out for other clues including: mannerisms, how they process information and tolerance for risk. This information will equip you to respond appropriately. Understanding yourself, your colleagues and your clients is essential, since making the right sort of connection matters.

The age of sensibility

Today, we need to integrate human understanding into each part of our organizations. For too long, we have relied on pure reason and rationality, and consequently, we have made mistakes – sometimes spectacular ones. This is hardly surprising. For example, in market research, individuals can indicate that they would definitely make a particular purchasing decision but when it comes to making that purchase in reality, they do not. This irrational world can only be properly understood by drawing on what neuroscience has to tell us. As an interdisciplinary field, it is well-placed to guide us through the labyrinth of human dynamics. The key lesson it has for us is that, rather than reason, our actions are largely based on our emotions, feelings and empathy. We now live in the 'Age of Sensibility,' and businesses need to wake up to this new reality. How can we hope to build brands, trust and client relationships or to engage employees and other stakeholders, etc., without basing our approach and strategies on a correct understanding of the way people behave and why they

FOR TOO LONG, WE HAVE RELIED ON PURE REASON AND RATIONALITY, WITH THE CONSEQUENCE THAT WE HAVE MADE MISTAKES – SOMETIMES SPECTACULAR ONES.

make certain decisions? This insight is crucial if we are to influence behavior toward the direction we wish it to go.

Any actions that we take, no matter how well-informed we are about people's behavior, rely on one critical factor: being genuine. Leaders need to be authentic. Reputation and relationships are earned and easily lost. As such, a leader should manage all relationships carefully, including how customers and external stakeholders perceive the organization.

Another aspect of taking personal responsibility is having the right mindset. In particular, adopting a 'never say never' attitude will prepare you for the unexpected. This can have significant ramifications given the volatile world we live in and especially, when faced with a black swan event. The extreme nature of these events can leave companies adrift and struggling to recover – or sometimes failing to. Having a mindset and approach that allows for uncertainty, including the possibility of extreme events, will strengthen your company. You should address any vulnerable areas, stay alert to any signs of change and be ready to act quickly.

Being personal in business is not a soft option – to be honest, it is not an optional extra at all; it is essential. Admittedly, it is difficult to get it right, and there is certainly a case to make for it being one of the hardest things we have to do since it goes right to the core of who we are and how we behave. This is understandable, as most people shy away from such an intense, personal focus; opening up, trusting, employing self-awareness, listening and empathizing can all leave us feeling exposed and uncomfortable. Furthermore, the breadth, depth, and complexity of human dynamics can be overwhelming and daunting. Having relied for so long on other methods that are more rational, sometimes impersonal and occasionally straightforward, many will find the transition a bumpy one. Yet, the transition must be made: future fortunes depend on it.

GETTING IT TOGETHER

Holism in business is about understanding how the parts fit together and function in the whole company, as well as in the external environment. Holism provides both a diverse and a unified view. It is all encompassing, enabling us to see how one thing affects another and revealing insightful information. We need to subject our companies to a series of questions.

- How do the various elements of the business – people, customers, products, resources, strategy and other elements – interconnect?
- Where are the interdependencies?
- Are there synergies that may be developed or exploited?
- What is the big picture?

A final thought about thinking holistically and acting personally: these behaviors require adaptability. If you are not at the forefront of change, or if you are unable to react to changes efficiently and effectively, then the future is bleak. The point is that we need to think in the widest sense, act and take personal responsibility. There's no point in wasting time by criticizing ourselves for being behind the curve in a particular situation; it's better to take the lessons learned and focus on the task of preparing ourselves and our companies for tomorrow. A key aspect of this is adopting the THAP framework and, critically, instilling it throughout the organization. How we do this for each element of the framework is the focus for the next two chapters.

Chapter Eleven

Think

"Stop and think. And then think on"

ROOSEVELT UNIVERSITY

THINK was a one-word slogan developed by IBM founder Thomas J. Watson, Sr. It appeared in IBM offices, plants and company publications in the 1920s and in the early 1930s began to take precedence over other slogans at IBM. It eventually appeared in wood, stone and bronze, and was published in company newspapers, magazines, calendars, photographs, medallions – even *New Yorker* cartoons – and it remained for years the name of IBM's employee publication. You can still find echoes of Watson's motto in the brand name of IBM's popular notebook computers: the ThinkPad.

"IF YOU DON'T THINK ABOUT THE FUTURE, YOU CANNOT HAVE ONE."

John Galsworthy, Swan Song, from The Forsyte Saga, 1928

"I think, therefore I am," observed René Descartes in 1637. This short diversion into 17th century philosophy is, perhaps surprisingly, relevant to the way we run our businesses today. This is because understanding the complexity of how we think is essential if we are to create strong, appealing companies.

To weave the six Rs into a framework capable of developing and delivering a successful strategy with 'stick-to-itivity', we must begin with the first element: THINK. This reflects how fundamental thinking is to all business activities. Far from stating the obvious, it is essential to examine 'thinking' in detail since it is much more complex and difficult to get right than we might assume. Taking Descartes' basic premise of thinking proving existence, consider how much more enriched and successful existence and, by implication, business decisions would be if the quality of thinking were improved: 'I think better, therefore I am more successful.'

Even today, thinking skills are often poorly understood. Thinking involves complex, multidimensional patterns and processes of identifying, analyzing and synthesizing information. For decision making to be of the high standard needed to deal effectively with today's business issues, we need to cut through this complexity and acquire the necessary skills. In essence, we need to relearn how to think.

CRITICAL THINKING

It is common to associate critical thinking with being negative. This is a mistake. Critical thinking is actually about approaching issues without bias, and it involves assessing information and considering situations rationally, fully and with an open mind.

Whenever a decision has to be made, an overwhelming number of factors – from facts and subjective beliefs to past experiences and uncertainty, can obscure the issue and cloud your thinking. We've all been there, struggling to find a way through a problem. The solution is to use 'purposeful reflective judgment,' which is the hallmark of critical thinking, to reach a conclusion or course of action. Logic and rigor guide critical thinking; problem-solving and questioning steer it. It explores. It teases out subtleties. It separates opinion from fact. Critical thinking is an intellectual approach that considers everything through a wide lens of accuracy, clarity, credibility, depth, precision, relevance and significance.

Edward M. Glaser, in the landmark study, An Experiment in the Development of Critical Thinking (Teachers College, Columbia University, 1941), defines critical thinking as, "The ability to reflect on problems and use logic and reason to solve them." This should be applied consistently, as Glaser notes, "Critical thinking calls for a persistent effort to examine any belief or supposed form of knowledge in the light of the evidence that supports it and the further conclusions to which it tends."

The Watson-Glaser™ Critical Thinking Appraisal is a popular way of testing skills in critical thinking. It involves a grueling array of statements that the candidate has to assess as true, probably true, probably false, false, or contains insufficient data. Knowing how to distinguish between true and probably true or false and probably false is astonishingly hard. Add insufficient data as another possibility and the intricacy of the test skyrockets. To cut your way through the possibilities and pick one option requires complex cognitive processing.

This is an immense challenge for a short test and applying it continually in our everyday lives is even more daunting. While that may leave us feeling that this requires too much effort, we should be mindful of the rewards. This level of hard work, dedication and thinking skills is essential to plotting an organization's path to sustained profit and growth. It is a critical form of competitive advantage and without it, a company is likely to be one of the also-rans that come in behind the leaders.

Why critical thinking, and why now?

Critical thinking strips away emotions and preconceived notions. It is a tool for gathering and exploring evidence at face value. This open-mindedness, in conjunction with in-depth cognitive processing, leads to appropriate and actionable ideas and solutions.

You may be wondering: why so much emphasis on critical thinking?

"SEEKING TO KNOW IS ONLY TOO OFTEN LEARNING TO DOUBT."

Antoinette du ligier de la Garde Deshoulieres, 1638-1694

While it has always been valuable, critical thinking is even more important today in these times of unprecedented volatility, complexity and opportunity, than ever before. In fact, precisely now, during this time of deep, rapid change, critical thinking goes hand and hand with decision making in organizations – and this need will certainly continue and most likely, intensify. Significantly, critical thinking skills are not just for top decision makers, they apply across industries, to jobs at all levels and in all areas of concern and specialization.

The reason is not hard to find: the marketplace has expanded. In fact, it has exploded. It is without question, global in scope. This includes spheres of influence and activities outside an organization's walls, as well as within. Diversity characterizes people, places, and roles – bringing a world of new ideas, influences, arguments and challenges to the fore. Transactions occur at an accelerated pace around the clock. Information flows at the same, seemingly non-stop basis. Logic, objectivity and reliability: we need them now more than ever if we are to navigate this new, complex landscape successfully.

The characteristics of critical thinkers

Critical thinking has a universal application. An interdisciplinary tool, it describes how a person addresses situations and tasks and resolves issues and problems. Critical thinkers ask questions and probe. They don't accept assertions or arguments without putting them through their own, detailed filter. They are independent and exceedingly rational.

In the essay *Critical Thinking: What It is and Why It Counts,* (Insight Assessment, 2010 Update, p.11) Peter A. Facione lists several attributes that define critical thinkers. These include:

- Inquisitiveness with regard to a wide range of issues
- Concern to become, and remain, well-informed
- Alertness to opportunities to use critical thinking
- Trust in the processes of reasoned inquiry
- Self-confidence in one's own abilities to reason
- Open-mindedness regarding divergent world views
- Flexibility in considering alternatives and opinions

- Understanding of the opinions of other people
- Fair-mindedness in appraising reasoning
- Honesty in facing one's own biases, prejudices, stereotypes or egocentric tendencies
- Prudence in suspending, making or altering judgments
- Willingness to reconsider and revise views where honest reflection suggests that change is warranted

To these attributes Peter Facione attaches the characteristics that 'the experts' would add, which include:

- Clarity in stating the question or concern
- Orderliness in working with complexity
- Diligence in seeking relevant information
- Reasonableness in selecting and applying criteria
- Care in focusing attention on the concern at hand
- Persistence though difficulties are encountered
- Precision to the degree permitted by the subject and the circumstances

A CRITICAL THINKER IS: ANALYTICAL, BALANCED, FOCUSED, INQUISITIVE, INTENT, NEUTRAL, ORGANIZED, QUESTIONING, RELEVANT AND RESPONSIBLE.

Now, we should apply all the information we have learned up to this point and build a profile of a critical thinker.

How to be a critical thinker

There is no disputing the fact that critical thinking can make an immense difference to a company's fortunes. It is a prime source of competitive advantage and in tomorrow's markets, this edge over competitors will be crucial. This leads to the obvious question: if we need it, how do we get it? So, can we acquire critical thinking skills? The general consensus is that critical thinking is a skill that can be learned. To be more accurate, it is a set of skills. There are a number of techniques to help us with this task. One approach, which is offered by Pearson Education, covers skills in six core areas: interpretation, analysis, evaluation, self-regulation, inference and explanation.

1. **Interpretation.** We are surrounded by an overwhelming amount of information. From all of this data we must be able to identify what is significant and relevant and what is not. To do this, we need to be able to sort and filter all the available information; make things clear by understanding and refining the evidence further, and interpret the information accurately.

2. **Analysis.** When analyzing and assessing all the information, arguments, data and viewpoints, it is important to notice any patterns, connections and correlations. Any assessment will highlight the core issues and illuminate incorrect or conflicting data and ideas.

3. **Evaluation.** The quality of critical thinking depends on how you evaluate the evidence. Your analysis will only be as good as your ability to assess the reliability, value and priority of the information and ideas presented. It is important, therefore, to scrutinize each piece of information critically and rigorously in order to test its validity and importance.

4. **Self-regulation (also known as meta-cognition).** As with any skill, self-awareness and the ability to scrutinize, check and improve your own thinking is necessary. This is to ensure that you do not arrive at erroneous conclusions due to thinking traps or flaws in your approach.

5. **Inference.** Once the ideas and arguments have been gathered and assessed, you can then glean further information from all this data by inferring more arguments, ideas and other details that, even if they are not known for certain, could be considered reasonable suppositions. This helps to broaden the reach of the existing data, to reveal useful information that might otherwise remain hidden.

6. **Explanation.** With the facts, arguments, ideas and suppositions gathered, interpreted, prioritized, assessed and evaluated, the task of explaining how you arrived at your

conclusion remains. By subjecting your methods and reasoning to this extra layer of criticism you will test the reliability of your conclusion. Clearly, the reliability of any decision is only as good as the quality of the evidence and reasoning it is based upon. Also, by correcting any thinking flaws, you will improve the quality of future decision making. Furthermore, by showing others how your analysis and treatment of evidence and ideas can be relied upon, you are more likely to persuade them to follow your recommendations.

Avoiding the pitfalls of critical thinking

Most experts agree that critical thinking can be taught but there is one significant caveat: it takes some doing! Although, like many other things, the more that we use critical thinking, the better we become at it. In *Critical Thinking Means Business: Learn to Apply and Develop the NEW #1 Workplace Skill* (Pearson Education, 2009) Judy Chartrand, Heather Ishikawa, and Scott Flander offer a helpful framework for sharpening these skills. They call it the RED Model, which stands for:

> "THE MORE ONE THINKS, THE BETTER ADAPTED HE/ SHE BECOMES TO THINKING."
>
> **Ernest Dimnet,** *The Art of Thinking*

Recognize Assumptions
Evaluate Arguments
Draw Conclusions

These are the principles of critical thinking. What's more, they are a sequence of steps to use when processing information upon which to base a decision. Challenge, check sources and find the most rigorous way to uncover the truth and arrive at the most appropriate decision. However, this is easier said than done. For further insight, it is useful to consider the halo effect, mentioned earlier. This is the theory put forward by Phil Rosenzweig in *The Halo Effect ... and the Eight Other Business Delusions That Deceive Managers* (Free Press, 2007). To review, the halo effect refers to a tendency toward cognitive bias. In other words, the halo effect extends a trait or judgment about one object or person to others. It could be positive or negative and exists beyond product marketing, pertaining to the entire commercial sector and everyday life as well. Rosenzweig wrote this book because during 25 years, he had seen, "so much nonsense – unsupported claims by famous gurus and self-described 'thought leaders,' sweeping assertions based on poor data, and simplistic stories that claim to be rigorous research. Worse, most people – including many very smart managers, consultants, and journalists – can't tell the difference between good and bad research. *The Halo Effect* is an attempt to raise the level of discussion in the business world, and to sharpen our skills of critical thinking about management." No wonder, then, that he dedicated the book to "clear thinking about business in management."

The message we can take away from this for developing our own critical thinking skills is watch out for the halo effect however subtle it may be, and guard against it.

Another tip comes from the article *Becoming a Critic of Your Thinking* (Criticalthinking.org, ©2009 Foundation for Critical Thinking) by Linda Elder and Richard Paul, who recommend the following points to improve critical thinking:

- Clarify your thinking
- Stick to the point
- Question questions
- Be reasonable

"Question questions" – what does this mean? The authors go on to explain, "Be on the lookout for questions. The ones we ask. The ones we fail to ask. Look on the surface. Look beneath the surface. Listen to how people question, when they question, when they fail to question. Look closely at the questions asked. What questions do you ask, should you ask? Examine the extent to which you are a questioner, or simply one who accepts the definitions of situations given by others."

Clearly, the way that people think, both as individuals and collectively within organizations, affects the decisions that they make in ways that are far from obvious and rarely understood. John Hammond, Ralph Keeney and Howard Raiffa in their article in the Harvard Business Review provided some of the most intriguing research and insights in this area (see John S. Hammond, Ralph L. Keeney and Howard Raiffa, *The Hidden Traps in Decision Making*, Harvard Business Review, September-October 1998).

Avoiding all of the following traps requires the recognition that they exist and an understanding of the traps that are the likeliest to cause you problems.

- **The anchoring trap** is where we give disproportionate weight to the first piece of information that we receive. This often happens because the initial impact of the first information, our immediate reaction to it, is so significant that it outweighs everything else, 'drowning' our ability to effectively evaluate a situation.
- **The status quo trap** biases us toward maintaining the current situation – even when better alternatives exist. This might be caused by inertia or the potential loss of face if the current position were to change.
- **The sunk-cost trap** inclines us to perpetuate the mistakes of the past, because 'We have invested so much in this approach that we cannot abandon it or alter course now.'
- **The confirming evidence trap,** also known as confirmation bias, is when we seek information to support an existing predilection and discount opposing information. It can also be shown as a tendency to seek confirming evidence to justify past decisions. Often, this tendency is manifest by people seeking to support the continuation of the current favored strategy.
- **The over-confidence trap** makes us overestimate the accuracy of our forecasts. Closely linked to confirming evidence, the over-confidence trap is when a decision maker has an exaggerated belief in their ability to understand situations and predict the future.

- **The framing trap** is when a problem or situation is incorrectly stated, completely undermining the decision-making process as a result. This is often unintentional, but not always. Clearly, how an issue or situation is seen is important in providing the basis for developing an effective strategy or decision.

- **The recent event trap** leads us to give undue weight to a recent, and quite probably dramatic, event or sequence of events. This is very similar to the anchoring trap, except that it can arise at any time – not just at the start – and cause a misjudgment.

- **The prudence trap** leads us to be over-cautious when we make estimates about uncertain factors. It is shown by a tendency to be extremely risk averse, and is particularly likely to occur when there is a decision dilemma: a situation when the decision maker feels that continuing with the current approach carries risks, and that taking an alternative course of action also carries risks.

As well as thinking flaws and coping patterns, there are two potential pitfalls resulting from the culture or environment of the organization. They can be thought of as extremes at opposite ends of the same spectrum: fragmentation and groupthink.

Fragmentation occurs when people are in disagreement, either with their peers or their superiors within the organization. Usually the expression of emerging dissent is disguised or suppressed, although it may appear as 'passive aggression.' Dissenting opinion can often fester in the background, for example, it can be mentioned informally in conversation, rather than clearly raised in formal situations, such as meetings. Fragmentation is corrosive, hindering effective analysis and decision making, and can worsen when the views of one grouping are dominant. It also feeds off itself in a self-sustaining cycle, with any move to break it cynically seen as one side's attempt to gain dominance. It can therefore become locked into the organization and be extremely difficult to reverse.

Groupthink is the opposite of fragmentation. It occurs when the group suppresses ideas that are critical or not in direct support of the direction in which the group is moving. The group appears to be in agreement or certain about something but is neither. This may be caused by many factors. For example, past success can breed the belief that a team is infallible and therefore produce complacency. Groupthink may occur because the group is denied information or lacks the confidence or ability to challenge the dominant views of the group. People may be concerned about disagreeing, either because of past events, present concerns or a fear of what the future might hold, and so will seek safety in numbers.

Groupthink is exacerbated by the fact that cohesive groups tend to rationalize the invulnerability of their decision or strategy, and this in turn inhibits critical analysis and the expression of dissenting ideas. The effect is an incomplete survey of available options, and a failure to examine the risks of preferred decisions.

Groupthink can occur in organizations where teamwork is either strong or weak. As with fragmentation, groupthink is also self-sustaining. Moreover, the longer it lasts, the more entrenched and 'normal' it becomes in people's minds and behaviors. After a short time, it is also very difficult to reverse.

Having explained the pitfalls, what are the solutions? A great deal has been written about the rational, process-driven approach to decision making but the psychological aspects are at least as interesting and are only recently beginning to be understood. In his book, 'Think on Your Feet' writer Jeremy Kourdi highlights several techniques for decision makers in turbulent times.

- **Be bold and don't fear the consequences of decisions** – we tend to overestimate the consequences, good and bad, of our choices. We also tend to discount our ability to make the right choice. This results from 'loss aversion': the view that a loss will hurt more than a gain will satisfy. Remember, the worst case scenario might never occur and even if it does, people invariably have the psychological resilience to cope.

- **Trust your instincts and emotions** – we have evolved to make good decisions and manage their implementation, so don't ignore our evolutionary advantage. Sometimes quick decisions work best precisely because you have picked up on the key pieces of information quickly and then responded. More time will simply lead to information overload and other distractions.

- **Be prepared to play the devil's advocate** – this search for flaws and failings will strengthen your decisions and illuminate the factors affecting a particular decision as well as other issues, such as biases. This means being aware of confirmation bias and using it.

- **Avoid irrelevancies** – when making a decision we can be faced with irrelevant information that distorts our perception, as described in the anchoring trap. The solution is to be ready to question the context of the information. What are you basing your perceptions on, and is it really relevant?

- **Reframe the decision** – this will help you view the issues from a new perspective.

- **Don't let the past hold you back** – the sunk cost highlights our tendency to stick with previous choices because we have invested so much already. Don't do it. It is invariably a mistake to stick with something just because it was a past choice, if other, better alternatives exist.

- **Challenge groupthink** – people are often afraid to comment or act because of social pressure. This is a poor excuse. Find out what people really think and use that to help you decide.

- **Limit your options** – this is the paradox of choice: the more options we have, the harder life can be. Choose the most promising options, this can help to remove pressure and clarify your thinking. This highlights the point that we are fixated with choice, believing more to be better. In truth, less choice can be more satisfying, or it may simply be worth delegating the decision to someone else who is better qualified. The challenge is to make sure that as far as possible, you enjoy what you are doing, and that the decision is made by the best person in the right way at the right time.

This has been quite an intense look at learning how to think critically. In summary, mastering critical thinking takes concerted effort. It entails thinking about thinking with an emphasis on truth and quality when making decisions. By adopting these techniques and this mindset, you will be better equipped to make the right decisions and lead your company to a strong, successful future. This is not the end of the story, however, when it comes to thinking skills. The next technique we will look at is strategic thinking.

STRATEGIC THINKING

We hear the term 'strategic thinking' often enough but what does it really mean? 'Strategy' is a very overused word but it simply means the plan that will move us from where we are now to where we want to be. Basically, it's thinking that goes above and beyond our everyday, working interests. It's big, it's broad. It's global, it's goal oriented. To get a fuller picture of what it is and what's involved we can look to how the experts describe it and then consider their views on how it helps and how we can become better strategic thinkers.

Strategic thinking at work

Rich Horwath, President of the Strategic Thinking Institute (at strategyskills.com), believes, "Strategic thinking is defined as the generation and application of business insights on a continual basis to achieve competitive advantage." He goes on to segment strategic thinking into three disciplines:

1. Acumen – perceiving and creating insightful business ideas and plans

2. Allocation – determining where and how resources should be directed and how they should be divided between activities

3. Action – taking the necessary actions to execute strategy to ensure goals are achieved

Next, any look at strategic thinking would be incomplete without a reference to Jeanne Liedtka whose ideas have stood the test of time. In *Strategic Thinking: Can it Be Taught?* (Long Range Planning, 1998, Vol. 31, no. 1, pp. 120-29), she attempts to clarify the meaning of strategic thinking. Why does she bother to do this? She points out that the expression 'strategic thinking' is used frequently – perhaps too frequently. The problem is that with overuse, it runs the risk of becoming watered down and indistinct. She makes a very important distinction between how the word is used and what it means, writing, "Most often, it appears that the term 'strategic thinking' is used to denote all thinking about strategy, rather than to denote a particular mode of thinking with specific characteristics."

To set the record straight, she developed The Liedtka Model of Strategic Thinking. This identifies the major elements that comprise the following process:

1. **Systems perspective.** This refers to the ability to take an end-to-end approach when processing information and evaluating actions. Analysis proceeds step by step along a continuum to identify trends, relationships and patterns of significance in order to create value.

"THE DIFFICULTY LIES NOT SO MUCH IN DEVELOPING NEW IDEAS AS IN ESCAPING FROM THE OLD ONES."

John Maynard Keynes

2. **Intent focused.** This element is defined as the ability to consistently channel efforts, avoid distractions and remain focused on the task. It combines elements of "direction, discovery, and destiny."

3. **Thinking in time.** Strategic thinking is about 'thinking in time.' That is, it traverses the past, the present and the future. For example, the past is a marker of what has gone, while

opportunities exist in the present, and the present is the jumping off point for achieving the goals of tomorrow.

4. **Hypothesis driven.** Strategic thinking combines critical and creative thinking in a sequential approach that develops and tests hypotheses.

5. **Intelligent opportunism.** An important aspect of strategic thinking is the ability to recognize new realities and capitalize on them. It scans information on an ongoing basis and assesses and reassesses positions along the way.

Figure 11.1: The Liedtka Model of the Elements of Strategic Thinking

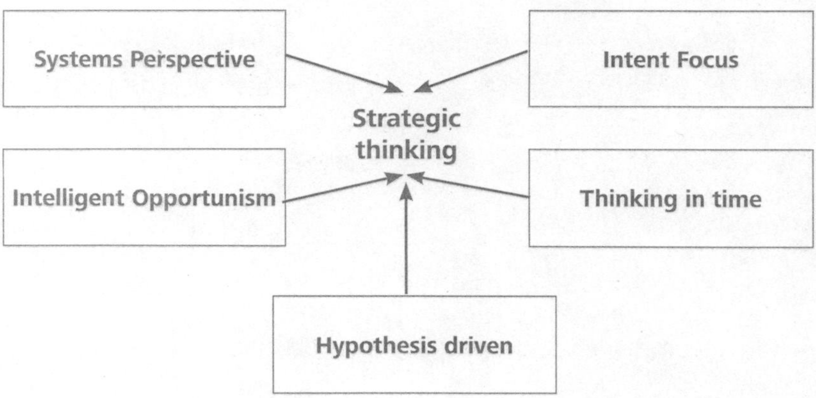

From Jeanne M. Liedtka: *Strategic Thinking: Can it Be taught?*

How to be a strategic thinker

The benefits that strategic thinkers bring to their organizations are considerable. For example:

- They help organizations and colleagues remain open to emerging opportunities. In fact, this 'intelligent opportunism' will make them more responsive to local opportunities.

- They have a holistic view – in other words, firms that succeed at embedding a capability for strategic thinking throughout their organizations create a new source of competitive advantage, because their system perspective allows them to redesign their processes for greater efficiency and effectiveness.
- Their intent focus makes them more determined and less distracted than their rivals.
- Their ability to think in time will improve the quality of their decision making and their speed of implementation.
- A capacity for hypothesis generation and testing enables creative and critical thinking to be incorporated into their processes.

"ACQUIRE THE WISDOM OF BIG-PICTURE THINKING."

John Maxwell,
Thinking for a Change

Strategic thinking addresses difficult matters; it is not the domain of easy answers. A complex process, strategic thinking has been likened to the scientific method, which consists of seven distinct steps. For example the Harvard Business School recommends a seven-step process for strategic thinking.

First in the seven-step process, you should be ready to extend your frame of reference from business-as-usual to a panoramic view. In other words: think big. That will prepare you for the next phase, which is to understand your organization's goals over time. Step three echoes Jeanne Liedtke's 'systems perspective': you should connect the dots and note any trends and accompanying patterns and issues. You are now at the point where you can apply your creative instincts to generate ideas that capitalize on opportunities and limit possible risks. Finally, steps five, six, and seven call for evaluating findings, prioritizing them into actionable points, and then making the hard decisions in light of available resources.

Strategic thinking is reflective and externally oriented: it scours the environment for meaningful events and developments and it seeks to connect the pieces into logical chains. It embraces and sprouts new ideas and it leads to new and more creative ways of doing things. Forward thinking, it aims to extend possibilities in order to create extra value and generate the right results. Without a doubt, it's a valuable weapon in the arsenal of thinking skills that drive sustained growth and profit.

A STRATEGIC THINKER IS ABLE TO EVOLVE THEIR THINKING AND IS: INSIGHTFUL, INTUITIVE, OPEN-MINDED, OPPORTUNISTIC, RECEPTIVE, RESULTS-ORIENTED, RIGOROUS, TOLERANT OF RISK AND VISIONARY.

In their book, *Thinking Strategically* (W.W. Norton & Co., Inc., 1991), Avinash Dixit and Barry Nalebuff define strategic thinking as, "[t]he art of outdoing an adversary, knowing that the adversary is trying to do the same to you." They added a further definition in their later book, *The Art of Strategy* (W.W. Norton & Company, Inc., 2008), "It is also the art of finding ways to cooperate, even when others are motivated by self-interest, not benevolence. It is the art of convincing others, and even yourself, to do what you say. It is the art of interpreting and revealing information. It is the art of putting yourself in others' shoes so as to predict and influence what they will do."

This is an interesting development. Our brief examination of strategic thinking has led us to the realization that there are now new and evolving needs that are changing the nature of strategic thinking. Today, strategy is about more than coming up with new and impactful ideas. It entails engaging and aligning resources. For example, Avinash Dixit and Barry Nalebuff underscore the role of game theory in developing inherent skills into those for effective strategic thinking. They also discuss the need to generate support and confidence to move forward. In essence, they bring into play what are widely regarded as the soft skills in order to achieve success.

Strategic thinking is dynamic and powerful. It helps executives to manage change and navigate uncertainty, both of which are sweeping over the business landscape and set to continue that way well into the future. There is no question that strategic thinking is the pathway to competitive advantage; creating value depends on it. Although learning these skills will require considerable effort, the payoff is well worth the effort. After all, strategic thinking culminates in strategic action. We have now reviewed critical and strategic thinking; in the next section we shall look at the last thinking skill: lateral thinking.

LATERAL THINKING

You could be forgiven for asking 'surely critical thinking and strategic thinking are enough, why do we need lateral thinking as well?' Apart from the obvious point that the more tools we have available to deploy the better equipped we will be to make decisions, there is another reason why lateral thinking matters now more than ever before: as we have continually said, the world is changing and it is changing rapidly.

In 2008, an article called, *Lateral thinking and agility are essential in a changing world* (The Banker, May 2008, pp. 156-59). In it, eight retail banking executives offered their views on how to succeed in their industry. Their views are summed up by the title, and it goes on to say:

"In many parts of the world, the global economy is being driven as much by trade in information, ideas and services, as by trade in physical goods. Organizations that were able to achieve success and predominance through sheer productivity and massive scale are now fewer and far between. Increasingly, it is the ability to think laterally, to operate on an agile basis, to react to global trends quickly and, above all, to innovate that will determine the sustainability of an organization in future."

"DISCOVERY CONSISTS OF SEEING WHAT EVERYBODY HAS SEEN AND THINKING WHAT NOBODY HAS THOUGHT."

Albert von Szent-Gyorgyi and Irving Good

This view is echoed among other business leaders and it is easy to see why. Lateral thinking, with its wide-angled view of the world and its challenging, creative and insightful approach, is perfectly suited to dealing with today's global markets, volatility and constant uncertainty. This vantage point is extremely valuable in good times and especially, in bad. Why? One major feature is that it approaches situations in ways that are off center. By seeing things differently, new opportunities are revealed that may never have been uncovered any other way.

What is lateral thinking?

- A heuristic for solving problems, where you try to look at the problem from many angles instead of tackling it head-on (see wordnetweb.princeton.edu/perl/webwn).
- Using reasoned thought in a non-standard or non-linear logical way to find a solution to a problem (see en.wiktionary.org/wiki/lateral_thinking).
- Attempting to solve a problem by using non-traditional methods in order to create and identify new concepts and ideas (see www.teach-nology.com/glossary/terms/l/).
- Methods of thinking concerned with changing concepts and perception (see india.smashits.com/wikipedia/Lateral_thinking).
- Escaping from habitual mind patterns (or logical sequential thinking) in order to solve problems or explore new ideas. Techniques include: deliberate and provocative challenging of preconceptions and a rejection of yes/no thinking (see securitybeyondborders.org/global-security-glossary/global-security-glossary-l/).
- Thinking that finds solutions in ways that do not seem obvious (see www.thutong.doe.gov.za/ResourceDownload.aspx).

What do these definitions tell us? Clearly, lateral thinking holds a prism up to a situation enabling us to peer through multiple panes and provocative points of view and perspectives. This is no place for those without the ability or desire to look beyond the obvious, to see more than others can see. It's bold, yet subtle. It is a place of logical imagination.

By comparing the three thinking skills, we will see why all are important and why lateral thinking in particular brings a unique and invaluable aspect to decision making.

- **Critical thinking** attacks an issue, situation, or problem front and center. It seeks to strip away bias, emotions and preconceived notions to determine the most appropriate response.
- **Strategic thinking** takes a forward looking, rigorously rational, yet innovative approach, to derive insights and ultimately decide on the most advantageous way to proceed.
- **Lateral thinking** shakes things up. It takes us out of our comfort zone to allow other perspectives and possibilities to surface.

Critical and strategic thinking reside in the realm of 'vertical thinking.' They get to an endpoint by stacking up information piece by piece and analyzing the sum total logically. Lateral thinking does not. It arrives at a solution sideways, as the word 'lateral' suggests. It deliberately seeks to break the mold, step outside the lines, so as to inspire creativity. In this way, it challenges convention and develops distinctly new propositions. It brings to mind the famous quote by Ford Motor Company founder Henry Ford, "If I had asked people what they wanted, they would have said faster horses." Progress is not made by adhering to what has gone, to past thinking and methods. Like Ford, we need to take our thinking to new places,

"I LIKE TO SAY THAT YOU CANNOT DIG A HOLE IN A DIFFERENT PLACE BY DIGGING THE SAME HOLE DEEPER. LATERAL THINKING IS FOR CHANGING CONCEPTS AND PERCEPTIONS."

Edward De Bono

push beyond the frontiers, to explore the unthinkable, imagine what others cannot – this is what lateral thinking gives us.

The term 'lateral thinking' was conceived by Edward de Bono. He explains that lateral thinking is concerned not with playing with the existing pieces, but with seeking to change those very pieces. It is concerned with the perception part of thinking. This is where we organize the external world into the pieces we can then process. So, while creativity and lateral thinking are linked, they are not the same thing. One important point is that lateral thinking leads to greater creativity. The benefits of acquiring this skill are clear, as de Bono says, "It empowers people by adding strength to their natural abilities, which improves teamwork, productivity and, where appropriate, profits." It enriches all business activities, elevating the quality of strategy and enhancing problem-solving skills. Crucially, Edward de Bono vehemently believes that lateral and creative thinking can be learned.

How to be a lateral thinker

A good starting point is to realize that lateral thinking can be used in many, many situations. It is particularly useful when facing change and uncertainty or when an issue or problem would benefit from a radically new approach. When you need to move your company from the traditional, business-as-usual onto a new path that fits it for the challenges ahead, lateral thinking has much to offer.

"IN THIS TIME OF INTENSE CHANGE, COMPANIES HAVE BEEN CONDUCTING LATERAL THINKING SESSIONS FOR TEAMS TO COME UP WITH A RESERVE OF BREAKTHROUGH IDEAS."

Edward de Bono

Edward de Bono has developed several techniques to help us acquire the necessary skills for lateral thinking. As in any process, lateral thinking sessions begin with the planning stage. This is where 'focus tools' are applied that solidify the state of current thinking, problems and wish lists. They help teams to gain agreement on the agenda and guidelines for lateral thinking sessions. The remaining steps in the process are: generating ideas, sorting and building/ assessing. For many people, the most useful and fun part gets underway with Edward de Bono's tools for generating ideas, which include:

- **Alternatives/Concept Extraction.** List alternatives and then find concepts to link them. This provides a base for developing new ideas.
- **Challenge.** Ask "why" repeatedly. This enables you to discard assumptions and to identify new vantage points.

"IMAGINATION IS MORE IMPORTANT THAN KNOWLEDGE."

Albert Einstein

- **Random Entry.** Choose objects and disparate information and associate them. This will help to form new patterns.
- **Provocation.** Use role reversal, hyperbole, and exaggeration. These 'triggering' methods will spark ideas.
- **Disproving.** Subject widely accepted ideas to extreme scrutiny, and see where that leads. This will help you see new options and will reveal new paths to take.
- **Word/Picture Mapping.** Start with one word or picture and add others, in order to extract new ideas. This creative tool is a clear and powerful way of developing understanding, linking concepts, exploring ideas and sparking imagination.

Edward de Bono's techniques have proven so popular that the field of lateral thinking has attracted many business academics. Paul Sloane is one of the most respected, and his insights have helped many companies. He opens minds to new possibilities and vistas with a range of techniques that can help us become better lateral thinkers. These include asking "what if?" questions. Briefly, these sessions begin with the facilitator posing a situation or a problem. Then the facilitator asks the "what if?" question – again and again, as if reluctant to see each answer as the definitive conclusion. These repeated inquiries push us beyond the traditional realm of thinking into a more radical realm – and ultimately leading us to useful insights and innovations.

The significance of lateral thinking to strategic development is emphasized by Paul Sloane in *The Leader's Guide to Lateral Thinking Skills*. Paul Sloane makes the point that, "The conventional leader is fine when what is needed is command and control of a well-defined process. But for rapid and discontinuous change, the lateral leader is better equipped. He or she focuses on developing the skills of the team in innovation, creativity, risk-taking and entrepreneurial endeavors. The lateral leader manages change by initiating it."

LATERAL THINKERS ARE PEOPLE WHO ARE: EXPERIENTIAL, FLEXIBLE, IMAGINATIVE, INNOVATIVE, INQUISITIVE, INTUITIVE, NON-JUDGMENTAL, OBSERVANT, PROVOCATIVE AND UNORTHODOX.

Another useful technique that Paul Sloane applies is to see the issue in a series of lateral thinking puzzles that take the form of 'fill-in-the-blanks.' You start with a statement that is realistic but improbable, and then you have to recreate the set of circumstances that led up to the situation. There are many possible explanations but only one that the originator had in mind. The answer is likely not the obvious one, rather it is the one that he describes as the most satisfying.

Not only is lateral thinking highly productive, there is also a strong element of fun. Just as comedians look at the world in different ways, lateral thinking sessions can lead to unexpected, often amusing scenarios. This isn't a trivial point: it is all about gleaning new ideas from seeing the world in a different way. This essentially comes from the same challenging, often irreverent and imaginative place as the humorist's vantage point.

IF YOU WANT TO OUT-COMPETE YOUR OPPONENTS, YOU HAVE TO OUT-THINK THEM.

THINKING AT WORK

Critical, strategic and lateral thinking all play a vital role. They help us build stronger organizations capable of generating more revenue. There is no doubt that thinking skills will impact all of the six Rs. More than that, the six Rs will improve our thinking skills by informing our judgments and providing a clear focus. All three approaches will reveal how to improve relationships and reputation; they will remind you why the company exists or even inject new purpose; and they will suggest ways of motivating others. Quite simply, by scrutinizing and challenging strategy (in fact, all business activities), and by identifying and developing new ideas, you will lead your company to a more resilient future. In essence, the power of critical, strategic and lateral thinking skills can be summed up with the following advice: if you want to out-compete your opponents, you have to out-think them. One question still remains: is it necessary to use all three styles? The answer is: sometimes yes; sometimes no. They are complementary. So the key is to develop all these skills and use them as needed.

By applying critical, strategic and lateral thinking skills to all of the issues facing the business, including external issues, we will be better able to develop and maximize new opportunities as well as avoiding potential problems and challenges. Crucially, successful businesses cannot succeed by operating in a way that is disconnected or fails to take account of all the issues influencing its future. It is the whole business that matters, including the external setting it operates in, and managing this challenge provides the focus for the next chapter.

Finally, we should end this chapter, as we started, with the words of René Descartes in *Le Discours de la Methode*, "It is not enough to have a good mind, the main thing is to use it well."

Chapter Twelve

Being Holistic

"I feel an indescribable ecstasy and delirium in melting ... into the system of being, in identifying myself with the whole of nature."

JEAN-JACQUES ROUSSEAU, 18TH CENTURY PHILOSOPHER

Thinking techniques of the sort described in the last chapter – specifically, critical, strategic and lateral thinking – require a context. In fact, by developing a precise focus on 'Think' you are better able to gain an appreciation of the world at large and in turn, position your organization to achieve sustained profit and growth. The reason for this is revealed by two questions: Why do we need this focus on thinking, and what does it give us? The first thing we notice about the purpose of thinking is seen in the phrase 'the world at large.' By applying the thinking skills we have just learned to all aspects of business, including external factors and with a global perspective, we are much better able to identify and draw together relevant information and reveal new opportunities. Successful businesses cannot operate in a disjointed, separated way, with distinct and unconnected activities. It is the whole business that

"MAN'S MIND, ONCE STRETCHED BY A NEW IDEA, NEVER REGAINS ITS ORIGINAL DIMENSIONS."

Oliver Wendell Holmes Sr., 1809-1894

matters including the external setting in which it operates. For this to happen, we need to cover the entirety of business operations, including the economic landscape at large, while also seeing the individual parts that make up the whole. Only by doing this can we fit everything together correctly and improve performance, build competitive advantage, ensure resilience and drive profitability. The time has come to merge our six Rs and critical, strategic and lateral thinking skills and enter the world of holistic business.

HOLISM: WHAT IT MEANS AND WHY IT MATTERS

Holistic comes from the Greek term 'holism' which means exactly what it sounds like: Whole. According to this concept, the properties of a cohesive grouping cannot be identified or understood through their individual pieces. It is the overarching umbrella – the super structure formed by uniting the different parts – that define how the constituents behave. This notion dates back over 2300 years to ancient times. The Greek philosopher, scientist and physician Aristotle articulated the natural end point of this belief as, "The whole is more than the sum of its parts." This view has significant implications for managing the way that individual parts of our businesses, by working together, can punch above their weight and build something that is much more than we might expect from each element in isolation..

The idea of holism, quite simply, is that when you observe the world through a holistic lens, what you see is unified and also diverse. You see how the whole structure is assembled, how all the pieces work together, and how the different parts and the whole are interrelated, with each one influencing the other. These formations are vast.

So, how should we begin to understand how large structures such as organizations, business models or strategies work: piece by piece or as a whole? Which aspect should we emphasize? Given what you have read so far, you will hardly be surprised to hear that the big picture supersedes the scope and results of the individual parts.

Why holism matters in business

So, why is there suddenly an emphasis on a holistic approach in business, and what can it accomplish? Albert Low in *Zen and Creative Management* explains, "A company is a multidimensional system capable of growth, expansion, and self-regulation. It is, therefore, not a thing but a set of interacting forces. When company organization is reviewed ... it must be looked upon as a whole, as a total system."

Today, medium-to-mega-sized organizations are mammoth configurations. They encompass a maze of departments, divisions, functions, products, lines of business, brands, locations and much more. Largely decentralized, companies have multiple offices, plants, satellite sites and operating units that extend across a region, country, and most likely, the globe. Each segment of the business has its own responsibilities and contributes in its own ways. Viewed individually, the parts pale in comparison to the overall effect created by an organization's people, products and services. This clearly illustrates the principle Aristotle proposed: that the whole is greater than the sum of its parts. However, the examples given, so far, only relate to entities inside the corporate walls. This is but a shard of the holistic point of view that we are seeking to establish.

What do I mean by this? Well, businesses are fluid and success relies on Thinking Big. How big? Our scope has to be so big that it captures all the interlocking elements, interdependencies and synergies of the commercial environment. We have to see and understand the broad picture. Understanding the holistic framework and the interactions that are involved is essential. This need is so vital that it has spawned its own field of study, known as 'systems theory.'

A SYSTEMIC VIEW

To introduce systems theory, I shall pass you over to Marilyn Ferguson, who, in *The Aquarian Conspiracy* (J. P. Tarcher, Inc., 1987), sums up why we have to view the business as a whole. She describes systems theory as "a related modern concept [to holism], that says each variable in any system interacts with the other variables so thoroughly that cause and effect cannot be separated. A simple variable can be both cause and effect. Reality will not be still. And it cannot be taken apart! You cannot understand a cell, a rat, a brain structure, a family, a culture if you isolate it from its context. Relationship is everything."

If I could just defy the premise of systems theory for a moment and divide the concept into its parts, we will be able to tease out more meaning. The word 'system' is commonly defined as 'a set of interacting or interdependent entities forming an integrated whole.' Being separate and connected reveals how this theory is a formula for building, part by part, a well-functioning, interrelated entity.

Systems theory views organizations organically and studies them from a holistic perspective. To do this, it uses the following elements as a basis for analysis:

- It provides an interdisciplinary and multi-perspective approach that provides relevant and valuable information.
- It looks for common patterns, behaviors, properties and principles that will better inform and guide decisions.
- It identifies the configuration of parts that are connected and joined by a web of relationships.
- It operates on the assumption that all systems are dynamic and complex and interact as a structured, functional whole.

"THE SYSTEMS VIEW LOOKS AT THE WORLD IN TERMS OF RELATIONSHIPS AND INTEGRATION. SYSTEMS ARE INTEGRATED WHOLES WHOSE PROPERTIES CANNOT BE REDUCED TO THOSE OF SMALLER UNITS. INSTEAD OF CONCENTRATING ON BASIC BUILDING BLOCKS OR BASIC SUBSTANCES, THE SYSTEMS APPROACH EMPHASIZES BASIC PRINCIPLES OF ORGANIZATION."

Fritjof Capra,
The Turning Point

Systems theory is certainly a huge topic with a specific vocabulary and its own subsets. It views companies as 'complex and adaptive' organizations. They are as 'complex' as they are diverse and have many parts that interact both with each other and with the environment at large. And they are 'adaptive' by virtue of their ability to change in line with experience.

Understanding systems thinking

The perception of organizations as complex social systems that react with the environment, and modify their course accordingly, provides the basis for 'Systems Thinking.' This offers a holistic approach to business management, planning, and problem solving and was pioneered by Peter Senge.

In his groundbreaking book *The Fifth Discipline* (Doubleday/ Currency, 1990), Peter Senge introduces systems thinking: "I regard systems thinking as a discipline for seeing wholes. It is a framework for seeing interrelationships rather than things, for seeing patterns of change rather than static snapshots. I also define it as a set of general principles – distilled over the course of the twentieth century, spanning fields as diverse as the physical and social sciences, engineering, and management. And, above all, I consider systems thinking as a sensibility – for the subtle interconnectedness that gives living systems their unique character."

To understand more about this approach, we have provided a question and answer session with Peter Senge:

Q. What is the significance of systems thinking?

A. Today, systems thinking is needed more than ever because we are being overwhelmed by complexity. Perhaps for the first time in history, humankind has the capacity to create far more information than anyone can absorb, to foster far greater interdependency than anyone can manage, and to accelerate change far faster than anyone's ability to keep pace.

Q. In light of the trends you describe, how does systems thinking help?

A. Systems thinking is a fundamental tool. In my view, it plays a major role in business strategy, especially in the area of organizational development. In case you're wondering why, I'll address that now. Systems thinking is the springboard for businesses to become what I refer to as 'learning organizations.'

Q. What exactly are learning organizations?

A. They are business entities where people continually expand their capacity to create the results they truly desire. They are where new and expansive patterns of thinking are nurtured, where collective aspiration is set free, and where people are continually learning to see the whole together.

Q. Aren't all organizations this way?

A. No. Learning organizations are flexible, integrative, engaging, and oriented toward long-term success. Open and receptive, they seek and obtain a continuous flow of information and feedback. They analyze and apply it. They adapt quickly and decisively. This enables them to innovate, to enhance their operations and performance.

Just to take a brief diversion from the Q&A, here's a question for you, the reader: do you know what putting the systems thinking loop into perpetual motion actually means for companies? These organizations that do this are able to excel at what they do and are on their way to achieving sustained, profitable growth.

Now, back to Peter Senge's Q&A session:

Q. What are the five disciplines that learning organizations implement and integrate?

A. I'll start with Systems Thinking, which is seeing the organization as a whole and understanding the web of relationships and interactions that drive it. Personal Mastery is another, which I define as committing to the ongoing process of viewing reality objectively, maintaining learning as a lifelong goal, and seeing the world at ever-deeper levels. Moving on, Mental Models refers to continuously surfacing, challenging, testing and improving deeply held assumptions that influence understanding about how the world works and what actions to take. The discipline that I refer to as Building Shared Vision is painting a broad picture that defines the articulated future for the organization, which internal stakeholders can address together and aspire to achieve. Finally, Team Learning is nurturing an environment where people learn together and embrace the same pattern of thinking.

Figure 12.1: Peter Senge's Five Disciplines

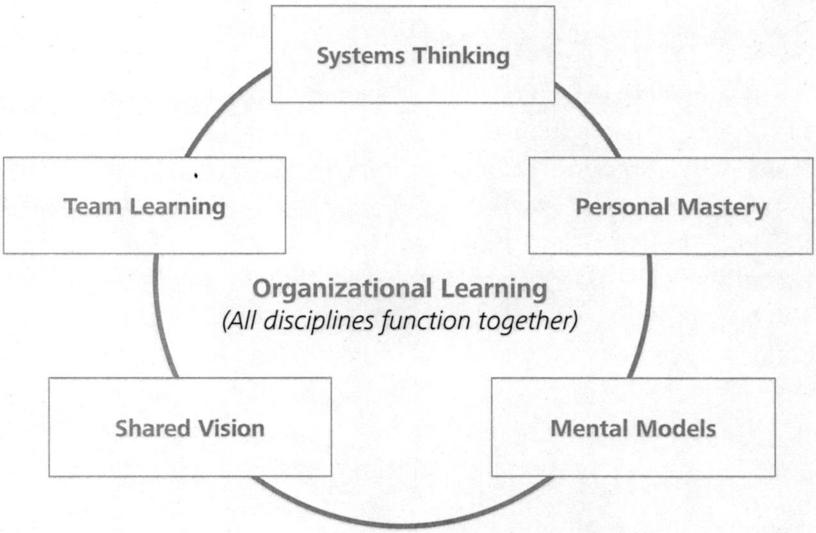

It's worth noting that systems thinking is first and it is also the foremost. It forms the foundation for the other disciplines and acts as the catalyst. It binds them, so they work in concert, as a whole. From this all-encompassing perspective, Peter Senge dubs systems thinking 'the fifth discipline' and uses it as the title of his book.

Q. The title of the first chapter of *The Fifth Discipline* is a quote from Archimedes, the ancient Greek mathematician and physicist: 'Give me a lever long enough … and, single-handed, I can move the world.' How does this relate to systems thinking?

A. The bottom line of systems thinking is leverage – seeing where actions and changes in structures occur that can lead to significant, enduring improvements. Often, leverage follows the principle of economy of means, where the best results come not from large-scale efforts but from small, well-focused actions. Our non-systemic ways of thinking lead us to focus on low-leverage changes; we focus on symptoms where the stress is greatest. We repair or ameliorate the symptoms. But such efforts only make matters better in the short-run, at best, and worse in the long-run.

Systems thinking in practice

It is clear that relationships and connections are distinguishing features of systems thinking. Anyone who has tried to identify the many people, groups, companies, suppliers, customers, employees, events and other issues affecting an organization will appreciate how difficult a task it can be to understand the complex web of interactions. Any attempt to understand these relationships and develop strategy and operations accordingly, is likely to miss the mark, especially if they are without a sound way of identifying them (and the relationships) in the first place. Fortunately, we have a useful conceptual tool to help us identify and plot these relationships: systems maps. Systems maps are diagrams that present the main components of systems and how they interact with one another. They may also incorporate aspects of flow charts that depict processes and movements of inputs and outputs. One particularly useful tool is the stakeholder map.

Stakeholder maps

It is a core premise of this book that we should think holistically. It is fitting, therefore, to introduce another tool, namely Stakeholder Maps. These 'living' charts illustrate the major constituents and patterns of business systems from a holistic perspective. To build one, you have to ask a series of questions:

- Who are the key players and influencers?
- What are their roles?
- How do they participate in the business process and interact with one another as well?

Figure 12.2: Stakeholders map

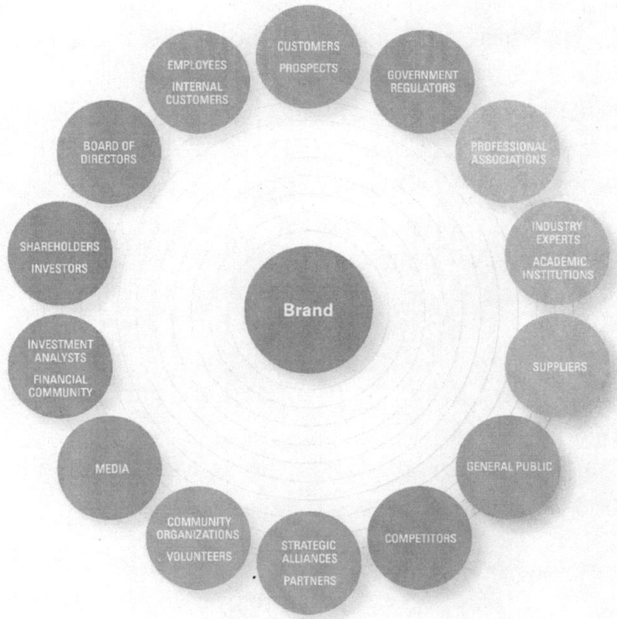

Stakeholder diagram from Designing Brand Identity © Alina Wheeler 2012

The usefulness of stakeholder maps is apparent as soon as you start the process of developing them, because they will help to fine-tune your systems-thinking skills. Also, once they are created, these charts contain a stockpile of valuable information. By analyzing and acting on the complex representation of webs and flows within a system, you will derive an array of benefits. You will gain insight into how best to position your company to derive an array of benefits.

Stakeholder maps:

- Assist in understanding the holistic, big-picture view of a business in terms of who's who
- Identify sources of power and interest, both inside and outside the business

- Include internal functions and departments, as well as those on the outside, such as:
    - Clients, targets, alliance/strategic partners, potential recruits
    - Academics, analysts, government/non-government organizations
    - Industry groups, trade associations, lenders, shareholders, suppliers/vendors
    - Media/press, opinion leaders, communities/public at large, special interest groups
- Record the effects and interactions of stakeholders on the system and each other
- Locate potential sources of support and conflict – clues about whom to engage and how
- Enable us to plan and manage initiatives, campaigns, change management programs

"EVERYTHING STARTS WITH THE CUSTOMER."

Louis XIV, King of France, 1643-1715

Zooming in on these bullet points, two things should be noted. First, internal players occupy a single line in this description. Yet their presence, roles and influence extend far beyond this brief listing. After all, they provide crucial roles in the lifeblood of a business. From an internal perspective, stakeholder maps define and illustrate the functions and interdependencies within a company's 'social' system. As a result, they are invaluable; nothing else you do will matter if you do not fully understand, manage and steer the internal players effectively.

Second, when it comes to stakeholder maps within the holistic framework of this book – and especially of this chapter – the scale tips on the side of the stakeholders identified as 'clients' (or customers, purchasers, patrons or patients, as the case may be). Let's face the most basic business truth, here – those who buy products and services pump vital money into the system. They are the raison d'être for the business in the first place.

The central role of the customer or client

Clearly, the centerpiece and ever-present underlying object of attention for an organization is the client. Many questions need to be answered if an organization is to succeed with client relationships. What are the client's needs? How do we, through specific functions as well as relationships with other stakeholders, make a positive impact on our client? Why do things happen the way they do (that is, why do clients and companies behave in certain ways)? How do we shape relationships, on a proactive basis, which will ultimately influence buying behavior? Does one isolated event create and sustain deep-rooted client loyalty? In all fairness, we shouldn't rule that last possibility out. Nonetheless, understanding a system and how it works identifies the key relationships and activities that build an effective, client-focused business strategy. This is where our multidisciplinary, holistic approach and stakeholder maps merge – they enable us to locate and leverage advantages, point the way to create synergies and minimize risk.

"THE ONLY WAY TO KNOW HOW CUSTOMERS SEE YOUR BUSINESS IS TO LOOK AT IT THROUGH THEIR EYES."

Daniel R. Scoggin, Founder, T.G.I. Friday's Inc.

"TO CONSISTENTLY SERVE THE CHANGING NEEDS OF CUSTOMERS FOR THEIR CONVENIENCE."

Mission statement, 7-Eleven, the world's largest convenience retail chain

This process of identifying and understanding stakeholders reveals the ways to deliver value and how to take those relationships even further to create more value. What may have initially seemed a hum-drum exercise, of plotting key players on a flat, two-dimensional diagram, suddenly reveals a complex, multidimensional world of possibilities. Take a moment to think about what has been achieved. We delineated and plotted the system, key players, flows and relationships of all kinds. We studied the inputs, outputs and feedback loops to distinguish the threads, drivers, hot buttons and landmines. Peer at it closely and pockets and paths of impact begin to emerge. Put it together and the stakeholder map serves as the blueprint for generating value on a broad scale. It's not value in the linear or static sense. It's the panoramic 'value constellation.'

From value chain to value constellation

"SUCCESSFUL COMPANIES CONCEIVE OF STRATEGY AS SYSTEMATIC SOCIAL INNOVATION: THE CONTINUOUS DESIGN AND REDESIGN OF COMPLEX BUSINESS SYSTEMS."

Richard Normann and Rafael Ramirez, *Designing Interactive Strategy: From Value Chain to Value Constellation*

Is the value constellation the same as the 'value chain' mentioned earlier? Yes, in essence, but there is a significant difference. The value constellation greatly expands the concept to a systems level. It uses the backdrop of the ever-exploding arena of global commerce and wide-ranging connectedness to develop an entire value-creating network. In their book, *Designing Interactive Strategy: From Value Chain to Value Constellation* (Wiley & Sons, Inc., 1998), Richard Normann and Rafael Ramírez put it this way: "Strategy is no longer a matter of positioning a fixed set of activities along a value chain. Successful companies do not just add value, they increasingly reinvent it. Their focus of strategic analysis is not the company or even the industry but the value-creating system itself, within which different economic actors – suppliers, business partners, allies and customers – work together to co-produce value. Their key strategic task is the reconfiguration of roles and relationships among this constellation of actors in order to mobilize the creation of value in new forms and by new players. And their underlying strategic goal is to create an ever improving fit between competencies and customers."

A HOLISTIC APPROACH

So, where does a holistic approach actually take us? Everything we have looked at in this chapter leads us to the intersection of Think and Holistic, and this is where our six Rs come back center stage. Like both Think and Holistic, the six Rs of Reason, Revenue, Rouser, Reputation, Relationships and Resilience are separate in that each is important in its own right, but they also draw even greater power when combined and integrated. When the six Rs combine with Think and Holistic, working in tandem as a system, the sum of the parts is so much greater than the whole.

Figure 12.3: The Six Rs Matrix

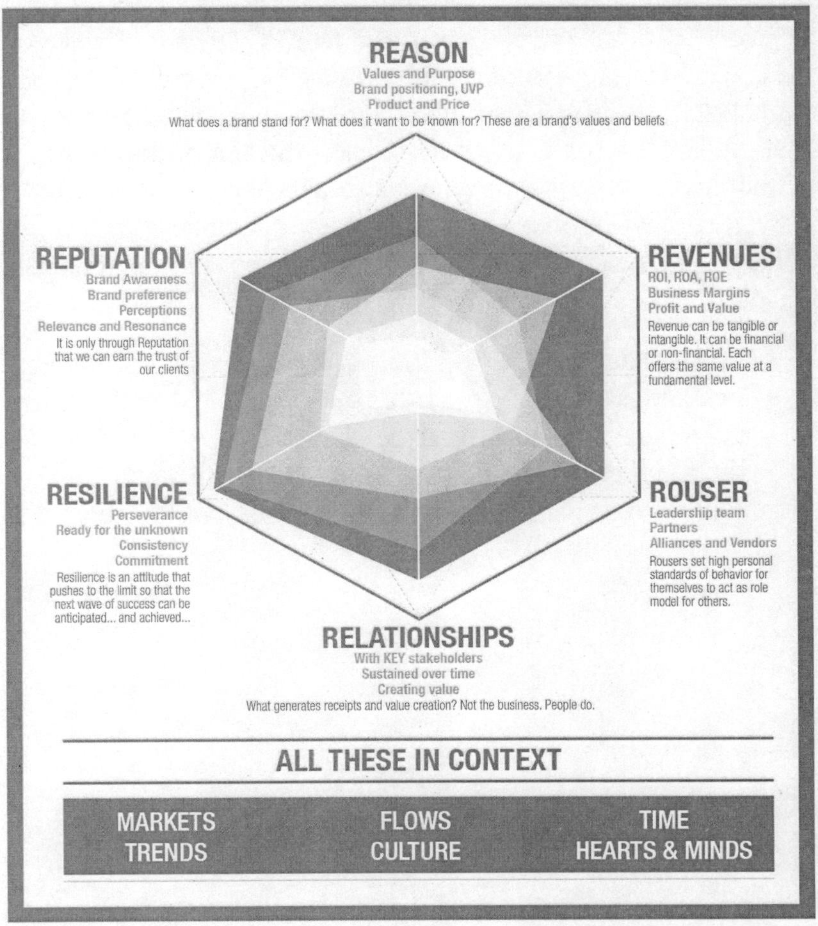

The case studies we have looked at in the book illustrate this point. When companies think holistically in terms of their Reason, Revenue, Rouser, Reputation, Relationships and Resilience, they derive success in every aspect of their business. When resolving problems and developing strategy successfully, these companies generally excel in all of the six Rs. In fact, in some instances, it can become difficult to discern which R predominates. This proves, yet again, the benefit of both the six Rs and the Think Holistic framework on the journey to sustained, profitable growth.

It is vital, therefore, that we see the six Rs as a whole and understand their interdependencies: identify them, leverage them and find and create synergies, so we can push our thinking further and achieve our desired goals and vision. The importance of this approach is clear. In the view of the late W. Edwards Deming in his book, *The New Economics for Industry, Government, Education* (MIT, 1994), "A system is a network of interdependent components that works together to try to accomplish the aim of the system. A system must have an aim. Without an aim, there is no system … A system must be managed. The secret is cooperation between components toward the aim of the organization. We cannot afford the destructive effect of competition."

Business strategy is multidisciplinary and spans many different functions and ways to create and derive value. It demands many new and different ways of thinking – in particular, we have to think as a whole and then act. And it is to this last point we now turn our attention, the next part of our THAP framework: Taking Action.

Chapter Thirteen

Taking Action and Making It Personal

"Talk doesn't cook rice."

CHINESE PROVERB

The last two chapters covered a great deal of ground and we are now up to speed on the Think Holistic part of our THAP framework. We have also seen that success hinges on the ability to carefully construct and consider the big picture and to look at things in different ways. While these have certainly given us much to work with, don't be fooled – we are not done yet! It is time to put all of this together and act. As the Chinese proverb says, "Talk doesn't cook rice."

"WHATEVER YOU CAN DO OR DREAM YOU CAN, BEGIN IT. BOLDNESS HAS GENIUS, POWER AND MAGIC IN IT!"

W. H. Murray, The Scottish Himalaya Expedition, 1951

As we embark on this chapter, the important thing to keep in mind is that the art of execution depends on the quality of our thinking and taking a holistic approach when we use the six Rs. Be warned though, the adjournment is over, things need to be done. It is time to Act.

MAKING IT HAPPEN

Overcoming the first hurdle: deciding to act

Despite this rallying call and the need to pick up the pace and step lively, we have to address a common problem that often happens at this stage: the problem of staying in the thinking and talking zone. It's human nature to enjoy musing about what will and can be. Thinking about an issue is gratifying. Talking about it can also be equally satisfying, assuring and even ego boosting. This is a nice, safe, fulfilling space to occupy but it is also a deceptive place and can lull us into a false sense of progress. Have you ever had the experience of not quite knowing at first glance whether an event, activity, or occurrence actually took place? This may sound a little odd, here, in black and white text, but for the many business leaders I have talked with it is a surprisingly common phenomenon. What makes it particularly pernicious is that you are barely aware of it at the time. Reality appears to blur ever so slightly when it happens. That's because thinking, talking, recommending, even dreaming about something can deliver a vivid impression as if it had actually transpired. It lulls us into feeling that all the discussing, presenting, lecturing and suggesting to Act are enough. Ideas, solutions and plans must all cross into the Act column, and we need to rally around the mantra of 'make things happen.'

You may be thinking 'surely, that goes without saying, we all instinctively know that we have to make things happen.' Well, that may be true, but what we don't know quite so instinctively is how and when to Act. In business, this has frustrated most of us at one time or another. Yet, we do this countless times on a personal level. In fact, we can learn a simple and important technique from our personal lives that is equally applicable in our working lives: the principle of testing. This will help us to know how and when to act.

KNOWING HOW AND WHEN TO ACT

Google

Organizations are increasingly getting our help, as customers, to test prototypes or outlines of service offerings before the company launches them on the market. This is the beta testing ring of product development, and one of the reigning champions in this technique is Google. Beta testing is a second-stage test where customers are brought into the equation to give a product a limited real-world test before launch. Google Labs draws participants into this online testing arena that they describe as a playground, and wait for the response. Products have the potential to become the next technology set to change our lives, or they can disappear in a flash if they don't test well. Some of the products that we all enjoy once started their lives in Google Labs, including Google Alerts, iGoogle and Google Maps, which has now become an indispensable part of many people's lives. The projects are not intended to be final products; they are showcased full of extra features because they are aiming to gather as much information and feedback as possible so that the final product can then be perfected. The feedback and data irons out kinks, improves features (and suggests new ones or the deletion of others) and reveals invaluable insight into how the market may react.

The most interesting aspect of this approach is how it complements and facilitates Google's philosophy on when to take action and launch: "early and often." Google's strategy of previewing potential products and soliciting responses, as well as launching early and often, epitomizes the taking action theme of this chapter. Google creates curiosity and invites those most likely to become stalwart users to participate in development decisions. This quickly gives Google the information it needs to know about whether something is worth the effort and cost. Essentially, Google gets a sense of 'if' and 'when' to act. Moreover, the company generates a buzz among members of its prime target population. In the best of all possible worlds – combining the online and in-person spheres – awareness and enthusiasm can go viral. And that is the holy grail of doing business today.

The next hurdle: where exactly is the tipping point?

Product testing and customer participation is such an important aspect of business strategy that it is the subject of intense interest. The power a few people wield was explored by Malcolm Gladwell in *The Tipping Point: How Little Things Can Make a Big Difference* (Little Brown, 2000). The tipping point is the defining moment when it is inevitable that an event will happen. Malcolm Gladwell describes it as, "The moment of critical mass, the threshold, the boiling point." It's when momentum builds to such an extent that it pushes past the place of no return into a new state. It is when change occurs en masse.

The premise of *The Tipping Point* is that some "ideas and products and messages and behaviors spread like viruses." They just take off. This sounds rather haphazard. Is it really as random as that? Not according to Gladwell. He believes that there are scientific principles at work:

- **The Law of the Few** is where an idea or behavior spreads because of the unusual qualities of a small group of key individuals. These include "connectors" – people who are supreme networkers with outstanding people and relationship skills. They excel at bringing people together, appear to know everyone, and are influential. *Mavens* – a Yiddish term, meaning trusted experts, these are people who possess in-depth knowledge in a field or discipline, who want to, and know how to, share information. They serve as the go-to points for any inquiries. "Salesmen" – superlative influencers, they have the gifts of persuasion and negotiation and are able to get others to follow. Their enthusiasm for a product can set it into a consumption orbit.

"PLANS ARE ONLY GOOD INTENTIONS UNLESS THEY IMMEDIATELY DEGENERATE INTO HARD WORK."

Peter Drucker, *The Man Who Invented Management,* Businessweek

- **The Stickiness Factor** is when carefully crafted content and images stay with you, like a tune that keeps playing in your head. These messages pique curiosity and inspire action, for example: watch it, consider it, read it and the ultimate – buy it.
- **The Power of Context** which emphasizes the impact of the environment and reigning conditions and issues that create a trend and influence behavior.

To understand why certain products and services achieve spontaneous exponential growth we need to appreciate that the underlying processes and players are interdependent. In other words, we need to think holistically. When the processes and players work in sync, they ignite infectious interest and a don't-block-the-door (or the keyboard) buying bonanza.

"AN ORGANIZATION'S ABILITY TO LEARN, AND TRANSLATE THAT LEARNING INTO ACTION RAPIDLY, IS THE ULTIMATE COMPETITIVE ADVANTAGE."

Jack Welch, Former Chairman and CEO, General Electric

It's a marketer's dreamscape, isn't it? The winners in this situation are those who keep their eyes open, watching for (or creating) new trends and opportunities. Do this and you are on the road to understanding and exploiting the evolution of trends and fads. Tipping points can occur naturally, without manipulation and intervention. Significantly, though, with knowledge of the players involved and the forces at play, you can engineer tipping points for your own products and services. This is the leap that takes us from Think Holistic to Act Personal – that is, knowing and planning the 'how to' and then swinging into 'to do' mode (or a 'do too' mode, if you are following others).

Figure 13.1: From 'How To' into 'To Do' or 'Do Too'

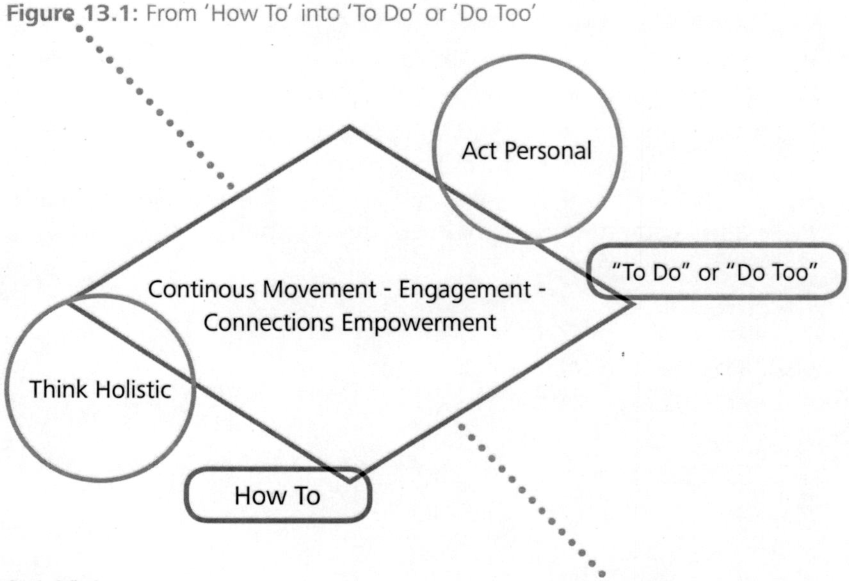

"THE PROFIT OF GREAT IDEAS COMES WHEN YOU TURN THEM INTO REALITY."

Tom Hopkins, consultant

To create a tipping point, you need to start with the premise that under the right circumstances, people can rapidly and fundamentally change their behavior, even their beliefs. Second, you should tap into the fact that we learn from what we see around us; to do this, you should create the right environment for your potential customers. As Malcolm Gladwell says, "If you want to bring a fundamental change in people's belief and behavior ... you need to create a community around them, where those new beliefs can be practiced and expressed and nurtured." He adds, "In order to create one contagious movement, you often have to create many small movements first." If all this sounds familiar it's because it is. Terms like the 'Ripple Effect,' 'Domino Effect,' 'Butterfly Effect,' or Chain Reaction are already well-known in the field of global commerce. Whatever you call it, the upshot is the same: profitable growth.

Finally, to achieve a tipping point, it is essential that our actions are capable of delivering results. For this, we need to understand the triggers, the causes and effects, and other elements that cause tipping points. And to understand this, we now need to turn to behavioral economics for further insights.

Understanding the power of behavioral economics

This relatively new discipline explores how stakeholders make financial decisions. What roles do social, cognitive and emotional factors play in buying behavior? Are our spending patterns reasonable or logical? Or do certain influences cause us to act in other ways? Dan Ariely, behavioral economist and academic, has focused on these issues, and he sets out his conclusions in his landmark book, *Predictably Irrational: The Hidden Forces That Shape Our Decisions* (Harper/HarperCollins Publishers, 2008). His aim was two-fold: to combine psychology and economics to reveal behavior, and then to understand the decision making that led to those behaviors.

With regard to the decision making processes, Dan Ariely says, "We are really far less rational than standard economic theory assumes. Moreover, these irrational behaviors of ours are neither random nor senseless. They are systematic, and since we repeat them again and again, predictable."

He concludes that there are traps that trigger predictably irrational economic behavior. These include:

- **Relativity** – this exposes the tendency for people to compare things. Understandably, people like to do this, as it indicates the value of one thing over another. Interestingly, though, people lean toward products and services that are easily comparable, while ignoring those that are not. This means that companies can use 'decoy' products to sway decisions in a predictably irrational way – as this provides customers a point of comparison for the 'real' product and consequently, draws them in.

- **The Fallacy of Supply and Demand** – although the theory of supply and demand prevails in traditional economics, in reality, certain factors may transcend these market forces. These factors include 'Arbitrary Coherence" – a phenomenon with a long reach. When a price becomes fixed in our perception, no matter how arbitrary the setting of the price was, it can be very difficult to change that perception. All future pricing can then be constrained by the fact that customers now associate your product with a definite price. This coherence between present and future pricing happens because of the Anchoring Trap (explained in Chapter 11), where people can anchor their thinking to the first price that will then stay with them, influencing all future decisions to buy. Clearly, it is important to consider pricing carefully before launching a product.

  Another factor that can undermine the theory of supply and demand is 'Herding.'. This happens because people tend to follow others. Seeing others 'doing this' or 'owning that' triggers a belief that the products or services being used must be good. Conversely, if they don't see others using it, the assumption is often made that the product must not be all that great. Therefore, getting a lot of people (or the right people) to use a product or service is critical to creating a buzz and turning your product into a 'gotta have it' amongst customers.

"ACTION IS THE FOUNDATIONAL KEY TO ALL SUCCESS."

Pablo Picasso

  Similarly, 'Self-Herding' can also negate theories of supply and demand. In addition to following others, we also make decisions based on our own past behaviors. These attitudes and actions lead us to buying decisions that reflect what applied in the past rather than reflecting the opportunities in the present. For example, when we are faced with buying something, we tend to fall back on past purchasing decisions we made or on an act that is memorable in some way. This behavior can blind customers to alternative products, so companies either need to counter this or tap into it.

- **The High Price of Ownership** – owning something is not as straightforward as it may appear. Deciding whether to buy a product or get rid of something is affected by our perception of what it means to own it – that is, what that product will make us feel about ourselves and what we think others will think of us. There are three, irrational reasons why this happens: we tend to be attached to the things we already own; we are afraid of what we may lose, should we get rid of something; we believe that a purchase will be seen by others in the same way that we perceive it.

The library of literature on behavioral economics continues to grow and as a result, there's much for us to take into account in the 'Act' and 'Act Personal' realms. What we have learned, so far, about tipping points and behavioral economics leads us to an important question: How can we create an environment that scouts for such ideas and translates them into actions? The first thing we should do is establish a culture of innovation within our organizations.

CREATING AN ENVIRONMENT FOR ACTION

Building a culture of innovation

In *The Starfish and the Spider* (Portfolio/Penguin, 2006), Ori Brafman and Rod A. Beckstrom show us how to construct a culture of innovation. The title alludes to two different business approaches; one that resembles a starfish and the other, a spider. While the starfish and spider have similar shapes – a central core from which tentacles radiate – their internal structures are considerably different. Attack a spider's head and it dies. A starfish has no head; chop a leg off and a new one forms. Cut a starfish in half and two grow in its place. What's more, a severed leg alone can generate a new starfish.

Moving from nature to the business world, it is clear that the spider represents the traditional, centralized command-and-control hierarchical organizations. At the other end are the starfish, with their decentralized, flatter, open systems. (The advent of the Internet has certainly fostered this latter model.) Here, power and knowledge are distributed throughout the organization. As a result, starfish organizations can mutate more quickly, that is, grow, take shape, make changes, invent, and reinvent – all at accelerated speed.

Organizations are not stuck in these categories. A spider can become a starfish by adapting and restructuring. To grow a resilient, innovative organization, we need to mimic the starfish. Just as a starfish has five legs, we need to make sure that the following five attributes are firmly embedded in our organizations:

1. **Circles.** Decentralized businesses resemble circles. They function autonomously and independently, yet are fluid, flexible, mutually supportive and revolve around norms which over time, breed trust and cooperation. Essentially, this helps to build the R for Resilience.

2. **Catalyst.** Decentralized organizations are not without leaders. However, those in leadership roles act as a catalyst: they generate and advocate ideas, inspire and lead by example. If this reminds you of something, think back to Chapter 6. It is one of our six Rs: R for Rouser.

3. **Ideology.** The corporate philosophy, its values and mission, all bind the organization and move it forward. A shared vision and set of ethics drive mutual support and achievement of goals. This is yet another place where our R for Reason comes in useful.

4. **Pre-existing network.** A building and by inference, an organization, need a platform. The Internet represents an open platform for decentralized companies and in itself, has been (and continues to be) the launching pad for numerous pursuits and businesses. A platform can take many forms, such as a company's customers or its reputation, that act as platforms from which to operate or launch initiatives. Here, two Rs come to the fore: Relationships and Reputation.

5. **Champion.** It's all well and good to talk about what needs to happen, but organizations need resources to make plans a reality. An implementer focuses on action and dedicates efforts to mobilize groups and troops. This is exactly what a Rouser does.

Most importantly, when all five attributes align accordingly, the organization is primed to 'Act.'

Following on from this, it is important to keep in mind the example of Google Labs, which engages the brainpower of those outside its organization to test and comment on a stream of potential ideas and products. This begs a vital question: are there other sources and applications of mass brainpower that can foster innovation and better inform our actions?

To explore this possibility consider the successful television game show called *Who Wants to Be a Millionaire*. Contestants have three lifelines should they need help answering questions. One lifeline is to 'ask the audience' and another is 'phone a friend.' Imagine that you are in the hot seat. Which one would you rely on more? You may wish to go with the friend, who you probably chose because you consider them intelligent. Statistically, you have just made a mistake. You should have gone with the audience, because the group is much more likely to choose the right answer. The difference is quite marked. While the studio audience reaches the right answer 91 percent of the time, the friend (the supposed expert) deliberating in isolation, only gets it right 65 percent of the time.

You would be in good company if you find this surprising. It also captured the attention of James Surowiecki, a journalist, who describes it and similar accounts in *The Wisdom of Crowds* (Doubleday, 2004). This is an interesting addition to the bookshelf in the behavioral economics section, because it illustrates a seemingly counterintuitive effect. Its message is astonishingly accurate; a group is smarter than the smart people who comprise it. Just as crowds are smarter, as a whole, than their individual members, this really shows just how important it is to take a holistic view of business.

However, there is an important caveat to be aware of: there are exceptions. Success, as James Surowiecki tells us, relies on certain criteria that must be in place: diversity of opinion, independence, decentralization and an ability to aggregate results accurately and effectively. In essence, group members have some sense of the subject and they form their own judgments. The process takes all the responses and then balances the different opinions so that the group's decision tends to weigh heavily toward the correct answer. Recently, this phenomenon has evolved into a new concept: Crowdsourcing.

"ACTION MAY NOT ALWAYS BRING HAPPINESS, BUT THERE IS NO HAPPINESS WITHOUT ACTION."

Benjamin Disraeli, 1804-1881

Crowdsourcing

As the potential power of groups gained greater awareness and influence, the concept of 'crowdsourcing' entered the business lexicon. Quite simply, crowdsourcing is a variation of outsourcing. Both invite external resources to perform functions traditionally done by those within an organization.

As its name suggests, crowdsourcing casts a wider net and outsources actions to the crowd. It issues a call-to-action to large groups, also known as communities, and to the global public at large. It's similar to an open-casting call, but staged on the Internet through the collaborative opportunities provided by Web 2.0.

The advantages of crowdsourcing are immense. The organization expands its talent pool and by extension, its pipeline of innovations. In fact, crowdsourcing is also referred to as open innovation. Problem solving occurs more rapidly and more successfully, with a consortium of minds focused on an issue. Ultimately, production and commercialization also proceed more rapidly. Costs are likely to fall given the voluntary nature of participation – and even when payments are made, these are usually minimal. What's more, crowdsourcing piques the interest of the informed and potentially influential public, and those engaged have a vested interest in the outcome.

Crowdsourcing has become an indispensable tool for organizations of all sizes as well as being useful to us on a personal level. Facebook, Dell, Kraft, Netflix, Peugeot, Unilever and Vodafone and countless others all use it for a variety of purposes. Wikipedia is another example of what crowdsourcing can achieve. The tributes for crowdsourcing are abundant and mounting. One accolade comes from MIT Professor Eric von Hippel, a respected authority on innovation management. In *Crowdsourcing Turns Business On Its Head* (NPR, August 20, 2008), he offers this testimonial: "Crowdsourcing is really the biggest shift in innovation since the Industrial Revolution."

SUCCEEDING WITH OPEN INNOVATION

Procter & Gamble

When Procter & Gamble needed a way to achieve its goal of organic growth, open innovation met this need. Today, as James Joia in the External Business Development team confirms, "Procter & Gamble's radical strategy of open innovation now produces more than 35 percent of the company's innovations and billions of dollars in revenue." This program expands the home-grown, internal, invention model to one that leverages external connections. The company also invites outside suppliers and technology entrepreneurs to contribute to the development process. This has seen a major shift from R&D to C&D – that is, the process has moved from Research and Development to Connect and Develop. This C&D initiative reels in promising ideas and then applies internal skills to make them even better. Now, half the company's new products come from its own labs, while half come from external participants.

So how does Connect and Develop work? James Joia explains it for us. "Connect and develop is about finding good ideas and bringing them in, to enhance and capitalize on internal capabilities. To do this, we collaborate with organizations and individuals around the world, systematically searching for proven technologies, packages, and products that we can improve, scale up, and market, either on our own or in partnership with other companies."

In the Procter & Gamble model, success relies on: pinpointing needs, translating them into problems explained in technology briefs, targeting 'adjacencies' or product-line extensions, and having effective decision making tools. And there's one more: building a network around the world and knowing how to use it.

Making your networks work

"THE CURRENCY OF REAL NETWORKING IS NOT GREED BUT GENEROSITY."

Keith Ferrazzi and Tahl Raz, *Never Eat Alone*

We have all heard about the power of networks and networking. Given that they are now an indispensable part of doing business, we need to develop a networking strategy that keeps our organizations poised to act, so they are always moving along the path of profit and growth.

Borrowing again from Procter & Gamble's Connect and Develop initiative, we discover that the company set up proprietary networks with technology entrepreneurs and suppliers to drive innovation activities. It uses open networks – as well as having its own – and it has joined others, including InnoCentive, YourEncore, and Yet2.com. What can we learn from their experience that will help us to erect a network and gain a legion of followers, influencers, customers and targets? There are several key points and when implementing each one, we need to keep in mind that the emphasis should always be on taking action.

What needs to happen ...	... and how to ACT
1. Provide Thought Leadership. Build awareness and credibility by disseminating information of value in the form of white/position papers; post on the organization's website, send alerts and links via social media; present at external meetings. Do the same at internal meetings to advise and encourage employees to share with clients and other stakeholders.	**ACT:** Overcome information overload by applying the six R framework when conceiving, creating, and circulating content. Relate it to people/problems/purpose/profits/big picture. Punch it up. Market it. Build interest and audience by developing a microsite.
2. Use Social Media. Social media tools touch the universe of stakeholders in a multitude of ways. Having a solid social media strategy makes an immense difference. It drives engagement, boosts customer satisfaction, retention and profits, as well as multi-stakeholder advocacy.	**ACT:** There is much more to figure out to arrive at an effective social media strategy. This really is the time to Think Holistic. Use the six Rs as the centerpiece. Plan the best way forward and then execute your strategy to the fullest potential by using all the social media tools at your disposal. Interacting with clients, recruits and all other stakeholders through these tools will have a massive impact on your organization.
3. Act Personal. It is important to recognize the importance of face time. It is likely that no one would dispute the value of this. Understandably, however, it can be hard to know how to find the time that face time demands to make appreciable inroads into networking and building networks. Again, this is where Think Holistic and the six Rs come in: they will help you devise a strategy to evaluate the efforts and costs involved and to develop an appropriate solution.	**ACT:** Go East, Far East... A substantial part of western manufacturing has already migrated to this region. Also, the vast Asian expanse has grown far more important in other ways, such as sales increases from resident consumption as well as innovation from regional product development with local business partners. The article *Top Executives Say It Pays to Spend Time in Asia* (The New York Times, September 23, 2010), reports that more western companies understand the need to be in Asia and China. This transition has included splitting headquarters, in order to have a presence in the region, and relocating high-level managers and executive board members. This increased amount of in-person contact has made an incredible difference, greatly benefiting the organizations involved. For many, the benefits that accrue from working face-to-face are worth the extra cost and effort.

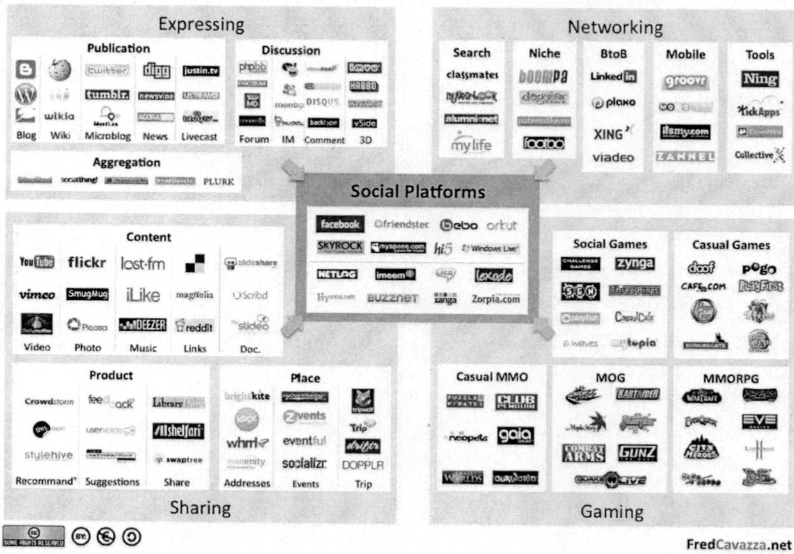

Figure 13.2: Social Media Landscape

Finally, instead of traveling around the world yourself, how about inviting the world to visit you? Take a leaf out of Larry Ellison's book. He and his colleagues at Oracle extend an invitation to attend its weeklong Open World conference in San Francisco. And do interested parties accept this offer? In 2010, an estimated 41,000 people came to this annual event to engage in business discussions and connect with each other in a face-to-face, personal way – and, quite frankly, to enjoy the experience. There is no doubt that bringing Oracle's own network together with Dell, Fujitsu, Lego and others, provided a rich environment where the network was made even stronger. Without question, this initiative extended the company's sphere of influence and networks and networking.

MAKING IT PERSONAL

Taking action is vital, but the final part of our model is the need for this action to be personal. In other words, each individual needs to take personal responsibility for making it happen. This brings two questions to mind: how can you take action and make the changes that are needed? And how can you as a manager make this happen with others?

Overcome the fear of risk

The conventional, controlling business approach to managing risk predominates. However, rather like viewing the glass as half-empty rather than half-full, it is only one perception, and a fairly limited one. In business, prudence and conventional logic demand that although there may be an advantage to taking a risk and winning, the dangers of failure are so great that it is probably better to either do nothing, or else to minimize the risk as much as possible. This limited approach may occasionally be valid, but it is far from adequate on its own. It takes no account of the complex nature of risk. Certainly, insurance and prudence have their place, but they need not always be the default options in situations of uncertainty, or the best approaches to take most of the time.

Unfortunately, organizations take the fun out of risk. It is seen as a necessary evil and as a result, suffers from being perceived as bureaucratic and stifling – which frequently it is. Organizations fail to see that risk is both desirable, providing new opportunities to learn, develop and move forward, and necessary, compelling people to improve and meet the challenge of change.

Create a positive climate

By itself, simply recognizing the need for audacity is inadequate: the ethos of the entire organization must embrace a culture that emphasizes and rewards any behavior that actively manages risk. This requires a commitment by senior managers and the resources (including training) to achieve it. Also, if we are to be audacious ourselves and expect others to follow, then there are several techniques to use proactively and determinedly to ensure success. These are not intended as a linear process but rather techniques and areas of focus that are important at specific moments when we are pushing back the boundaries of risk and audacity. These techniques are:

- Establishing a compelling vision.
- Handling conflict and emotions.
- Communicating, influencing and negotiating.
- Dealing with stress.
- Coaching and teamworking.
- Decision making and problem solving.

Develop audacious thinking

Becoming successfully audacious requires three elements: awareness, self-confidence and a compelling vision.

- **Increasing awareness.** Successfully audacious people have high levels of awareness – in particular, self-awareness – that enable them to reflect on and question what is going on. This insight allows them to recognize their own role in terms of their abilities and their impact on others. They are also aware of other people, objectively evaluating their strengths and weaknesses and judging what their likely responses and actions will be.

- **Building self-confidence and taking control.** Many situations, activities and opportunities possess a dangerous edge, a point at which we perceive that trauma may occur. To approach this point we need a protective frame, a way of viewing the situation so that we can deal with it. If such a frame exists, we can view the risk with excitement; without it, we are filled with anxiety. There are three levels of control necessary for being audacious: control of the situation; control of contribution; control of reaction.

- **Establishing a compelling vision and motivational connection.** A vision does not mean simply a goal, if a goal is simply a destination to be measured and dispassionately achieved. A vision describes the journey to be taken as well. It is motivationally rich, meaning that it appeals to a broad range of values in those who take part.

Stepping into the danger zone

When taking risks, we need to feel the presence of danger but not to focus on it. This heightens our senses and ensures that the three critical components of an audacious mindset – awareness, confidence and motivational connection – come into play.

Stepping into the danger zone requires us to have a protective, 'confidence frame' that is built on a firmer foundation than simply knowing the odds. Audacious individuals build their confidence frames from three overriding emotions:

- A sense of self-mastery.
- A feeling of rebelliousness – willfully defying convention.
- These two feelings then lead to a third: a sense of control.

Most people distinguish between two sorts of control: controlling the situation and controlling one's reaction. Audacious people seem to be able to add a third element to their control strategy: they know how to control the way they contribute to a situation.

Stepping into the danger zone also requires each individual to develop and heighten their personal awareness. This works when the danger is not simply in our minds but is real and tangible. One of the great insights into sporting performance in recent years has been the understanding of the role of awareness in high performance. Elite athletes seem to have a heightened sense of awareness, not just on what is going on around them but of their own internal world. Moreover, they seem to be able to change this focus to deal with an unfolding situation. This situation is highlighted by Nideffer's Model of Attentional Focus:

Figure 13.3: Nideffer's Model of Attentional Focus

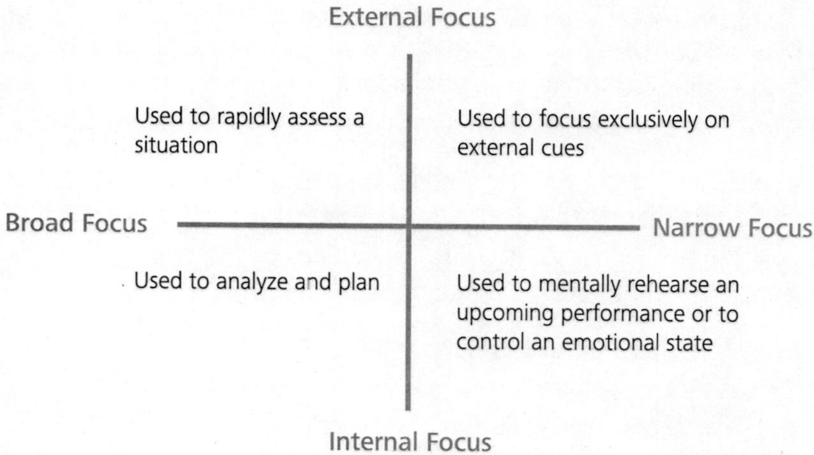

Nideffer's model is about concentration and has been used to highlight the role of attention in performance. Successful, adventurous performance depends on:

- **A high degree of self-knowledge:** How am I doing? What assumptions am I making? How am I emotionally and motivationally responding to the world?
- **An external focus,** sensing what is going on in the environment and what its impact might be. What is crucial is how self-knowledge of our changing and dynamic internal world leads us to interpret the broad and narrow features of our external world.

Almost any sort of audacious activity will require this ability to change attentional focus. A would-be business will need to really understand what their market is doing (broad external), identify specific opportunities to exploit (narrow external), maintain a winning strategy (broad internal) and develop and utilize specific capabilities to achieve it (narrow internal).

Handle changing and contradictory emotions

To this attentional model, we also need to add motivational and emotional factors – our own and from the others around us. For example, successful audacity requires that we move back and forth, consciously as well as subconsciously, between opposing emotions:

- Feelings of seriousness and playfulness.
- A focus on ourselves and an emphasis on others.
- A desire to conform and a desire to rebel or challenge.
- An emphasis on mastery and a desire to support.

Audacity relies on awareness, and this in turn depends upon our emotional versatility – our ability to be in the right frame of mind at the right time. And if we are on a team, others need this ability as well. Individual awareness is important if we are to avoid being fooled by false protective frames. It also matters if we are to seize opportunities by challenging our assumptions about the true nature of a risk. While some people are more naturally self-aware than others, this is also a skill that can be developed and a discipline to be followed.

Key questions when taking action

- What are the main assumptions you make in your work? Which of these are central to the way you work and could be usefully reevaluated?
- Are you aware of other people's assumptions? What are they, and how can they best be challenged?
- Which areas of work would benefit from greater awareness, confidence and a guiding vision for: a) yourself b) your team and c) your organization?
- Review the list of coping and thinking flaws; which ones are most significant for: a) yourself b) your team and c) your organization?
- Where do you need to take greater risks? Where would you gain the greatest benefit, and how can you minimize the risks? Answer this question for your team and your organization.

- Motivation and confidence are vital for developing audacity and avoiding mistakes. How can you increase your motivation and that of your team (remember, money is rarely sufficient!)?

Bringing your talents to work: what organizations need to do

It is time to talk about talented organizations and how the workplace can encourage people to bring all of their talents to work, so that they take action themselves. As far as possible, this means that people are not only realizing their potential but stretching their abilities in new, enjoyable and fulfilling directions. Several issues can help:

- The need for organizations to segment their workforce and understand the priorities, character, strengths and weaknesses of different groups of employees
- The importance of their moving beyond groups and aggregation to personalize each individual's contract of employment (informally as well as formally)
- The value of recognizing these psychological contracts with each employee – this means understanding issues of behavior, personality and self-awareness, notably including emotional intelligence

Above all, talented organizations recognize that everyone is in the talent team: top executives, people management professionals, each individual leader or manager and each employee. It recognizes that the best employees want work to be more meaningful – stimulating, worthwhile and accountable. For leaders this means answering a vital question: 'how can you make work more personal for your team?'

Focus on the head, heart and guts of people

So, how can leaders keep pace and succeed in the fast moving world that we have described? Our search for a solution brings us to the focus on head, heart and guts. The difficulty is that leaders often rely exclusively on a single quality: data and rational analysis, emotional connection or courage – but not all three. Concentrating on just one of these dimensions means they ignore other aspects necessary for enduring success. If you rely on your analytical rigor, you may be seen as insensitive or unethical or you may lack the ability to respond outside a narrow range of situations. If you try to create a compassionate culture, you may miss opportunities that a more strategic leader would have seen. Relying solely on the courage of your conviction and toughness may lead you to underestimate the negative consequences for the people you are trying to lead.

Worse than that, taking just one of these approaches to leadership rather than blending and deploying them at the right time has damaging consequences. In particular, leaders often intimidate people with their intellect, confuse matters by complicating issues, or dominate conversations. They change direction without being transparent, fail to connect other people's experiences to the company's direction, and drive for performance without incorporating other necessary values such as honesty, compassion and trust.

More than ever before, leaders are managing complex situations and constituencies that require a broader range of leadership attributes. They are faced with decisions to which there are no 'right' solutions. They will have to learn how to manage paradoxes rather than try to resolve them. Sometimes they will have to act counterintuitively and at other times they will need to trust their instincts. Dealing with these difficult and ever-changing situations is not possible without head, heart and guts working together.

A systemic, integrated approach to developing leadership provides a useful solution. Today, many companies still cultivate their leaders the way they did when leadership demands were different. For example, they often use traditional classroom training, focusing almost exclusively on cognitive learning. Even when more effective and imaginative methods are used (such as project work or temporary assignments), the danger is that people revert to their old way of doing things when they return to the workplace. To develop capable leaders, however, organizations need to move away from this traditional approach and instead embrace a more holistic way of working.

A final thought: finding the meaning in work

In most organizations, people wish to leave it better than when they arrived: they aspire to deliver quality as well as achieve recognition and reward. This should come as no surprise; after all, very few successful people are content simply to work on a pointless endeavor for long.

The challenge, therefore, is to help people find the meaning in their work; the element that they value and enjoy as well as the recognition of where they fit within the organization's work. The six Rs provide a great framework for this: they can help people understand what they do, why, and its wider impact and benefit. They can connect with other people, both inside and outside the organization, and work with a common purpose.

WHICH OF THE 6Rs PLAY TO YOUR STRENGTHS, WHAT ACTION WILL YOU TAKE YOURSELF, AND HOW WILL YOU ENCOURAGE OTHERS TO ACT?

It is worth reviewing the six Rs and understanding that while they work together in a holistic system, making it personal may mean focusing on one (or a few) in a single role, rather than all six. The question, therefore, is which of the six Rs play to your strengths and crucially, what action will you take yourself and how will you encourage others to act?

To help you answer these questions we have summarized the six Rs:

Reason is the most fundamental part of any organization. Why all the other Rs must come together in pursuit of Reason and why this R supports all the others is understandable: it is the raison d'être, the very soul of a company, without which the company would be directionless. Clearly, this matters enormously. Everything springs from intention – it sets the tone for the whole business.

Revenues are the financial capital of a company, including its portfolio of clients. To improve this portfolio and increase income, the other variables in our six R list must work together, mutually reinforcing each other.

Rouser involves being goal oriented, committed to common objectives, being adaptable, innovative and seeking the opinions of others. It requires inner strength and encouraging this strength in others.

Reputation operates at an internal level, affecting your own people, as well as externally (affecting clients, investors and opinion leaders and others). Clearly, internal reputation is affected by (and also affects) the other Rs.

Relationships are divided into internal and external relations. As well as affecting the other Rs, they also affect each other. For example, customer perceptions of the company motivate employees, while engaged employees improve the service to customers.

Resilience has to be a total, companywide activity, which means that it calls on capabilities in all aspects of the business. Resilience should operate at a personal, team, and company level, which requires all six Rs to support each other. When all six Rs work well together, not only is a company ideally placed to cope with problems, it is in a position to fix things before they actually break, circumvent threats and take advantage of opportunities.

Everything we have learned leads us to the conclusion that success comes from:

- Being curious and exploring
- Understanding the forces around us
- Receiving and cultivating ideas
- Engaging … Aligning ... Changing
- And never standing still….

As Winston Churchill once said, "I never worry about action, only inaction."

Chapter Two

1 See Journal of Marketing, May 1, 2009.

Chapter Five

1 Deloitte *Connecting the Dots: Trends & Opportunities for Service Development (Draft for Discussion)*, March 2010, www.cpsi.co.za/conferences/past/Top_20_Mega_Trends_1.pdf.

Final Thought

I invite you to share and write your own view of Brands & Rousers by visiting **www.BrandsRousers.com**. The website serves as a platform in which best practices can be shared among communication and marketing experts, strategic concepts can be discussed and new ideas can catch fire.

You can contact me on twitter: @lgallardo

I look forward to hearing from you soon.

Luis Gallardo